Contents

Introduction

The development of National Criteria for Business Studies has provided a golden opportunity to extend the teaching of Business Studies from the few schools and colleges in which it has been taught into the general curriculum of most. This book follows the content requirements for GCSE and is firmly based in the objectives stressed by the national criteria which are:

1 To develop knowledge and understanding of:
the environment in which business activity takes place.
the way in which changes in that environment influence business behaviour.
the major groups and organisations within and outside business.
the ways in which such groups are able to influence business objectives, decisions and activities.
the roles and purposes of business activity in both the private and the public sector.
the ways the main types of business and commercial activities are organised, financed and operated.
how business relations with other organisations, consumers, employees, owners and society are regulated.
the factor inputs and product outputs of business and of the forces which help to determine and control them.
the co-operation and interdependence which participation in society entails.
the language, concepts, techniques and decision-making procedures in business behaviour.
the nature and significance of change within the context of business activities.

2 To give opportunity for the development of skills and competencies relating to numeracy, literacy, research, interpretation and analysis.

3 To encourage the confidence and awareness of students in their approach to participation, particularly through group work in the classroom and direct experience outside it.

In pursuit of these objectives this book is structured to cover all the core content as outlined in the criteria, being of use to those studying similar courses or in the introductory stages of higher ones. It is aimed at all students who may be following such courses and is additionally designed to be used in conjunction with support materials for teacher and student which are produced by the Cambridge Business Studies Project.

The major thrust of teaching for the GCSE will be to create opportunities for students of all abilities to learn from their own activities in the classroom, and from positive investigation and observation outside it. The book is written to enable this approach, and the focus of that effort is the **Things to Do** sections at the end of each chapter. They are divided into three.

SECTION A

Short answer questions will enable a distance learning approach in that it tests understanding of the main ideas which have been the subject of a particular chapter, and relates back to previous chapters where it is thought that reinforcement of learning is desired. It can be omitted by those who wish to reinforce or test learning by more direct means.

SECTION B

Essays and structured questions may involve calculations or any other skill which the chapter particularly supports.

SECTION C

Coursework and assignments; the active part of the section and the one which is likely to be of most lasting value. These are open-ended activities of the kind which may be undertaken as learning activities or as coursework assignments for an examination. Many combine work outside the classroom with opportunities for learning activities within it and all can be undertaken either as group exercises or as individual ones.

Those who wish to do so may see the Things to Do sections as the focus of their teaching, using the chapters as information bases for their students rather than in the traditional ways.

Throughout the book words commonly employed in business or in talking about business are freely used. Where they are central to understanding they appear in **bold** and are defined in a Glossary at the end of the book, in addition to any explanation which may be given during the text.

The book starts with a birds-eye view of the centre of a typical small town which we have called Culmford. The purpose is to introduce in an informal way most of the ideas and relationships which are discussed throughout the book. We consider that this chapter can be read as an effective introduction to the subject. We feel that, in a book about business studies which aims to look outward rather than to stay locked in a classroom, it is appropriate to begin with a typical community at work on the busiest day of its week.

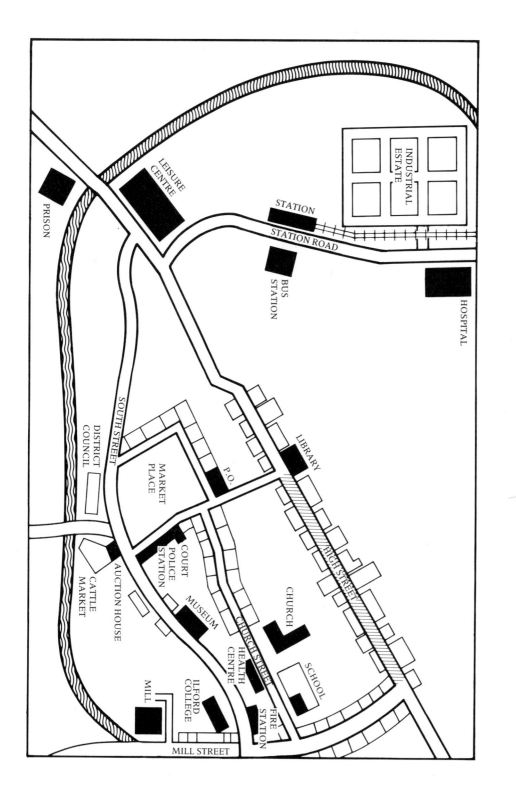

Figure 1.1 Sketch of the centre of Culmford

Chapter 1
Business at work

1.1 Introduction

Figure 1.1 is a map of Culmford, a typical small town which could be seen anywhere in the country. It compares with small towns everywhere, having a population of about 15,000 people and a role as market town for a number of villages and farms. Its business, commercial and industrial activity meets the needs of the area and some tourists are attracted during the summer months. Most of the inhabitants of the town and the surrounding villages work within it but there are many who live there and work in larger towns up to twenty-five miles away.

We are visiting Culmford in order to see something of the nature and range of its activities. It is market day, so all the facilities and services are being used to the full and we have a very good idea of the way the community operates. Most of the usual businesses are here and each of the streets we visit seems to have its own special character and role in the life of the town. We begin with South Street, closest to the banks of the River Culm, which never really features as an attraction in the life of the town but which is important to leisure and tourist activities outside it.

1.2 Business at work

South Street

The most impressive building in South Street contains the district council offices. Here, full-time officials administer the local services which help the people and businesses of Culmford. Collecting refuse, maintaining the roads, looking after the parks and recreation centres, protecting consumers, and many other services are provided to the whole town, and paid for mostly from the **rates** collected from households and businesses. The council does not try to make a **profit** from its activities – it aims to provide a public service. Many decisions which councils make are similar to those made in businesses.

The council is spending money provided by the community and the people of the town vote at local elections for councillors who will make decisions about how that money is spent. A mayor will be chosen from this group of councillors each year. The council is an important employer in the town, with accountants, lawyers, managers, and clerks who work in the council offices, and refuse collectors, rent collectors, and gardeners who provide the council services.

As well as the council, there are some **commercial** activities in South Street. An auction house sells household goods, houses, cars, land and even businesses on behalf of clients at a weekly auction. Unlike the shops in the High Street, no price is fixed for the product being sold at the start of the sale, but customers bid for it and the highest bidder is able to buy it. Behind the auction house there is an open cattle market where every Friday local farmers bring in their cattle and sell them to other farmers or butchers. There has been a cattle market in Culmford since medieval times, and farming is still an important business activity in the area. The cattle are sold in an auction, and the speed of the auctioneer is worth watching if you have the chance to visit such a market.

The main garage for the town is in South Street, and not only sells petrol and other motoring products, but also services and repairs vehicles, and sells new and second-hand cars. The owner is **franchised** by Nissan to sell their new cars – it is interesting to note that five years ago they sold British Leyland cars. The garage has suffered a fall in petrol sales since the High Street has been pedestrianised, and since two large stores opened outside the town attracting shoppers away from the town centre. A small garden shop next door to the garage has also found that its sales revenue has fallen with competition from a large garden centre outside the town.

A small museum of the town's history has been set up by the local council in a sixteenth-century building that was the town's gaol. It provides a service for local schools and has attracted a number of visitors from outside the town. Judy Ng saw the market opportunity of this museum, opened a small Chinese restaurant next to it and has now established a good lunch-time trade. In the evening she has found it more difficult to attract customers, but having introduced a take-away service she hopes to expand.

Further along South Street, opposite Mill Street, you will find the sixth-form college. As with the other schools in Culmford this public service is provided free of charge and is paid for by households and businesses mainly through rates. Education is administered by the country council. As well as providing education and training for the young people of Culmford, the college also provides employment for teachers, secretaries, cleaners, kitchen staff and caretakers. In helping to produce a well-educated workforce, the schools and college do an important public service for businesses and employers. Both public and private enterprise are closely linked. Opposite the college is the fire station, providing a valuable service in protecting the community's property, and again paid for through the rates.

Station Road
You will find the railway station to the north of the town. It is a branch line which connects to the main line to London. British Rail, a **nationalised industry** owned by the state, has reduced the number of passenger trains on this line to eight a day to stop the line making too large a **loss**. The line is an important one for freight trains, but they cause a lot of disturbance at night to those living close to the line. Such a problem is known as the **social cost** of living near to a railway. Although some local people commute by train to London, most people use their car to travel to work or for shopping. People without cars, especially school children and the elderly, rely on the bus service.

The bus station is opposite the railway station and is particularly busy on market days with passengers coming into Culmford from the local villages. Buses are no longer run by the local council, but the routes have been taken over by two local private coach firms, Coles and Archers, who run services to the surrounding villages and nearest large towns. At night and on Sunday, however, there are no bus services as there would not be enough passengers to make it profitable, so the taxi firm next to the station provides the only alternative to the private car.

Several businesses have set up in Station Road. A road haulage firm with a number of branches in the region has a depot there, and a builders' merchant sells materials and hires out machinery from its yard. A tyre and exhaust-fitting business provides a specialist service in competition with the garage in South Street and the Railway Hotel offers real ale and pub lunches. A brand new factory unit has just been finished on a vacant site where Gerry Loader, a local carpenter, is planning to make double-glazed windows and doors as he has found a steady market for the product among both house builders and house owners.

At the far end of Station Road, on the way out of town, you can see the Memorial Hospital. Along with the local general practitioners and health visitors it helps to ensure a fit and healthy community, as well as providing employment for medical and other staff. It forms part of the National Health Service, paid for out of the contributions which people in work make from their wages and salaries. Culmford hospital does not have an emergency department – this was closed as part of spending cuts in 1984 – but there is a local ambulance service based at the hospital and all major cases are dealt with in a larger hospital twenty-five miles away.

High Street
The streets are crowded and the overall impression is that there are many more small shops than would be seen in large towns. The variety of businesses represented in the High Street is much greater too. The street begins with a modern library which is much more than a source of reading material, catering for a range of leisure interests and being an important source of information. One person in there is researching for a book she is writing on the wildlife of the area; two people are planning a holiday and find the booklets from the English Tourist Board very useful. Another person is reading a variety of newspapers and some young people are looking through a library of records and tapes.

The library is a business, it must organise its activities and it has objectives which those who run it will try to achieve. Those objectives are largely concerned with the needs of the people of Culmford, and the library does not seek to make a profit because it is a service provided by the local council and paid for out of the rates.

Next to the library is the town's only independent supermarket. It is small by most standards and is a **private limited company** run by a family who have been in business in the town for many years. It has to compete with several shops in the same line of business, some of them in the High Street. Competition has been increased lately by the opening of two new **hypermarkets** on the outskirts of the town. In all of these busy shops people can buy most of the things they want, but the High Street shops find they are less popular because it is quite a walk to the nearest car park. Three banks compete with each other in the town and they are all close together as if watching each other's daily activities. Two of them are standard high street names, and you will find at least one of them in your town. Culmford does not have enough banking business to attract them all but today there are queues everywhere and it would take you a long time to cash a cheque. Even the cash dispensers on the walls of each bank have queues but they do reduce the pressure on the counter staff inside.

As we walk up the street our attention is drawn to two newsagents opposite each other. There are two things which are noticeable about them. One is small and clearly run by its owner whilst the other is managed on behalf of a national chain. Both of them do very much more than sell newspapers in order to make a profit. In the larger shop there are several staff, all in uniform, and a self-service series of shelves on which a range of goods is displayed, from office equipment to toys and from books to computer software. The shop on the other side of the road is smaller and sells wallpaper and a range of do-it-yourself products as its way of increasing business. All the workers inside are members of the family and the atmosphere is a social one with customers chatting to each other and to the staff. For the stranger this may be irritating because it takes a long time to get served, but for the owner the friendly service and time to talk are the reason why people come into the shop.

We see this competition all the way up the High Street between butchers, and chemists, and ironmongers. In many cases a local shop is vying with one which is part of a national chain and it might be interesting to find out from the customers of each why they shop at one of them rather than the other. The two chemists are interesting, one reminds us of the nineteenth century with its coloured bottles in the window and its concentration on prescriptions, drugs and other chemist-shop goods. The other is much more familiar to those who come from larger towns. It is much bigger and is more like a department store than a chemist's shop, with a very wide range of goods – most of them found by self-service.

Woolworths is immediately recognisable a long time before we can see its name because of the familiar shop front. It is small but the layout inside is the one common to all branches and space is very carefully used. Today it is very difficult to get through the crowds and we think that perhaps the smaller shops of Mill Street will be easier to buy things in.

Culmford has only one **department store**, and from the outside it looks more like the 'Crazy House' at the fair. This is because it has been gradually built up by buying shops next door as they became vacant and simply linking them together as one. An interesting jumble of levels and stairs is evident inside and on a less busy day this must be quite an attraction, persuading people to look all round the store. It sells all the usual things in separate departments and in fact two departments, carpets and glass and crockery, are in two further shops in Church Street.

The way the store operates is not at all old-fashioned. Like most department stores it is aimed at people who have a long time to shop and don't have to buy the cheapest goods. It has a wide range of services and attractions and through its coffee shop is a common meeting place. Much of its business relies on **credit purchases** and customers may use all the leading credit cards as well as one which the store has provided for use in its shop alone. The sales staff do not try to push sales but they do watch keenly and are expert in realising exactly the right moment to offer their help. Overhead and watching for those who prefer not to pay for the things they take home is a closed-circuit television camera.

Our overall impression of the High Street is that a lot of well-known stores are missing and that all these small shops would not be able to afford to do business in the high street of a large town or city. There are even some homes and some personal service businesses in the street. Nevertheless the shops are doing the same sort of business and satisfying the same sorts of need as would be the case elsewhere. This is not the case in Mill Street into which we turn next.

Mill Street

Streets with names like this can always trace their origins to a mill of some kind and this is true in Culmford where the mill is still a working part of the street, although its activities are now carefully screened off from the street and all the traffic for the mill goes via a side street. The main product of the mill is animal feedstuffs and it is the only processing activity in the centre of the town entirely different from the rest of the activity of the street.

Until very recently Mill Street was nearly all small cottages and now most of them have been turned into small shops. This has proved very attractive but it is unlikely that anyone wishing to pull the cottages down to build modern buildings would have been given **planning permission** by the local council. It is in this street that we discover the meaning of the word **entrepreneur**, for most of the shops are **sole traders** and have adopted an amazing combination of activities to make a living.

The corner shop is an OXFAM shop receiving and selling things which people do not want to keep, and sending the proceeds to head office for charitable purposes. The shop reminds us that the way the economic system works does not provide equally for everyone and that many are in need. It also reminds us how much of the economic activity in our lives is done without payment. On this market day there will be several activities for charitable causes and a flag day because today is the one which sees people pouring into the town from all the villages. The second shop is more familiar and one of three in the town selling fish and chips. There isn't really enough business in the town for three shops doing this and each of them finds different ways to stay in business. This one sells fresh produce for a local farmer and also acts as a notice-board for all the small businesses and leisure activities of the town. One of the others has a large shopfront and also opens as a fishmonger.

Further down the street is a small delicatessen which has been there for several years, but the owner recognised the changes in taste which were happening and has changed the main direction of the business to the supplying of health foods. She has added facilities to cook food and now offers a range of ready-cooked take-away health foods. It took her some time to make this change because there are strict regulations about cooking food which had to be kept and her kitchens are regularly inspected to ensure that standards are maintained. The owner likes to create and build up new businesses and the town already has a motel and a hotel and restaurant which she began, developed until they were profitable, and then sold to somebody else. She has an instinct for the kinds of new business which are needed in the town and a preference for doing new things all the time.

Four small businesses follow specialising in bakery, fashion dresses, photography and confectionery and all adding to that speciality because, on its own, it is not enough. Over the dress shop there is a small Indian restaurant run by the family and making good use of surplus space. In the back of the bread shop there is a small coffee shop, very busy most mornings and all day today. The photographer gives over half his space and business time to an interior decorating business. He gives advice and accepts some commissions for people's homes. The two women who own the business next door also run a taxi service. They do it as an agency. The drivers own their own cabs and the women run the switchboard with a radio link to the cabs. The business is very much in demand and perhaps they should think of themselves now as a taxi service which also sells sweets and chocolates.

Small businesses find it difficult to compete in the main lines of activity but are often successful if they specialise, particularly if they can do it in a field in which they are experts or enthusiasts. Mill Street has two shops which are examples of that. One of them is a hobby shop owned by a model railway enthusiast who gets business from all over the country. The other is a motorcycle shop with a workshop at the rear. The owner is a former speedway rider.

Mill Street can teach us a lot about how businesses begin and why they survive. It is not a street which is ever crowded with shoppers or in which the shops themselves are ever full. It is one in which buyers take their time and browse, it is one in which most of the owners are experts in their field and in which advice and service are as important as the goods that are sold. It is above all a street of survivors whose business skills and instincts are very important.

Church Street

A quiet street in which there is a lot of business activity but very little evidence of it. There are probably more businesses here than in any other street but even a very careful look will miss some of them.

The street is dominated by the parish church, one of about twelve churches in the town. Even churches have things in common with businesses. They have an organisation which keeps them going, much of it on a voluntary basis, and a marketing task to do in getting people to church, spreading their beliefs and raising money which they either use for their own needs or give to a charity. It is a weekday and there is no evidence of activity in the church although the vicar will have two weddings and a funeral later today. Across the road in the church hall members of the congregation are running a bazaar for the church funds.

Most of the businesses in Church Street provide professional services. Next to the church is to be found the offices of the Clerk to the Justices who administers the work of the local magistrates court and collects fines and other payments which people have to make. There are two solicitors offices, two dentists, three accountants, three estate agents, one architect, an insurance broker and an optician all in the space of a few yards. Each of them is a **partnership** and this suggests that partnership is particularly appropriate to these kinds of business. You might like to think why this is so.

At the end of the street is a school. You will be familiar with the way in which a school organises its activities although you may think about that in a different way as you read each of the chapters of this book.

Opposite the school is a public house – one of the oldest in the town and probably linked with the building of the church. Inside there are several reminders of the history of the town and an opportunity to talk with local people over a pleasant and inexpensive lunch. This publican is a tenant. This means that he pays a rent for the pub and makes his living in his own way. Some of the other pubs in the town are managed, being owned by one of the national breweries. The pub shows three of the changes of taste in recent years. It sells real ale; it has taken away the barriers and has one long room instead of several small ones; and wine is now a popular drink.

Next to the pub is another reminder of the way things change even in small towns like this. It is the health centre. Doctors used to work on their own and mostly from their own homes. Now, in Culmford, they work together at the centre with a team of nurses and other staff to help them. All the services they need are there and they can support each other.

The health centre is, of course, supported by the National Health Service and much of the work undertaken there is for patients who pay through their contributions and taxes rather than directly for the services they need. But some of the patients are private, paying for the treatment they receive. This mixture of both ways of doing things is another way in which we say that we live in a **mixed economy**. Some of the goods and services provided by the state and paid for through rates and taxes and some provided and paid for privately.

The market place

A noisy and busy place. We have arrived here quite late. Business always slackens in the afternoon and much of the best fruit, vegetables, and other things for sale have gone. The bargain hunters are beginning to come into the square because stallholders want to get rid of their perishable foods before they go home and so they drop the price of the things they have left. Most of the stallholders are regulars who stand in the same places each week and have a loyal following, a few are casuals who have something to sell this week and have paid for a pitch for the day.

The centre is usually a car park on other days of the week, but there is room for nothing but people today.

Around the square are some of the most important business outlets of the town. It is here that we have further evidence of our mixed economy because the shops of the electricity board and the gas board are side by side. Just down from them is the local water authority. The post office is here too and so are a row of telephone boxes, one of them modernised by British Telecom so that it takes phone cards rather than cash, and one vandalised so that it does nothing at all. Some of these businesses remind us that the state sells off the business activities it runs from time to time in a process called **privatisation**. British Telecom has been privatised and British Gas and you may well live in a town in which the local authority has invited private businesses to do jobs they used to employ their own staff to do. Examples are collecting refuse and providing the meals in schools and hospitals.

Not surprisingly, there are two small cafes and a pub in the market square. The pub is an example of the way in which the law makes provision to meet the needs of special occasions. It is now the middle of the afternoon but, because it is market day, the pub is still open. The frozen food shop reminds us that convenience foods are much more important then they used to be. People often buy food in large quantities from this and other shops in the town and store it in freezers at home. The shop owners encourage this by offering discounts for large orders. Once more, in this shop you can see the entrepreneur at work because the owners have realised that microwave ovens are a convenience which more and more consumers wish to have, so they sell them together with all the special dishes which go in them and a range of books which tell you how to use them.

The shop next door was empty last week but today it has opened up again meeting a new need for video equipment and video tapes. The main business is in hiring out tapes for a day or two rather than in selling them. The square also has a computer shop selling some hardware and a range of games and other software. To the casual observer its main function seems to be as a sort of entertainment hall in which several young people are playing with the models on display.

In the far corner of the square are two clear reminders that one of the duties of the state, which both provides employment and uses tax payers' money, is the maintenance of law and order. Side by side are the magistrates court and the police station. The police station is a regional one which means that the police working from it have duties which take them well beyond the town.

The industrial estate

The local council, in order to attract more businesses to the town, set aside land for an industrial estate during the 1960s. The largest employers in Culmford are now to be found on this estate, which is over the railway bridge to the north of town. A firm making petfoods has a mainly unskilled workforce of about 350, producing tinned dog and cat food which it sells through major supermarkets. It is part of a **public limited company**, one with many shareholders, which has several production plants in the country. Although sales of petfood have been steady recently, the company has reduced its workforce from 600 over the last three years by increasing its use of labour-saving machinery and installing a production line.

Electroware Ltd, another business on the estate, has 300 skilled and semi-skilled workers making electrical components for telephones. It has been running a **Youth Training Scheme**, giving training to twenty school-leavers who have a chance of being taken on by the company at the end of their course. Electroware is a private limited company, owned largely by two friends who went to school together in Culmford. The third large employer in the estate is Bailey Textiles Ltd, an expanding business which makes ties and belts for Littlewoods.

Culmford is a market town at the centre of a large and fertile dairy and arable farming area. Two businesses on the estate are closely linked to this industry: a seed merchant which also has a large mail-order business with amateur gardeners; and a company which rents out or leases agricultural machinery to local farmers. Most of the farms surrounding Culmford are family businesses with ownership going back several generations. But an increasing number are now owned by large companies based in London, with the farm looked after by a manager. Like any private business, farms aim to be profit-making. If you visit the area in May you will see a lot bright yellow fields as many of the farmers now grow oil seed rape, attracted by the price that they can sell the crop for inside the Common Market. It is interesting to note that the prices which Culmford farmers get for their produce are decided in Europe as a whole rather than locally.

Several small firms, some of them one-person businesses, are also to be found on the industrial estate. The town's only printer, who will do any job, however large or small, from posters for a local election to the invitations for an eighteenth birthday party, has a small workshop, and next door there is a picture-framing business. These are further examples of entrepreneurship in Culmford. A cash-and-carry warehouse occupies another of the units, and a furniture removal firm set up by a brother and sister uses the estate for their office and overnight storage.

New shopping area

Two years ago Sainsbury's opened a very large supermarket, with plenty of free parking, on a site next to the industrial estate. This has attracted many people from the town who drive out to do their weekly shopping, and has certainly taken business away from the shops in the High Street. More recently a large do-it-yourself discount store has opened close by, which has again proved popular. Both shops are very large, self-service outlets where customers are faced by a wide range of goods, many on special offer. The shops are also backed by a national advertising campaign run by their companies. They both open from 8.00 a.m. to 8.00 p.m. Monday to Saturday, in contrast to the shops in Culmford, and the DIY store also opens on Sunday. The local chamber of trade, which represents the town's shopkeepers, has complained to the local council about these developments, but further out-of-town shops are planned and it is rumoured that McDonald's might open a fast-food restaurant there.

Leisure and recreation

The leisure industry is a growing one for Culmford as people have more time and money to spend on recreation. A new leisure centre, which offers swimming, aerobics, weight training, badminton and squash has been built and financed by the local council and can be used by the whole community. It is located next to existing football, cricket and tennis clubs. These are financed by the subscriptions of the clubs' membership and usually have the objective of making a small **surplus** each year. Nearby parkland offers visitors the chance to go walking and horse-riding, while a small lake provides for fishing, sailing and windsurfing. Culmford is a good centre for touring the local countryside, and many businesses in the town are benefiting from an increased number of visitors. The local library now contains an information centre, with maps and guides readily available. Only the prison, a castle-like building on the west of the town, stays out of the promotion for the area!

The trip round Culmford has taken the best part of a day and public transport from the town finishes early with the last train to the mainline station at 5.00 p.m. The trip has introduced most kinds of business and most kinds of activity. We have learnt something of both the businesses which make their living in the town and the consumers they must serve if a profit is to be made. Some businesses are small, some are large. Some are run by private individuals and others by the state. All have problems of management and organisation, all employ people, all have to live and work in the knowledge that the interests of other people and other organisations are important.

In Chapters 2, 3, and 4 we look at the way the economy works and the different ways in which businesses may be structured to operate within it. In Chapters 5 and 6 financial aspects of businesses behaviour are discussed and we look at organisation and management in Chapters 7 and 8. Chapters 9 and 10 are about the people who work in businesses, and Chapters 11 and 12 about the two major activities of marketing and production. At the end of the book we come back where we started and look at the way that businesses have to respond to the needs of others and can be helped by others. Throughout it all you will be able to relate what is said to your own community – look for the things that are the same but also look for the differences and try to discover why these differences exist and what they tell you about business behaviour.

THINGS TO DO

1 Some of the words and phrases used in this chapter will be unfamiliar to you and will occur again in the chapters which follow. Find out what some of them mean and look for examples in your own community.

2 Working as a group, go out into your town or to one near you. Each of you take a street in the same way that we have in this chapter, and see what you can discover about the businesses in it.
Write a report about your chosen street along the lines of those in this chapter.

3 As a result of your investigations, can you think of any business activity which seems to be lacking or insufficient in your town?
Explain why and work at a way in which this might be put right.

4 Did you discover any businesses of which there seemed to be rather a lot in the town?
What is the explanation for this?

5 What can you learn about the nature of your community, and about the needs and wishes of the people in it, from your survey?

Chapter 2
Organising the economy

2.1 The purpose of business activity

We are wanting beings and the purpose of economic activity is to provide us with the things we want. Such wants will vary from person to person, each of us seeking different things at different times. Those who are very poor will want the basic necessities – food, drink and shelter. Luckier people who never need to worry about their basic needs will want luxuries such as cars, television sets or things to do in their leisure time. We are seeking the satisfaction of our needs all the time.

Think about all the things you would like to have and then about your **resources**. Unless you are either very undemanding or have unlimited resources you will discover the problem all of us have to face – the uses for our limited resources are far greater than we can imagine. A **choice** must be made; some wants can be satisfied, but others cannot. Such a choice always means that something we would have liked must be given up for something which, at the moment, we think is more important. One way of looking at this choice is to say that the cost of the want we decided to satisfy is the one that has to be neglected. Economists call this kind of cost **opportunity cost** and it is the central theme of economics.

Figure 2.1a Business activity

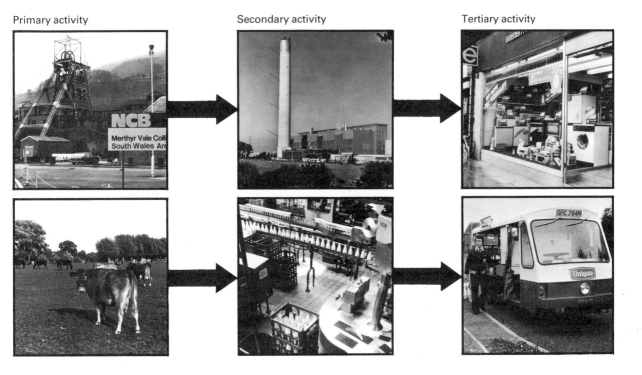

Primary activity   Secondary activity   Tertiary activity

> *a* You have limited pocket money to spend in a week. A choice to spend your money on a new LP may mean that you cannot go to the cinema.
>
> *b* Suppose a manager wants to open a new branch of a retailing business in your town. He asks questions, looks around, and then comes down to three possible sites. He seeks a lot more information about these. You might like to consider the kind of information he would need and where he is likely to get it. Finally, he makes a choice: Site A is better than Site B which is better than Site C. The opportunity cost of selecting A is the next best alternative rejected, Site B.
>
> *c* A county council is setting its budget for the coming year. The transport department would like to spend £800,000 on a new ring road, whilst the education department would like to spend the same amount on two new primary schools. Choosing one will mean that the other one will be cancelled. How do you think such a decision would be made?

Figure 2.1b Examples of opportunity cost

2.2 Free and economic goods

We have to work to survive. Some things we can get freely and easily such as the air we breathe, the wild fruits in the hedgerows or a beach at the seaside. These are called **free goods**. Other goods are not so abundant that everyone can have as much as they want; they are scarce and this gives them **value**. Such goods are called **economic goods**.

> *a* In most country areas in September blackberries are free as long as we are prepared to go and pick them. But if we want them picked and available in our local greengrocers, or if we want them in July, we have to pay for them and so they become economic goods.
>
> *b* Sunshine is free, but when everyone wants to go to the same beach on the same day then usually there are charges for parking, for deck chairs and even sometimes for swimming. The seaside has become an economic good.

Figure 2.2 Free and economic goods

2.3 A country's resources – the factors of production

The resources of a country are available to help satisfy the needs of its residents, but these resources are limited and so some of the wants will remain unsatisfied. The resources we have available are:

Land
At its simplest the ground we stand on and all that grows on it, but we must also include resources in the sea, in the air and under the ground.

Labour
We have ourselves; the skills we were born with and those that we have learnt; the strength of our bodies and the dexterity of our hands; our intelligence and our memory.

Capital

This is a manufactured resource. Using our skills we make things which make jobs easier – tools, machines, computers. We set some of our resources aside to provide goods for the future. All capital comes from the effort, time and skill we apply to the natural resources we have.

Enterprise

Among the skills we develop are making judgements and taking risks; managing and using resources towards a set purpose. The person exercising these skills is called an **entrepreneur.**

> John James Sainsbury, the great-grandfather of the company's current chairman, was a man with a passion for order and detail. When he set up as a dairyman in 1869 he brought to the business his own ideas of how a food retailer should operate. He believed that high quality would go with low prices so that however poor the housewife she could still have the choice of buying the best quality available. He also believed that cleanliness and freshness were what people wanted if only they had the chance of getting them. Sainsbury's today are still aiming for low prices and cleanliness; the current board still personally taste every new product and the stores are open and airy. When he died, John James Sainsbury's last words were 'Keep the shops well lit'.
>
> Adapted from *The Wining Streak* by Walter Goldsmith and David Clutterbuck

Figure 2.3 Entrepreneurship at Sainsbury's

2.4 Satisfying our wants

The things we do to satisfy our wants are called **production** and the process of actually satisfying them is known as **consumption**. The goods which we consume are called **consumer goods** and may be either single use or durable, i.e. they are used only once or are used and last for a long time. The goods which allow us to produce are known as **producer goods** and again there are two kinds; they are either used up in the process of production or they are more permanent and are used to keep on producing in the future. These are known as **investment** or **capital** goods.

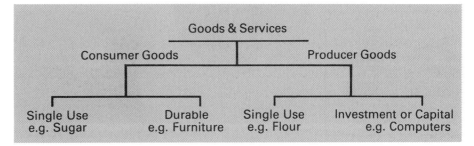

Figure 2.4

If we try to classify all the goods we use in this way some will be difficult. For example, a desk bought for someone's work at home is a consumer durable good, but a desk bought for a school or office is a capital good. How do we deal with public transport? Although buses run all the time, each time we use them is an individual trip which can't be repeated, and so public transport is a single-use good. The sugar or milk which we put in our coffee is a consumer good, but used by a baker to make bread or cakes it becomes a producer good.

2.5 Production

Production is possible through the contribution of land, labour and capital. These three kinds of resource are called the **factors of production**. Throughout the world these resources are used in different ways and quantities to satisfy needs. Farming in the United States, where land is plentiful, spreads widely across the prairies, while in the Netherlands, where land is scarce, it is very concentrated in small, but very productive, dairy farms. Textiles are made in India by many individuals working at home because labour is so plentiful, while in Yorkshire and Lancashire fewer are employed as the textile mills become more mechanised. By attracting large amounts of capital countries like Singapore and Taiwan have been able to compete successfully against countries with many more natural or human resources.

2.6 Specialisation

In a very small business each person has to do many different things, some which they are good at but some which they would rather leave to someone else. In a larger business the chance to get on with the things they can do well and leave the rest to others is much greater, and so each person makes a better contribution to the running of the business. This use of the factors of production is called **specialisation**.

Figure 2.6 Specialisation in a business

We can see many examples of specialisation all round us and everybody specialises in some way. Many jobs can be broken down into a series of quite small steps. This is particularly true of manufacturing jobs, especially those involved in producing cars and electrical goods. This extension of specialisation is called **division of labour** and you should be able to see many examples of it in any factory or workshop you visit.

2.7 Distribution

If we were living in a very simple (**subsistence**) economy in which each person or family did everything for themselves we should spend all of our time doing those things necessary to satisfy our own wants. However, economies like the UK are very specialised so that we all rely on others to produce the goods and services which will satisfy our wants, expecting to **exchange** the results of our efforts for the things we need. Because it would not be possible to buy all of our wants directly from the producer we have developed a varied and international system of **distribution** from producer to consumer to make sure that goods and services appear at times and in places where the consumer needs them. Some of the economy's resources are therefore used to support rather than add to production. The most important of these **commercial services** are shown in *Fig 2.7*. The more an economy develops, the more important these services become.

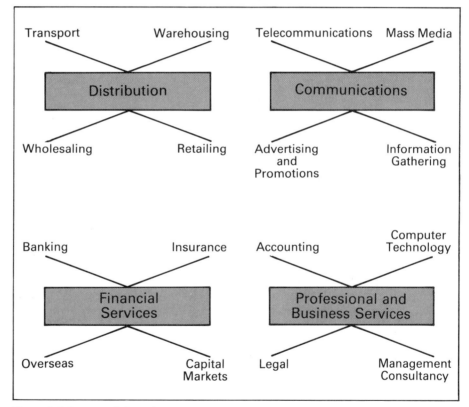

Figure 2.7 Commercial services

2.8 Exchange

If we exchange or **trade** the results of our efforts for the things we need we have to attach a **value** to both the things we have and the goods we wish to obtain. How many loaves of bread would a baker have to give for a meat supply from the butcher for a month; a holiday abroad; the services of a doctor? In our economy we use money as a **measure of value** so that the baker will be able to find out the value (or **price**) of his bread and compare it with the price of meat or the holiday. We also use money as a **means of exchange** so that by selling his bread for money the baker can use that money to buy meat or to buy a holiday for himself. But the services of a doctor are usually provided free by the state and this shows that there are different ways of organising trade in an economy. We will consider these ways in the next sections.

2.9 The general structure of the economy

Our basic needs are for food, drink and shelter. The nature and extent of these needs vary from one part of the world to another and so does the ability to satisfy them. However, the general structure of activity which takes us from natural resources to final consumption is the same in all economies. There are three stages:

Primary
Extracting the natural resources so that they can be used. Good examples of this type of activity are agriculture, fishing, forestry, and mining. With careful production some of the resources we extract are **renewable**, e.g. food crops or animal products. Others are **non-renewable**, e.g. coal or oil where the deposits are limited. But we can lose our renewable resources by soil erosion, by over-fishing or by not replanting the forests.

Secondary
Most primary goods need some further work on them before they can be consumed. Milk has to be pasteurised and bottled, or turned into cheese or butter. Oil has to be refined and processed to become petrol. Iron ore is converted into steel which in turn is used to **manufacture** motor cars or washing machines. Other secondary production uses resources to make manufacture possible, e.g. in the construction industry or in making investment goods.

Tertiary
Surrounding and helping both primary and secondary activity are the commercial **services** we considered earlier. There are also a number of activities provided directly for the consumer, e.g. transport, retailing, entertainment, and **public services** provided by the state on behalf of everyone, e.g. defence, law and order, health care, and the supply of electricity and water.

2.10 The market economy

The market economy allows resources to be organised by the wishes of consumers. Money plays an important part in showing what these wishes are. If we think of each pound coin as a vote, then each consumer has a number of votes which can be spent on those goods and services most wanted. The goods and services with the most votes will be produced. The factors of production are owned by private individuals who will organise them to produce those goods most wanted.

It is at the **market** that the activity of exchanging the goods produced for other goods or for money will take place. You will be used to the idea of a market as a place in a town for buying and selling or as a shop where the goods of many producers are brought together for the consumer to choose from. But markets can also exist over the telephone or by post where buyers and sellers never meet. It is the activity of exchanging goods or services which makes a market and not the place where it happens.

Figure 2.10 A range of markets

Many buyers One seller

Buyers and sellers bargain face-to-face

No bargaining – retailers selling many goods on behalf of producer

No visible product Services cannot be stored

Transactions only exist on paper

Buying and selling over telephone No face-to-face contact

2.11 The price system in action

In all the markets shown in *Fig 2.10* it is the **price system** which brings the buyer and the seller together. To show how this system works let us look at two very similar goods – tinned strawberries and frozen strawberries.

Suppose a report by a group of doctors says that frozen strawberries are good for your health. Consumers will buy more frozen strawberries and fewer tinned ones. Shopkeepers will order more frozen strawberries from their suppliers, and less of the tinned ones. But suppliers will find that their stocks of frozen strawberries are falling low, and they know that they cannot replace them until next season. What will they do? And what will they do about the tinned strawberries that are now piling up in their warehouses?

The answer is that they will increase the price of frozen strawberries and these higher prices will be passed on to the consumers. And they will lower the price of tinned strawberries to try to reduce their stocks. The effect of these price changes may be to slow down the increase in **demand** for frozen strawberries and make consumers think about buying the reduced-price tinned ones.

If we continue this story into the next year, strawberry growers will find that firms freezing strawberries are offering higher prices than those tinning them and they will **supply** them first. More frozen strawberries will now be available in the shops and the price will fall. On the other hand tinned strawberries will now be less common and their price will start to rise again. *Figure 2.11* shows step by step how this market for frozen strawberries was disturbed and how the price system moved it back to a more stable position.

What happens	Demand	Price (per lb)	Supply
Start	0000000000	£1.00	0000000000
1 Report 'strawberries are good for you'.	0000000000 0000000000	£1.00	0000000000
2 Suppliers must raise price so some of the demand goes.	0000000000 00	£1.50	0000000000
3 Suppliers bring in more strawberries in new season.	0000000000 00	£1.50	0000000000 00000
4 With more available prices will fall and some of the demand will return.	0000000000 00000	£1.25	0000000000 00000

Figure 2.11 The market for frozen strawberries

2.12 Market forces

We can produce a model showing how a market works. This model takes the form of a graph with the price of the good on the vertical (y) axis and the quantity of the good on the market on the horizontal (x) axis. This outline is shown in *Fig 2.12a*. On this graph we have to show the customers' demand for the producers' supply of the good.

In general, if the price of a good was to fall, then consumers will buy more of it, and if the price was to rise then consumers will buy less of it.

We can show this on the model by drawing a **demand curve** which normally slopes downwards and to the right. *Figure 2.12b* shows this. On the other hand retailers will be keener to sell if prices are high, and less willing if prices are low. We can show this on the model by drawing a **supply curve** which will rise up from left to right. *Figure 2.12c* shows this.

When these two curves are drawn on the same graph we will get a model of the market for a particular good. This is shown in *Fig 2.12d*. The price (p) and quantity (q) at which sellers will have available exactly the amount that buyers want to buy is called **equilibrium** and is the ideal position for the market. If the price was higher than that then suppliers would be willing to sell, but consumers less willing to buy, so there is a **glut** of the good on the market. Prices will then fall to get rid of the glut. If the price was lower than the equilibrium, customers would want to buy, but there would not be enough

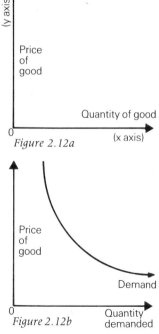

Figure 2.12a

Figure 2.12b

goods on the market, and the result would be a **shortage**. Prices will rise to encourage producers to reduce the shortage. Market forces will gradually move buyers and sellers towards equilibrium.

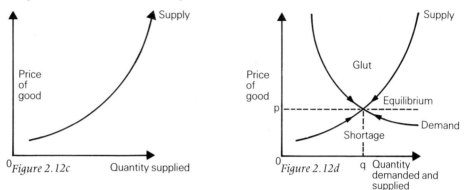

Figure 2.12c   Quantity supplied

Figure 2.12d   q Quantity demanded and supplied

2.13 Market forces at work

These forces can be seen at work every day in any market place. A stallholder selling fruit and vegetables will lower prices towards the end of the day to get rid of all the stock by closing time. Supermarkets make sure they have a plentiful supply of Christmas turkeys and puddings to stop any shortages on their shelves in December. Travel firms often cut the price of package holidays which have not proved popular enough. On the Stock Exchange the movement of share prices is based on how many people are buying and how many people are selling a particular share. And at an auction in the beginning there are usually several people wanting to buy a picture, but as the price rises people will pull out until only one is left – so demand is matched to supply.

In a market economy therefore, price shows the wishes of consumers. If demand for a good or service starts to increase, prices will follow and suppliers will devote more resources to producing that good or service. If demand falls, and prices fall, suppliers will devote fewer resources to that good. The price system decides how the economy's resources are allocated.

2.14 The planned economy

In some countries it is considered that it is best to exercise state control over economic activity. In a **planned economy** the state owns most of the natural and manufactured resources of the country. Most of the workers are employed by the state, and consumers buy goods in state-owned shops at prices decided by the state. Decisions about what to produce and how to sell the goods are made by the government on behalf of the people. It makes it possible to make decisions quickly and to be sure that these decisions will be carried through. If the government decides that more cars should be produced but fewer motor-cycles then it can make sure that resources are moved from the motorcycle industry to the car industry.

The fact that a government can do these things does not mean that they are easy to do. Many people will be involved in collecting and studying information about what the country has and what it needs, and in making and carrying out the decisions. Think of a basic producer good like steel. *Figure 2.14a* looks at some of the information needed in making a decision about steel production.

Demand information	Supply information
– who needs steel?	– how much can be made?
– in what form?	– what types of steel?
– where?	– where are the factories located?
– when do they want it?	– what raw materials do we produce?
– in what quantities?	– what raw materials should be
– what transport is there?	imported?
– how important are delivery	– how quickly can output be changed?
dates?	– what are the opportunity costs of such
	change?
	– what transport is available?

Figure 2.14a Information needed by the steel maker

Decisions of this type will also affect what is likely to be produced and needed for several years ahead. Often planned economies produce a five-year plan to cover this, although economic conditions can easily change to disrupt this plan. Once decisions are made people also have to make sure that things are going according to plan. Targets for steel output, for example, would be set. But how does the state encourage the workers to meet these targets?

Money is used as a measure of value and a means of exchange, but prices and wages are fixed by the state. They are not changed by market forces. If consumers want more shoes they can get them only if the state decides to produce more within their plan and there is likely to be a delay before this can happen. And so there will be a shortage of shoes. If factory managers want to hire more workers they can do so only if the state allocates them more workers. They cannot use the offer of higher wages to attract them. In both cases, in a market economy the price system would operate to meet these demands.

There are examples of the problems faced by a planned economy in the UK. The number of tickets for the FA cup final or for the Wimbledon centre court are fixed, and people who wish to buy them have to queue and hope to be lucky. Each buyer will be **rationed** to a certain number of tickets and a **black market** may arise where people are willing to buy their tickets at a very much higher price than the original admission price.

Figure 2.14b Cup Final and Wimbledon tickets

2.15

We have, then, two different types of economy; the planned economy with decisions about how resources are used taken by the state, and the market economy where the price system is used to decide how resources are allocated. There is no complete example of either in the modern world and every country has its own mixture of planning and free-market decisions. Some, like the USSR and Eastern Europe, are largely planned and some, like the USA, are largely market economies. The majority like the UK, France and West Germany, have significant elements of both and can be described as **mixed economies**.

THINGS TO DO

Short answer questions

1 Why is business activity needed?

2 You are given £5.00 for your birthday. Write down three items which you could buy with this money and explain which one you would choose to buy.

3 What is the opportunity cost of this choice you made in Question 2?

4 Give three examples of free goods which you have consumed in the last week, and three examples of economic goods.

5 What do you understand by the term 'a country's resources'?

6 Consider the list of items below and decide whether they would be examples of land, labour, capital or enterprise in a country:
   a the skills of an engineer
   b a microcomputer
   c a harvest of wheat
   d a factory unit
   e a coal seam
   f a railway line
   g the owners of a football club
   h spanners and hammers in a workshop
   i students at school or college
   j a shopping centre.

7 How do consumer goods differ from producer goods?

8 Consumer goods might be either single use or durable. Find five examples of each which you might use at home.

9 Why do you think the division of labour is greater in a large business than in a small one?

10 Give two examples from your local area to show the difference between production and exchange.

11 Which type of commercial service are the following companies involved in?
   a Marks & Spencer   *d* Sinclair Research
   b National Westminster   *e* British Telecom
   c Saatchi & Saatchi   *f* British Rail

12 In our economy, what is money used for?

13 Match the terms on the left with the type of business activity described on the right:
Primary   – the manufacture of goods and services from natural resources
Secondary – services provided to support production
Tertiary   – the extraction of natural resources.

14 Give examples of six different kinds of market that you can find in your local area.

15 Why do we say that market economies are run by the wishes of consumers?

16 Explain what is meant by demand, and draw a diagram to show how demand may change when the price of a good changes.

17 Explain what is meant by supply and draw a diagram to show how supply may change when the price of a good changes.

18 Who owns the factors of production.
a in a market economy?
b in a planned economy?

19 Who makes decisions about what to produce in a planned economy?

20 During World War II the UK had virtually a planned economy. How was it decided what consumers were able to buy?

21 If tickets for the Wimbledon centre court were available on an open market how would you expect their price to be affected?

22 USA and USSR both face the same economic problems. What are they?

SECTION B   **Essays and structured questions**

1 Look at the photographs in *Fig 2.1a*. Explain the different types of business activity which each picture is illustrating.

2 *a* What are the four factors of production?
b Describe how an industry in your local area uses the factors of production to help produce a good or service.

3 *a* What is meant by the division of labour?
b By looking at *Fig 2.6* explain how the activities of a business can be divided up.
c What are the advantages and disadvantages for a business of the division of labour?

4 'It is not easy to decide whether a good or service can be called a consumer good or a producer good.' Why is this so? Use plenty of examples to illustrate your answer.

5 *a* What is the major function of the price system in a market economy?
  b In recent years there has been a trend by consumers away from buying white bread towards wholemeal bread. Outline the way the price system will operate to help the market respond to this change.

6

Some main sectors of UK economic activity

	A % share of output (1983)	B Change in output per year % (1975–84)
Agriculture, forestry, fishing	2.1	+2.5
Energy and water supply	11.4	+7.7
Manufacturing	24.0	−1.2
Construction	5.9	−0.7
Distribution, hotels, and catering	13.5	+0.4
Transport	4.4	
Communications	2.7	+1.3
Financial services	12.0	
Education and health	9.2	
Public administration	6.9	+2.5
Other services	7.9	
Total:	100	+1.2

  a On a graph show the percentage share of output in the UK arising from primary, secondary, and tertiary production.
  b What does your graph show you?
  c Column B shows the average change in output per year between 1975 and 1984. Which of the three sectors have been growing larger, and which of the three have been declining?
  d Why does energy and water supply show such a large average increase?
  e Why do you think service industries are becoming more important in our economy?

7 *Figure 2.14a* shows some of the information that would be needed by a government of a planned economy making decisions about steel production. Make out a similar list of demand and supply information in order to make decisions about:
  a coal production
  b the production of video recorders
  c providing a bus service for a town.

SECTION C　　　　**Coursework and assignments**

1 Survival

Your group has crash landed on an Arctic island with little hope of rescue. Your objective is **survival.**

In order to survive you will need *food, clothing and shelter.* In the Arctic, that means *fish, a poncho and an igloo.* Each member of your group will need one unit of each item if they are to survive.

Here are examples of each (not to scale):

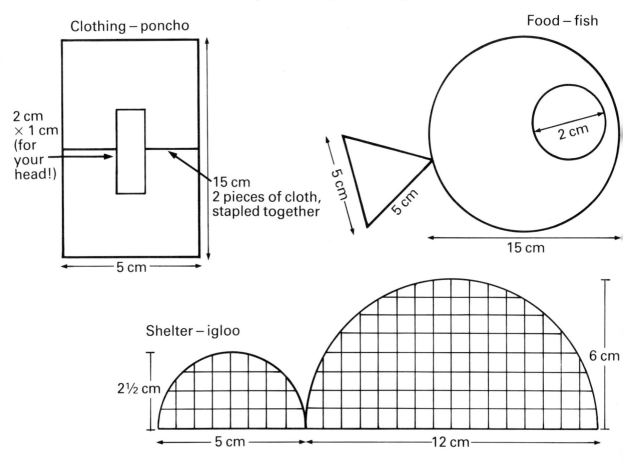

And now *the complications.*

1 Only a very limited amount of equipment and materials survived the crash

2 The Arctic night is fast approaching – and it lasts nine months! So you have only limited time.

Remember – if you fail – you perish!

2 In *Fig 2.1b*, there are three decisions which are outlined. Write down a list of factors which would be important in each decision, and explain how you think a choice would be made in each case.

3 Find out about an entrepreneur who is important in your area or who is well known nationally. See if you can answer these questions:
  a What was the entrepreneur's background?
  b How did the business start?
  c What product or service did the entrepreneur develop?
  d What skills does the entrepreneur show?
  e What problems has the business faced?

4 Choose a product that you are interested in, and find out how that product is distributed from the producer to the consumer. Draw a diagram to show the types of distribution that are used, and explain each stage.

5 *a* Choose a good and carry out a survey in different retail outlets to discover the prices which are being charged. Can you explain the differences you find?
  b Continue this survey over four to six weeks and record any price changes over this period. Present your findings in a graph or table.
  c Try to discover the reason for any change that you notice, and explain whether the price change was due to demand or supply changes.

6 From your local library or local council find out:
  a the pattern of production in terms of primary, secondary, and tertiary stages in your local area
  b the number of people employed in these sectors locally
  c any significant changes which have occurred in the last fifteen years.
Present your findings as a report to a business manager who is thinking of moving to your area.

Chapter 3

Business activity in the private sector

3.1

In the UK economy we have many decisions which are made by private individuals. How much fish to land in Hull; how many cars to produce at Dagenham; what price to charge for a new chocolate bar; what a plumber will charge to mend a leaking pipe; how much a bank manager lends to a customer. The part of the economy in which these and many other decisions are made is the **private sector**. The sector of the economy in which decisions are made by the state or by an organisation which the state has set up is called the **public sector**. Decisions made here will include how much coal to mine in Yorkshire; where a new power station will be built; what price to charge for a train trip from Bristol to London; how much schools can spend on textbooks; what wages to pay to nurses. Because we have decisions made by both private individuals and the state the UK is a **mixed economy**.

3.2 The private sector

Here all factors of production are owned by individuals and companies motivated by monetary reward. We discussed three factors of production in Chapter 2 and a fourth activity called **enterprise** which managed and controlled the others. The activities of the **entrepreneur** can be seen most clearly in a one-person business since that one person must make all the decisions. In doing this he or she takes **risks**, relying on his or her own judgement that consumers will want what the business is producing, at the price being asked and in enough numbers to cover **costs** and provide a living. If the entrepreneur produces the wrong product, sells it in the wrong way or at the wrong price, then he or she will not be in business for long. If the business is successful it will make a **profit** which is the reward for good judgement and successful risk taking. In the private sector the role of profit is very important as it persuades people to take risks. Good profits are a signal of success and poor profits are a signal of failure.

3.3 The business

The word most commonly used to describe a business unit is **firm** although this says nothing about the size or nature of the business. Very large businesses may have many factories all over the world but be only one firm, while small local organisations can also be called a firm. Obviously the way such different firms are controlled and organised must vary and there must be laws to enable firms to be organised in the way which is best suited to their purposes and resources. In fact the law recognises several different kinds of structure and we look first at the simplest of them all, the **sole trader**.

3.4 The sole trader

The oldest and most common of business structures, the term **sole trader** means that decisions are taken by one person even though many may be employed. The finance almost always comes from the personal savings or borrowing of the owner and other private funds. Often many of the staff come from the owner's family working a number of hours per week which few employees would be prepared to do. Even if a sole trader gets some funds from family and friends they do not share in the decisions and risks. The owner is totally responsible and may have to use personal belongings to meet the **debts** of the business in times of difficulty. The owner may chose to give responsibility to some workers for parts of the firm's activities, but in law he or she is still responsible if things go wrong.

Small firms face a number of difficulties which are common to most of them. The most important of these are shown in *Fig 3.4a*.

> **Limited amount of specialisation** The owner may have to be book-keeper, store keeper, manager, assistant, typist, clerk, and salesperson all in one.
> **Slow growth** Few outside sources of finance are available and annual profits are not large. They do not always want to grow, but it is a disadvantage when a good opportunity has to be missed.
> **Unlimited liability** The owner is entirely responsible for the debts of the firm.
> **Little scope for** *economies of scale* Small firms do not attract discounts or free delivery from their suppliers so their **unit costs** are high and it is difficult to compete with larger firms.
> **Lack of continuity** The business is personal to the owner so that it ceases to exist with the owner's death.

Figure 3.4a Problems faced by small businesses

Despite these problems there are a large number of sole traders, particularly in the tertiary sector of the economy, and they outnumber their larger competitors. Most businesses have to start small and there are always some in the early stages of their life, but there are also some advantages which the sole trader enjoys. These are shown in *Fig 3.4b*.

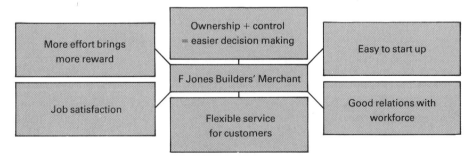

Figure 3.4b The advantages of running your own business

Sole traders are unable to grow to any great size because of the risks involved for the owner, and because extra capital is not easy to find. So **growth** usually means that the firm will have to change its structure by opening its doors to finance from other people.

3.5 The partnership

This is one of the first means of growth which a firm may consider. The attractions of a partnership are shown in *Fig 3.5a*.

Increased *finance* This is probably the major reason.
Increased *business* Particularly when two existing firms come together.
Increased possibility of *division of labour* **and** *economies of scale*
Shared decision making may be welcome.
Increased *security* The risks are shared.
Maintenance of *ownership and control* Partners work together.

Figure 3.5a The advantages of a partnership

These advantages are likely to mean that partnerships are popular in the service industry, especially in personal services such as medicine, the law, and estate agency. Partnerships, however, are not always the best way to grow. The disadvantages of partnerships are shown in *Fig 3.5b*.

Each partner has the right to make decisions on behalf of the firm; although partners should discuss and agree they do not always do so and this can lead to serious problems.
There is still unlimited liability and if one partner cannot bear a share of the risks the others have to cover it.
The job satisfaction of being your own boss is reduced.
Partnerships are unlikely to be very large because only small amounts of capital can be raised and profit will not be great.
There is no continuity since it is ended whenever a partner wishes to leave or dies.

Figure 3.5b The disadvantages of a partnership

Partnership can be informal, but it is wise to agree a **contract** in which the partners can decide their own terms. *Figure 3.5c* shows a typical Contract of Partnership. If a business seeks further funds it can form a **limited partnership** which lets people provide money but without any participation in the business. Ordinary partners with unlimited liability will manage the firm and take the risks. The limited partners simply receive a return on their capital. It is because such partners do nothing in the business that they are often called sleeping partners.

A CONTRACT OF PARTNERSHIP

Partnership agreement of Kew and Baker, Industrial Painters of Warwick Road, Leamington Spa.

Capital   £20,000 is provided by J Kew and 10,000 is provided by M Baker.

Profits   These will be shared two-thirds to J Kew and one-third to M Baker. Each partner will contribute towards any loss in the same proportion.

Management   Both partners have a right to participate in decision making and major decisions must be agreed.

                Both partners have a right to inspect the books which are kept at the business premises.

                Each partner is bound by the decisions on behalf of the partnership that the other may take.

                Partners must act in good faith; they must not conduct themselves in a way damaging to the business.

End of   Will occur on the death of one of the partners or on the
Partnership   agreement of both partners.

Figure 3.5c A contract of partnership

3.6 Registered companies

Sole traders and partnerships make up the majority of businesses, but it is **registered companies** which account for the largest part of economic activity. *Figure 3.6a* shows that in the manufacturing industry small businesses which employ less than 20 workers are very numerous, but it is the large businesses which employ the majority of the workforce.

Figure 3.6a Size of firms in manufacturing in UK (1983)

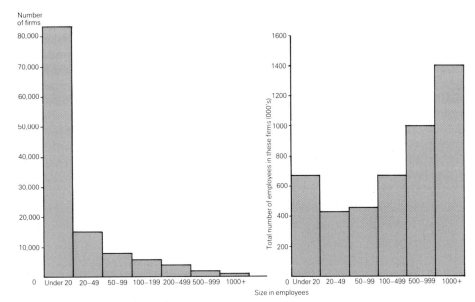

Source: Census of Production Central Statistical Office

These are the three main reasons why a firm may wish to become a registered company. Firstly, it gives the business access to more funds and makes growth possible. Secondly, the firm now exists in its own right and is separate from the people who have formed it. Thirdly, shareholders have **limited liability** which means that if the company fails they will lose only their personal stake in the company. They will not be liable for any other debts.

The state takes a keen interest in the way companies are formed and the way they work, and controls them by a series of Acts of Parliament. *Figure 3.6b* shows how the 1980 Companies Act divides up companies. Approximately half a million companies exist but only about three per cent are public limited companies, although these are the majority of large businesses in Britain, e.g. ICI, Ford, Sainsbury's, Barclays Bank, Marks & Spencer.

> *REGISTERED COMPANIES*
>
> *Public Limited Company (plc)*
> is one which
> *a* is registered in accordance with the Act
> *b* has the required minimum authorised capital
> *c* has a business title ending with the letters 'plc'
> *d* has at least two directors.
>
> *Limited Company*
> is any company which does not meet the conditions for a plc.
> In addition it
> *a* is limited to 50 shareholders
> *b* cannot offer its shares for sale to the general public.

Figure 3.6b Registered companies under the Companies Act (1980)

3.7 Becoming a company

Anyone wishing to form a new company will find that the law lays down clearly what he or she has to do. Most importantly a new company must be registered. Let us suppose that a sole trader making educational toys has decided to 'go public'. What the **registrar** will require is:
a the names and addresses of the founding directors and the company secretary
b the **memorandum of association** of the company. *Figure 3.7* shows the main parts of this document
c the **articles of association** which contain the day-to-day rules of how the company will operate
d a declaration that the requirements of the various Companies Acts have been followed
e a registration fee.

The registrar will check that all is well and then issue a **certificate of incorporation** which means that the company exists. A limited company can now start business, but a plc will first want to offer its shares for sale to the public by issuing a **prospectus**. The registrar will check the way the company issues shares and once he or she is happy that the money has been properly obtained will issue a **certificate to commence business.**

> *a* The name of the company is 'Play-Learn plc'
> *b* The company is to be a public company
> *c* The registered address of the company will be 32 Skittle Street, Nottingham
> *d* The objects for which the company is established are to manufacture and trade in toys and similar items and to carry out other activities needed to support this objective
> *e* The liability of the members is limited
> *f* The share capital of the company is £200,000 divided into 200,000 ordinary shares of £1.

Figure 3.7 The main clauses of the memorandum of association of Play-Learn plc

One of the most important aspects of becoming a company is that the business is now **incorporated**. This means that it has a legal personality, separate from its owners. Suppose you bought a new cassette player which in the first week eats up your favourite Madonna tape. You would like some compensation to make up for the loss, but who do you claim it from? The shop assistant who sold the cassette player? The shop's manager? The workers who assembled the cassette? The directors of the company who made it? Because of incorporation you would be able to sue the company itself because it has a separate legal identity (just as though it were a person). It has a set of rights and duties. This means that it can:

a buy, own, and sell assets in its own name
b make contracts
c be taken to court by customers or suppliers or protect itself against others through court
d be taken over by new owners through transfer of shares
e be liquidated by legal means brought by its owners or creditors.

3.8 Ownership and control of companies

A company is owned by **shareholders**. They will provide **capital** in two ways: by buying shares and by agreeing that profits may be kept and used in the business. A company is controlled by the **board of directors** who are normally shareholders and who are elected at the **annual general meeting** (AGM) of the company. They will sometimes be major shareholders and this will maintain a link between ownership and control. In many companies, however, most of the shareholders will not be involved in the day-to-day running of the business and so there will be a separation of ownership and control. Again the law tries to protect these shareholders' rights. An AGM must be held so that the directors can report to shareholders and can be questioned by them.

Where a major policy issue is being voted upon, each shareholder has one vote per share, and, if he or she cannot attend a meeting, may transfer these votes to other shareholders. The shareholders also have a right to call for additional meetings of the company.

This protection may not be as effective as it sounds for it depends upon the willingness of those who think something is wrong to do something about it, and they often do not. If you belong to any club or society you will know how few people bother to turn up to the AGM. This means that a few active and interested people may control decisions. The AGM of a company is often very small even when there are hundreds of shareholders who could attend. It takes a crisis to persuade more people to come.

Once shareholders have elected directors, it is the directors who are responsible for the overall management of the company. A typical board of directors is shown in *Fig 3.8*. The Board makes policy decisions and sets the aims for the firm. It also ensures that a capable **management team** is appointed to make sure the company achieves these aims.

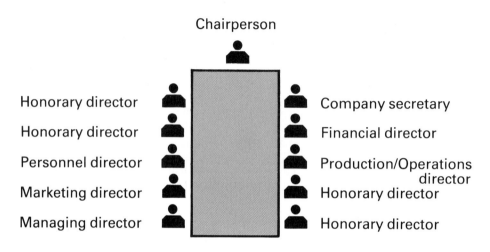

Chairperson

Honorary director

Honorary director

Personnel director

Marketing director

Managing director

Company secretary

Financial director

Production/Operations director

Honorary director

Honorary director

Figure 3.8 A board of directors

3.9 Winding up a company

Since a company is created by law, it is also ended by law. This may happen because;

a   it has no further reason to exist, e.g. a company set up to sell something for a royal wedding will wind up after the event is over
b   its owners accept that there is no real future for it
c   it is in difficulty and its creditors (people to whom it owes money) want it to be wound up.

Most of the cases we hear about are of the last kind, when a company is brought to court by creditors, banks, shareholders or the government. If the court accepts the request the company passes into the hands of the **official receiver** who runs the company in the best interests of the creditors and shareholders until **liquidation** takes place. This normally sees the sale of the assets of the firm, the payment of its debts, and the payment of any money left to the shareholders.

3.10 Co-operative organisation

Most people will know co-operatives as retail shops in the main shopping areas of most large towns. This is an important example of co-operation but by no means the only one. There are examples in production, in marketing, and in research and development.

Joint ventures

These are the simplest kind of co-operation involving two or more businesses but not affecting their organisations. The major examples get into the news, for example the development of Concorde and the European space programme, but there are many more which we become aware of when we see them advertised or use their products.

> *a* Mini-holidays in which British Rail co-operate with major hotel chains to provide a combined travel and accommodation package for the customer
> *b* Two or more farmers get together to buy an expensive piece of equipment like a combine harvester
> *c* Small retailers co-operate to buy goods in larger quantities and enjoy lower prices
> *d* Major construction firms have combined to produce plans for a Channel tunnel in the hope that the government will give the go-ahead.

Figure 3.10 Some examples of co-operation

Arrangements similar to those in *Fig 3.10* allow firms to share the risks of a venture, to share the costs, or to enjoy **economies of scale**.

Employee co-operatives

In these the people who work in the firm also own it. Large-scale ones have not been very successful in Britain, often suffering from a lack of finance as they have to rely on the savings of the workers. But smaller-scale co-operative ventures, where a group of craft workers, for example, join together, are proving more popular, especially as employment in large organisations becomes more difficult to find. Worker co-operatives, as these organisations are often called, offer the chance for employees to become more involved and interested in the day-to-day running of a business.

Retail co-operatives

The shops of the co-operative societies that exist throughout the country offer a range of services which tends to be wider than most retailers and which some claim to be able to meet every consumer need from birth to death. However, they are best known for their supermarkets. A co-operative society is rather like a registered company in that there is a limited liability for the owners, but there is a major difference in that each owner (or member) holds only one share and therefore has only one vote. Not all those who use the shops are members of the society, and in normal situations the ordinary member has very little interest in what is going on and does not attend meetings.

As with worker co-operatives, the retail ones have suffered from a lack of capital to modernise their shops and selling operation, but recently the retail co-operatives have begun to work together to promote a better national image for their shops through advertising and promotion.

3.11 Other friendly societies

Other organisations are registered by the state to give it some measure of control over them, and to give the society limited liability. These include:

a some insurance firms
b some building societies
c some trade unions.

Insurance companies and building societies both work in the interests of their members to provide them with important economic services. Trade unions also work in the interest of their members both at their workplace and in providing a range of services and benefits of help in everyday life.

3.12 Multi-national companies

In recent years, particularly since Britain joined the European Community (Common Market) there has been a substantial growth in the number of international firms operating in this country. A multi-national company will sell its products in a large number of countries and produce them in those which are an important part of its market, or which offer favourable conditions such as cheap labour or plenty of land. In some cases the stages of production will take place in different countries, and this extends the principle of division of labour to a world-wide basis. Some examples of multi-national activities are given in *Fig 3.12*.

a General Motors, an American company, will design a car in the United States, make its engine and transmission in Germany, make its electrical parts in Canada, and assemble the car in Luton.
b In 1984 the one millionth Nissan car was imported to the UK from Japan, making it the top-selling foreign car in Britain. But by 1986 Nissan will be producing cars in Sunderland with the aim of making it their base for selling to the whole of Europe.
c Some of the largest companies have a value of sales greater than the output of countries like Denmark and Holland.
d Multi-nationals control over one-third of total world production, and are especially important in the production of oil, cars, tyres, chemicals, drugs, food and drink, computers, banking, finance, and accounting.

Figure 3.12 Multi-national business activity

The fact that multi-nationals operate in different countries makes the problem of management and control of the firms very complex. Laws and taxes differ between countries and multi-national firms try to make sure that they operate where the laws and taxes are most favourable to them. Although they can make efficient use of limited economic resources some people are worried that governments can no longer control them.

3.13 Summary

We end this look at private sector organisations by summarising the differences between the types of business we find operating in the UK.

Feature	Sole trader	Partnership	Company*	Co-operative
Regulating Acts	None	Partnership Acts	Companies Acts	Friendly Society Acts
Owners (members)	One	Two–twenty	Minimum two – no maximum	Anyone who wishes to join – usually customers
Legal personality	Owner is legally responsible	Partners are legally responsible	Company is a legal person	Friendly society is a legal person
Liability	Unlimited for owner	Unlimited for ordinary partners	Limited to shareholding	Limited
Capital	Provided by owner	Provided by partners as stated in agreement	Provided by share-holders as stated in memorandum. For plc, minimum £50,000	Provided by members, one share per member
Profits	At disposal of owner	Divided as partners agree	Retained in company, or shared among owners as agreed by AGM	At disposal of members. Partly retained. Partly returned to members as dividend in purchases in shops
Management	By owner	By partners	By board of directors elected by share-holders. Board appoints professional managers	Through meetings and professional managers
Life	Limited to life of owner	Ends either by agree-ment or by death	Ends only by legal proceedings (liquidation)	Ends by agreement of members

Figure 3.13 Comparisons

*Multinationals in the UK are usually plc's.

THINGS TO DO

Short answer questions

1 What is meant by the phrase 'a mixed economy'?

2 Which of the following decisions are taken largely by private individuals in the UK economy, and which by the state?
   a how much a driving instructor will charge for lessons
   b what price a new LP will sell for
   c the level of grants for students
   d how many vacuum cleaners will be produced
   e how much money will be spent on painting schools
   f how many postmen or postwomen will be employed
   g where in a high street a new clothes shop will open
   h how much gas will be produced from the North Sea.

3 What role does profit play in a business?

4 State and explain five difficulties which small firms commonly face.

5 Despite the number of supermarkets that exist, many small shops still survive. What benefits are there for the customers using these small shops?

6 In what kinds of activity are partnerships most commonly found and why is this so?

7 What is meant by 'limited liability' and why is it important for the owners of a business?

8 What are the two types of registered company?

9 What do the memorandum of association and articles of association tell a shareholder about a business?

10 On the left is a list of people involved in a company, and on the right is a list of jobs that are carried out. Match the people to the activities:

   the shareholders   responsible for the overall management of the company

   the board of directors   makes day-to-day decisions about running the business

   the management team   owns the company

11 How is a company wound up?

12 Below is a list of co-operative ventures. Say which are examples of joint ventures, which are worker co-operatives, and which retail co-operatives.

a the John Lewis Partnership

b textile workers who have lost their jobs when a cotton mill has closed setting up on their own

c apple producers joining together to promote British apples

d young school leavers forming a co-operative to produce computer games

e a supermarket chain where customers receive a dividend when they shop there

f the building of a European space shuttle.

13 What is a multi-national company?

14 Find out the name of three multi-national companies whose products you buy, and the countries in which they are based.

SECTION B

Essays and structured questions

1 *Figure 3.6a* shows the size of firms in manufacturing in the UK in 1983.

a How is the size of a firm measured in *Fig 3.6a?*

b What type of chart do we call this form of presentation?

c From *Fig 3.6a* how many people does the most common type of firm employ?

d What does *Fig 3.6a* tell you about the number of large firms in the UK in comparison to the number of small firms?

e From *Fig 3.6a* how many people in manufacturing are employed by firms which employ more than 1,000 people?

f What does *Fig 3.6a* tell you about the importance of large firms as employers in the UK in comparison to small firms?

g This information is about the manufacturing industry. Would you expect the service industry to show a different pattern?

2 Have a look at the comparisons shown in *Fig 3.13*, then answer the following questions:

a Which organisations have unlimited liability, and which have limited liability?

b Which organisations are managed directly by the owners?

c Which organisation would you expect to have the most capital?

d In which organisation will the customer have the opportunity to become an owner?

e In which organisations are dividends issued when profits are made?

3 Discuss the advantages and disadvantages for the owner of a business having unlimited liability.

4 When paying a bill by cheque in a supermarket the assistant asks you to write 'plc' after the name of the business.

a What do these initials stand for and what does this tell you about the business?

b How would this business differ from one which is called 'Limited'?

5 A friend has an accident when the bicycle she is riding fails to stop due to faulty brakes. She decides to seek compensation for the injury she received when she ran into a lamp post, and for the two weeks of pay that she lost through missing work. She would like to sue the bicycle makers 'Fast Wheels Ltd.' but she is not sure that she can, for who should she blame? As a Business Studies student, what advice could you give her?

SECTION C   # Coursework and assignments

1   A small business survey:
 a Make a map of your local community, and by walking around the area mark on your map all the small businesses that you spot (shops, garages, farms, small factories, solicitors, etc.).
 b Make a separate list of the businesses, and describe the type of activity they are involved in. Also state, if possible, whether they are sole traders, partnerships, limited companies, plc's or co-operatives.
 c Go and talk to the owners of a small business. Ask them:
    How did the business start?
    How is it organised?
    What are the advantages of being a small business?
    What are the disadvantages of being a small business?
    Why do they think that customers like to deal with a small business?
    How is the business capital raised?
    How much time do the owners put into running the business?
You will be able to think of other interesting questions.
Write up your interview for presentation to the class.

2 Imagine that you are going into partnership with one or more of your classmates. Decide what you might do together, and draw up a partnership agreement (see *Fig 3.5c*) to cover your activities. Discuss any differences that you had in reaching the agreement. Compare your agreement with those that others in the class have reached.

3 Choose a company that is important in your local community, or a nationally known one, and find out from the information they publish:
 a what type of company it is
 b what business activity the company is involved in
 c how the company is controlled
 d what markets the company sells in and the value of its sales
 e the number of its employees and where they work
 f any other information which helps describe the company.
Write up your report for your local newspaper or radio.

4 If there is a retail co-operative society in your area find out:
 a the area over which it operates
 b the range of goods and services it offers
 c how the customers are involved in the co-operative
 d what type of people use the co-operative
 e what problems the co-operative faces
 f how the co-operative organisation differs from that of a public limited company.

Chapter 4
Business activity in the public sector

4.1 The public sector

In the **public sector** factors of production are owned or employed by the state at national or local level. Decisions about which goods or services to produce and how they will be allocated are not made by private individuals but by organisations controlled by the state. There are two different ways in which goods and services are provided by the public sector, and this is illustrated in *Fig 4.1.*

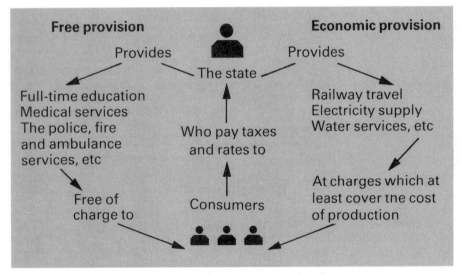

Figure 4.1 How public sector goods and services are produced

In practice this distinction between **free** and **economic** provision is not clear. For example, most people are charged for medicine but some groups of people are not. Children, students, and pensioners can travel cheaply on the railway and buses. People who are unemployed may get their electricity or gas bills partly paid for them by the state.

4.2

What kinds of goods and services are provided by the public sector?

a those which cannot or would not be provided by the private sector. Individuals would not be able to defend themselves well enough and so the state provides an army and a police force. These services can not be withheld from someone just because he or she refuses to pay for them.

b **merit goods** These are things which the state thinks everyone should have, but which if left to a free market would not be provided in the right quantities or at the right price. Education, health, and social services are good examples.

c those which could be provided by the private sector but which have come under the control of public bodies. Examples are water, transport, postal services, coal, electricity, and steel. All of these are provided by public corporations often created by the taking over of private companies, which is known as **nationalisation**.

The best-known elements of the public sector are the large public corporations which supply many of our daily needs like energy and transport. But the sector is wider than this and *Fig 4.2* gives a better idea of its extent.

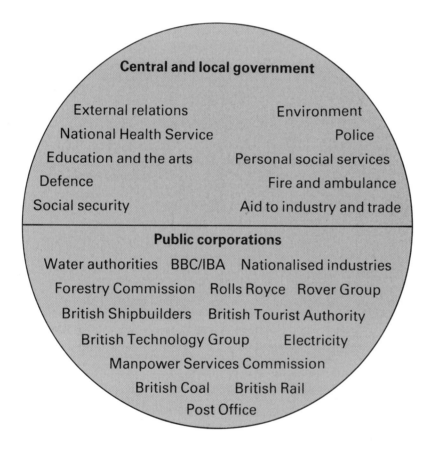

Figure 4.2 The public sector in 1985

The structure and aims of all the organisations in *Fig 4.2* are different, ranging from defence, which is run directly by the state, to firms like British Leyland, which still operate as companies but which receive the financial assistance of the state. To show how the operation of a public sector organisation differs from a free market one we will look at the way nationalised industries are run.

4.3 Nationalised industries

Most of our nationalised industries were brought into public ownership after the war. Industries such as electricity, the railways or coal had been controlled and **planned** by the government during the war and it seemed sensible to continue public control in peace time. *Figure 4.3* shows a comparison between the way these three large industries have been organised by the state, and as you can see the ways they have been structured are not the same.

Electricity	*Railways*	*Coal*
The Electricity Council set up in 1948	British Rail set up in 1948	The National Coal Board set up in 1947 (now British Coal)
In charge of the generation of electricity and its distribution in the national grid	In charge of the transport by rail of passengers and freight	In charge of all the coal fields in Britain
Two levels of organisation; a Central Electricity Generating Board supplying power to several regional selling organisations	Organised into a number of regions which are roughly the same as the old private railway companies	A more centralised form of organisation with a National Board controlling its 200 collieries although these are grouped into areas
Sales Turnover (1981–82) £8,057 m 150,000 employees	Sales Turnover (1981–82) £2,899 m 225,000 employees	Sales Turnover (1981–82) £4,727 m 225,000 employees

Figure 4.3 A comparison of three nationalised industries

However, there are common features in the way nationalised industries are set up and operate:
a An **Act of Parliament** lays down the important rules and gives the state power to run the industry.
b A **minister** is given responsibility for the industry. He or she will lay down the central policy which the managers must follow, and will bring about any changes that are necessary. For example, the Secretary of State for Energy will be responsible for coal and electricity while the Minister of Transport will be responsible for British Rail.
c A **board** similar to the board of directors of a private company will be responsible for carrying out the policies set down by the state and will appoint the top managers. A **chairperson** is also appointed who often appears to the public as the main representative for the industry.
d A **consumer organisation** is set up. This is really a 'watchdog' to make sure that the activities of the industry do not act against the interests of consumers or the general public. For example, the Gas Council will try to make sure that the price of gas does not increase by too much.
e **Politicians and civil servants** are very closely involved in the way these industries run, as the **Treasury** provides the finance for the activities of nationalised industries and **parliament** watches closely over their day-to-day operations.

4.4 Why should some industries be nationalised?

There are a number of good reasons why a government may want to take an industry into public ownership.

a The industry is **essential** both to the consumer and to a large number of other industries and activities.

b To stop the **abuse of monopoly power**. In essential industries it is often wasteful to have more than one firm. For example, it would be costly to have two railway lines between the same town or two firms digging up the roads to lay gas pipes. A **monopoly** where only one firm provides the supply will come about. But a firm in this position could charge higher prices, or produce poor quality goods unless the state takes some control.

c Where **the public interest** would not be met by private enterprise. A private company would find it unprofitable to run a railway service to small villages, or to deliver post to remote houses.

d Where the **financial support of the state** is needed. In industries such as aviation and the railways any purchase of new planes or trains is likely to require some aid from the government and in return the government would want some control over the running of the industry.

e Where the industry is needed for **the economic planning of the state**. The Bank of England is vital for the government's economic policy and an industry like steel is essential to activities such as defence.

f Where there are major economies and advantages to be enjoyed because there is only one operator in the industry. *Figure 4.4* gives some examples.

a The development of North Sea gas fields by British Gas required very large amounts of capital which only a government could supply, and also did not give any return for several years until the gas started to come ashore.

b Inter-city travel by train across the country would have been very difficult if the journey involved using different railway companies.

c London Regional Transport has been able to develop an integrated system of bus and tube travel and has been able to introduce combined tickets for both forms of travel, thus encouraging more passengers to leave their cars behind.

d A national electricity grid, where different parts of the country can swap electricity has been possible because of the existence of only one electricity generating board.

Figure 4.4 The benefits of a nationalised industry

4.5 What are the arguments against nationalisation?

Nationalisation creates a monopoly and there are arguments against this even when the state is running the industry.

a Public operation by one firm **reduces the choice** for the consumer. If coal supplies are cut by the National Coal Board, the customer cannot go elsewhere for coal.

b Nationalisation **interferes with the free market** so that there might not be in these industries the best use of resources. Country bus services have to be **subsidised** by local government, using money which could be spent elsewhere.

c Public enterprises **are usually very large** and may suffer from problems found in any large business, such as slow decision-making, poor industrial relations and too much **bureaucracy**. Also the lack of direct competition may make the organisation inefficient.

d Despite the existence of customer watchdogs the public often find that it is difficult to get complaints dealt with, but at the same time they cannot take their custom elsewhere.

Many of the arguments for and against the public sector are about the kind of society that we want. Do we want to allow the free operation of the market which should lead to the most efficient allocation of resources? Or shall we control the free market in the interests of those who would suffer if the price of a service was too high or if private owners decided to shut down a service?

4.6 The aims of public corporations

Public corporations are concerned with areas of economic activity which are very important to the nation, and their aims will be different from private companies. *Figure 4.6* sets out some of the aims which a public corporation might follow.

a To provide a service for the community in the public interest even where costs are greater than revenue. A railway line is kept in service for social reasons even though it makes heavy losses.

b The industry should **break even** over a period of time. This may mean that losses in one year are made up for by profits in the next, or a loss-making service is kept going by the profits from another service.

c The industry should achieve a target level of profit (or loss) laid down by the government. This might mean that prices have to be raised, or costs, especially wages, reduced. The 1984–85 dispute between the National Coal Board and the National Union of Mineworkers arose because the National Coal Board intended to close down many pits to help it reach its financial targets.

Figure 4.6 Some possible aims for public corporations

Different governments have used different policies towards public corporations, but the Conservative government from 1979 insisted that they should follow the aim *c* in *Fig 4.6* and therefore behave more like private sector companies. With the first two aims, the result will be that the industries will make a loss and have to be **subsidised** by the state out of taxes. With the third aim, the industries should move towards a **surplus** of income over expenditure and this will allow them to finance their own plans for long-term development without having to rely so heavily on money from the state.

4.7 Privatisation

With more nationalised industries showing a profit and behaving like private companies the Conservative government from 1979 sold parts of the public sector to private individuals. This is known as **privatisation**, and the most important decision made in this area was the privatisation of British Telecom in 1984. This was done by selling shares in BT on the stock exchange, which the public were able to buy. *Figure 4.7* shows an example of the advertising the government used to try to persuade the public to buy British Telecom shares.

Privatisation can also be seen at a local level in different ways:

a   selling council houses to private owners

b   allowing private firms to run services like refuse collection, school catering, and local buses.

Privatisation is both an economic and a political issue. The fact that it is being debated clearly shows that the arguments over which part of the economy should be in public control and which part in private hands is a continuing one.

Figure 4.7 British Telecom advertisement

4.8 Is there any other type of business activity?

Before leaving this area it is important to remember that many people are involved in voluntary activities which make a vital contribution to the provision of goods and services for the community. From the secretary of the local angling club to Bob Geldof and Live Aid; from visiting the elderly to playgroups for children; from Poppy Day and the Royal British Legion to a charity disco at school. All these activities are non-profit-making but exist within the private sector. They are often not considered to be forms of work or economic activity, but without them everybody's standard of living would be much lower. And, as we consider in later chapters business activities like marketing, accounting, and production, remember that these are carried out not only by companies and small businesses, but also by charities, churches, clubs and societies, local councils, and even schools.

THINGS TO DO

Short answer questions

1 Is it true to say that all goods and services provided by the state are provided free of charge? Give your reasons.

2 Why do you think the following goods and services are provided by the public sector in the UK?
   a lighthouses
   b street lighting
   c primary and secondary education
   d wheelchairs for the handicapped
   e bus services
   f electricity

3 Give three examples of public corporations which are nationalised industries, and three examples of other public corporations.

4 How do politicians have a say in how nationalised industries are run?

5 What is meant by the following terms which are often used in the discussion of nationalisation?
   a abuse of monopoly power
   b essential industry
   c in the public interest
   d financial support of the state
   e economic planning
   f major economies.

6 My electricity bill arrives and it is £50.00 higher than last month. A letter from the electricity board says that the prices have been increased by 30 per cent. As a consumer who can I complain to?

7 Give four examples of the problems that can occur when the state runs an industry.

8 What is meant by privatisation?

9 Give two examples of nationalised industries that have been privatised.

10 Write down a list of non-profit-making activities that your school is involved with.

SECTION B   **Essays and structured questions**

1 Look at the examples of nationalised industries given in *Fig 4.3*.
   a In which sector of economic activity does each of the three industries operate?
   b Which is the largest of the three industries?
   c Looking at each industry, can you say why it was nationalised?
   d How would the way these industries are run differ from a private sector company?

2 A branch line of about 25 miles connecting a seaside town in Suffolk with Ipswich is being considered for closure by British Rail. The line breaks even in the months of July and August, but loses money for the rest of the year. The main users are business commuters and college students during the morning and evening, and shoppers without cars during the day. An alternative bus service exists, but the bus journey takes 30 minutes longer and the last bus leaves Ipswich at 4.00 p.m. The town council has protested against the closure but British Rail say that they cannot keep the line open because the government has reduced its subsidy.
   a Why does British Rail want to close the line?
   b What does the term *breaks even* mean?
   c What would be the social costs to the town if this line was closed?
   d What alternative to closure might the town council suggest?
   e How can the government influence the decisions British Rail takes?

3 *a* Explain the major arguments for and against nationalised industries.
   b Is privatisation of nationalised industries in the public interest?

SECTION C   **Coursework and assignments**

1 *a* From your local area, make a list of all the activities that go on which are part of the public sector (you may be able to start with your school). Find out whether the activities are controlled by central government, by local government or by a public corporation. Draw a diagram similar to *Fig 4.2* which illustrates these activities.
   b Which of these activities are provided free of charge, and which are customers charged for?

2 Choose one of the nationalised industries and find out the following information about the industry:
   a When was it nationalised?
   b What does it produce?
   c How is it organised?
   d How large is it (sales revenue and number of employees)?
   e What problems has it faced in the last five years?

3 Do other countries have a mixed economy? The United States, Japan, West Germany, and France are our major trading partners. By using the library find out which industries in these four countries are publicly owned and compare your list with the UK. What conclusions do you reach?

Chapter 5

Financing a business

5.1 Finance

Suppose a hotel owner decides to extend the business by buying the house next door and linking it in with the present property. There are several ways in which the capital for this can be found.

a If the money is available the house can simply be paid for – a **cash purchase**.

b A deposit can be paid now and the rest paid at a later date. This is still a cash purchase, but with some time to find the rest of the money.

c The owner can take a partner, or become a limited liability company and issue shares.

d The owner can borrow in any one of a number of ways and from several possible sources.

e The owner can take out a **mortgage**, a special form of hire purchase which most people use when they decide to buy a house.

Whatever decision is made, and it may be more than one of the possibilities we have suggested, the hotel owner needs **finance**, i.e. someone else's help in finding the money to make the purchase.

The way this help can be given is different in each of the five ways of solving the problem.

a No help is needed because the cash is available, but when it is used to buy the house it is no longer there for other use. In other words there may be an **opportunity cost** in using it.

b Some of the money is paid now and the hotelier is given **time** to find the rest. Some of this may come from other sources, but some may come from the earnings of the business up to the time that the final payment has to be made.

c If this method is used, the owner is **sharing the risk** by finding either shareholders or partners who will contribute capital to the purchase. Partners may be easy to find, but becoming a limited company may take quite a long time. If the hotel owner shares the risks in this way then both the ownership and the profits must also be shared.

d Borrowed money has to be paid back and those who lend it will also expect to earn interest. The hotel can be extended quickly, but profits must be good enough to pay back the loan and the interest on it.

e The mortgage will mean a deposit and the firm must use some of its own money. It will be repayable over a long period of time, at agreed amounts per month or quarter and including interest payments.

Finance, then, involves support by:

using your own resources for which there may be a better use

or

relying on others to wait for their money until you are in a better position to give it to them

or

borrowing for an agreed time and then paying back the loan as well as an agreed amount of interest

or

sharing the risk and therefore the ownership and the profits of the business.

Big businesses with good reputations often find it easier to get the finance they need, even though it may be a considerable amount of money, whilst little businesses often have to struggle to find the small amount they need.

5.2 Cash flow

If a business is to survive it must make a **profit** and part of that profit can be used to provide finance for the activities of the business. In this country keeping profits in the business to allow it to grow, or to make it even more successful, is the main source of finance. But – think of some of the businesses near you.

a **Farmers** Those who grow crops for the market receive much of their **income** in the summer and autumn, but their expenses have to be met all the year round, and in the winter when there is little money coming in.

b **Seaside guest house owners** have the same problem. They are able to charge higher prices in **July** and **August** and can expect that they have few vacancies. At other times of year there will be less income. They too, have expenses all the year round and must do much of the repair and maintenance work in the winter months.

You will be able to think of many more who have an unbalanced pattern to their income and expenses and who have to plan so that the money they need is available when they want it.

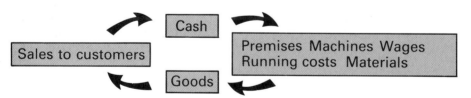

Figure 5.2 The cash flow cycle

The flow of money into and out of a business is called **cash flow**. If the cash flow is even and sufficient business is being done a firm will not have **cash flow problems**, but where this is not so, borrowing may have to take place – most often through an **overdraft**. *Figure 5.2* shows cash flow in a business, in the simple situation where goods and materials are paid for at the time when they are bought. It would be typical of a 'cash and carry' business or of a new one unable to obtain credit or to afford to give it.

5.3 Internal sources – making a profit

When a business is successful the amount for which its goods or services are sold will be more than the cost of producing them and sufficient to provide an income for those who own it. This surplus is called **profit** and is the reward for taking **risks**. Some of the profit will be paid to the state in taxes, some will be used to live on, some will pay **interest** to those who have lent the firm money or will pay off previous loans, some may be paid to employees as a **bonus** and the rest will be kept in the business to make further growth possible. If the business is small or new it is unlikely that the **retained profit** will be very large and the owner may choose to use it to reduce the need for outside finance.

The amount of profit which is made in a year will depend upon many things but two of the important ones are:

a **Mark-up** However a firm decides the prices for its goods or services it is obvious that the bigger the difference between the cost of producing one pair of shoes or one pullover and the price for which it is sold the bigger the profit made on each sale. The difference is called the mark-up.

b **Rate of turnover** Suppose it costs £9,000 to stock the shelves of a small shop. Suppose too that the sales value of all those goods, assuming everything is sold at the marked price, is £24,000. If it takes three months to sell all the goods it will take three months to make the profit of £15,000, but if they can be sold in one month that same £15,000 profit will only take a month to make. This speed at which a shop, or any other business, can sell its products is called the rate of turnover and is very important in helping to determine how much profit will be made in a year. *Figure 5.3* illustrates this.

	£
Firm A: *Slow Rate of Turnover*	
Shelf value of stock	81,000
Mark up ⅓	27,000
Sales value of stock	108,000
Rate of turnover 4	
Profit per year 4 × 27,000	108,000
Firm B: *Rapid Rate of Turnover*	
Shelf value of stock	81,000
Mark up ⅓	27,000
Sales value of stock	108,000
Rate of turnover 9	
Profit per year 9 × 27,000	243,000

Figure 5.3 The effect of rate of turnover on profits

A rate of turnover of four means that the shopkeeper has to replace stock completely four times a year. Obviously Firm B is selling more because it has to replace its stock about once every six weeks, whilst Firm A although it carries the same value of stock has to replace it only about once every 13 weeks.

5.4 The need for funds

Figure 5.3 shows how rate of turnover influences profit. What it also shows is that businesses in which the rate of turnover is rapid need less finance to operate profitably than ones in which that rate is much slower. In Firm A in *Fig 5.3* the trader took 13 weeks to sell all the stock, whilst in Firm B the other trader took only six weeks and so was able to buy new stocks more regularly using the money which the business had earned. The longer capital has to be used for unsold stock, the more is needed to keep the business going and this will be even worse when the rate of turnover is very slow because stock deteriorates with age or becomes less attractive to the customer.

5.5 Making use of profits

As soon as money begins to flow into the business faster than it is flowing out there is a surplus which can be used by the business. Skilled business people try to manage their **cash flow** so that this surplus is available when it is needed, and they can use their own funds rather than rely upon the support of others. There are several ways in which they can do this:

a by thinking carefully about the best use of funds at a particular time. As stock is sold it has to be replaced, but it may be wiser to spend money on a new till, on advertising, or on the employment of a new member of staff rather than on keeping stocks up to the maximum.

b by using funds more efficiently. This may mean shopping around for the best buy rather than always buying from the same source, or it may mean employing another person rather than pay overtime.

c by learning from experience. One of the best examples of this is in the decision about what items should be stocked and in what quantities. The more experienced a trader is, the more accurately stock is bought and the less danger there is of unsold stock.

d by careful management of credit giving policy. There are two parts to this, knowing to whom credit can be given so that business is increased and making sure that bills are paid as promptly as possible.

e by careful use of credit opportunities available from other traders since these give time to pay and may sometimes make it possible to sell goods before they have to be paid for.

5.6 Looking outward

In many cases wise management of cash and cash flow is not enough, particularly for those who have problems, or who are trying to find ways of doing more or of growing. These needs must be met from outside, from people and organisations having no direct interest in the business, but with funds available and a desire to use them.

From the point of view of the owners of a business this means finding out where the available funds are, what would be the conditions on which they could be obtained, for how long they would be available and whether a particular source is the right one to use.

From the point of view of the holder of the funds the problem is whether a particular organisation and the things it wants to do with the funds are attractive. Fund holders may be individuals with small amounts, other firms with an interest in the business, large organisations like insurance companies and pension funds or a government, and all of them will have other opportunities to invest and will want to choose the best. *Figure 5.6* poses the problem.

Firms	Fund Holders
Will this be worth the risk?	How much will I earn?
How much do we need?	How much do they want?
For how long?	Is it a good risk?
How quickly?	Can I get my money back?
What will it cost?	Are there better opportunities?
Can we afford it?	Should I wait for something else?
Who do we get it from?	How do I know they're right?

Figure 5.6 Finding outside funds – the key questions

5.7 The sources of finance

Suppose 'The Odd Job Shop' has been successful for a few years and there is an opportunity to open another shop in the next town. Although the firm has been profitable for some time the total amount of money earned has not been large and funds must be found from outside. There are three main sources:

a Finding other people to work as fellow owners of the firm by forming a **partnership**.
b Finding other people who will contribute small amounts to the capital of the business provided their liability is limited. This means forming a **registered company**.
c Finding some way of borrowing the money.

We looked at the first two ways in Chapter 3 and here we concentrate on borrowing. It is a way of getting money for present use with which we are all familiar, having both borrowed from and lent to friends and relations. From this experience we know the risks of borrowing and of lending. These risks are the same in business except that there is always a **cost of borrowing** as well. All firms have the possibility of borrowing and the bigger, the more successful the firm and the less it really needs the money, the easier it will be to find it. The other major difference between our borrowing and that of a firm is that we do not always have to give proof of borrowing, but a business does.

5.8 Debentures

The word debenture comes from a Latin word meaning to **owe** and in its simplest form would be a quickly scribbled IOU £10 with signature to seal it. A debenture which might be bought by a lender to a business is a much more formal document.
The important things about a debenture are:

a The amount borrowed will be repaid at a time stated on the certificate, called its **maturity date**.
b **Interest** will be paid at a fixed percentage per year.
c The interest must be paid whether or not the firm makes a profit.
d Buying a debenture makes the holder a **creditor** of the firm and not an owner.
e It is a **long-term liability** and not a current one, because it will not have to be paid back for a long time.

f Holders cannot get their money back from the firm until the maturity date but can sell their certificate to someone else.

g If a firm is in trouble debenture holders have the same rights as other creditors. They can buy safer debentures called **mortgage debentures** which because the risk is less, will be at a lower rate of interest.

Figure 5.8 sums this up and compares ordinary shares, preference shares and debentures as ways of providing funds.

	Ordinary Shares	Preference Shares	Debentures
Status	Part owner – risk taker	Part owner – little risk	Creditor – slight risk. No involvement
Receives Income	Dividend Only if profits sufficient	Dividend Virtually certain	Interest Certain
Rate of return	Varies – zero to very high	Fixed	Fixed
Rights in firm	One vote per share	Usually no vote	None
Repayment	Never	Never	When debenture matures
Disposal	May sell at will	May sell at will	May sell at will
Residual rights	Last to receive any payment Usually none	Next to last	Those of a creditor may be better if it is a mortgage debenture

Figure 5.8 Comparison of different ways of providing funds to a company

5.9 Banks as a source of finance

Banks may be a source of finance in one of two ways:

Overdraft usually with permission, and up to an agreed limit. Permission to draw from an account more than there is in it.

Loan negotiated with the bank. A fixed sum which may be borrowed and paid back either at the agreed time, or in instalments over the period of the loan. Most businesses use an overdraft facility some of the time and it is particularly important to those whose business and therefore cash flow is very variable. Most are granted loans at some time. In each case there is a **cost** to the firm which is an **income** to the bank. The amount which the bank will charge will depend upon:

The amount The greater the amount the greater the risk of losing all or some of it. Banks must make sure that a loan is large enough to achieve its purpose, because otherwise there will be little chance of success and therefore a high risk of loss.

The risk Sometimes it is the purpose for which the loan is to be used which is risky and sometimes it is the situation, perhaps because it is not a good time to choose. Sometimes the risk is more associated with the people and their ability or determination to do what they are trying to do. This is why being able to assess people is an important part of a bank manager's job.

The time The length of time before the loan will be repaid. Mostly a matter of how quickly the firm will make the profits from which the money to pay back the loan and the interest will have to come.

The facts A bank manager will want to see evidence to support the claims of the borrower to show whether or not the intentions are likely to be achieved.

Past performance will be an important part of these facts as will a sensible forecast of likely returns.

The collateral The risk can be reduced if a business can provide some asset which could be sold to repay the loan in event of failure. The deeds of the premises would be a good example.

5.10 Loan or overdraft?

From the point of view of the borrower an overdraft is preferable to a loan because it is flexible and much of the time when cash is flowing into the business rather than out little or nothing will be owed to the bank, whereas with a loan indebtedness and therefore cost in terms of interest is always there until the loan is repaid. Interest is normally calculated daily. Banks will not allow overdrafts for very long periods, or for very large amounts, preferring to do that kind of financing through loans.

5.11 Hire purchase

You will be familiar with hire purchase since opportunities for it can be seen in every shop which sells expensive durable consumer goods, like cars and washing machines. We will deal with it in detail when considering consumption. It is not a common method of finance for businesses, although it might be used to purchase expensive assets which can be used whilst they are being bought. The great weakness is its relatively high cost as compared with other methods. A calculation of hire purchase finance is shown in *Fig 5.11* to make this point.

Cash price of machine	5,000
Initial deposit 20%	1,000
Balance owing	4,000
Service charge 15%	600
Repayment over 1 year	4,600
Payment per month	383.33

Figure 5.11 Hire purchase calculation

The smaller the amount of the deposit and the longer the period of repayment the greater the total cost.

5.12 Mortgages

The majority of those who buy houses do so on a mortgage, which is a form of hire purchase over a long period of time. The sum needed is borrowed from a building society, local authority or bank and the deeds of the property are held by the lender until the loan is repaid. Such loans are for very large amounts of money and are repaid over long periods of time, rarely less than 20 years and often much longer. The borrower will pay interest often on a monthly basis. Businesses could buy premises in this way, or could borrow on the security of the premises in order to obtain a large capital sum. Mortgages are always secured against the asset, which means that if the borrower fails to meet payments, the building can be sold by the lender in order to recover the amount due.

5.13 Financing organisations

There are businesses which provide most services and finance is no exception. Most are groups of firms acting together and may include the Bank of England and the joint stock banks. They mostly want to provide medium- or long-term finance and large sums, rather than small ones.

5.14 The state and finance

The state finances a wide range of economic activity, partly because it is a major employer in its own right; partly through assistance to public corporations, but also by making funds available to private firms. Sometimes this help is linked with an important objective of the state, for example help given to encourage firms to set up their business in certain areas of the country where there is high unemployment and the underuse of resources. Help is given to firms wishing to export but lacking capital and unable to take the risks involved.

Firms most in need of help are small ones. There are considerable differences in the way in which small businesses find funds. In most cases they are working on very small margins and with very little long-term capital. Many might obtain more finance if they became companies and issued shares, but there is a lack of interest in this way of raising money because it means loss of control.

Small firms are likely to seek finance from banks as an overdraft or a loan. This is a short-term source since banks are not always prepared to finance for long periods of time. Since small firms don't like to become companies and yet need medium- and long-term capital, the state makes funds of this type available through a range of schemes.

The best known is the 'Small Businesses Loan Guarantee Scheme', intended to meet medium-term needs for ventures which have promise, but which are slightly more risky than the banks normally fund. The state also offers a range of 'start-up' and expansion grants and schemes. Some are available only in certain areas, where there is a need for economic development. Some are available only for certain purposes such as exporting whilst others are for particular industries such as micro-electronics. Some are designed to make British industry more creative and forward-looking by supporting research and development.

5.15 Making the choice

Suppose The Odd Job Shop needs money. You probably begin by trying to work out how much is needed and how quickly. Then perhaps you make a list of the sources putting down everything you can think of for the time being. Such a list of sources is given in *Fig 5.15*. You may not think it's complete; if you can think of some more add them to your list.

Figure 5.15 Sources of capital

Sell shop and lease back	Buy on HP	Find partner(s)
Sell off some stock	Mortgage shop	Form a company – issue shares
Get as many of the debts in as possible	Get a loan from the bank	Issue debentures
Increase overdraft	Get loan(s) somewhere else	Private grants
Buy more things on credit	Try for government grant	Mergers

You may be able to cross some of them out and perhaps put the rest into order of preference.

All firms go through this sort of decision-making process when they need finance. For them it may be a little quicker because they will know from experience which ones are the most likely. Things which will help them to make the choice will include:

a **The objectives of the firm** The most important objective of any business is to **survive**. It's often difficult to get money for this reason because those who might lend can see the firm is in trouble and may not like the risk of helping. If the amount is small the bank might help if they think it is the best way of looking after their own interests or think the firm's troubles won't last very long.

If the amount needed for survival is large the best hope is that another firm might take over the business and keep it going.

Alternatively, the state might help if it thinks it is in the national interest, as it did with Rolls Royce and British Leyland. Sometimes associations might help because it damages public confidence if a single firm is in difficulties it can't overcome. This sometimes happens with building societies and travel agents.

The Odd Job Shop is successful so **survival** is not the reason for money. Perhaps the firm is considering bigger jobs, for example moving away from repairs and small extensions and into new buildings. This would require a lot of money and being a small firm not much will come from inside. The **risk** will be high so that the firm may need to find partners in the venture.

There may be other objectives, but enough has been said to show that they are an important part of the decision.

b **Amount** The Odd Job Shop would have no trouble with really small amounts. The larger the amount needed the greater the problem will be and the fewer the likely sources. This is particularly true for small firms.

c **Time** How long before the money can be paid back? If it is a very short time then perhaps the money can be found by extended credit or through overdraft. If it is a long time, then other ways will have to be found.

d **Risk** How good is the idea? How likely is it to work? How much profit is it likely to bring in? Part of the risk will be the idea itself; part will be timing — is it a good time or a bad one to develop the business? But when those who might help look at the project they are likely to be most interested in the owner and the record of the firm, and they will be able to see the success of the shop and the repair and maintenance work over the years and they will make a decision looking not only at what has been done, but how it has been done, and whether the methods used and the organisation are likely to be able to support the bigger business.

All these factors have to be considered together since they affect each other. For example, the more money needed and the longer it is required the more risky the idea is.

e **Present position of the firm** This is important since it helps to decide what options are open. For example, a company cannot consider becoming a partnership, but it might find it much easier than a one person business to issue shares or debentures to be bought by someone. The healthiness of the business is also important. A firm that is doing well and wants finance to do better is more likely to get it than one which is in trouble; a firm with a good reputation is more likely to be helped than one with a poor one.

5.16 Cost of financing

You have heard that expression or one like it. It is true of all forms of finance. Overdrafts are charged for depending on their size and the length of time you have them; loans carry a rate of interest and in *Fig 5.11* we calculated the cost of HP. If a firm decides to raise money by a share issue, the cost of setting this up and letting people know there are shares on offer and what the money is for is very high.

What about using your own money, what is the cost of that? It is easy to think that using your own money costs nothing because all you do is take money which belongs to you out of a current account. But there is a cost. What could be done with that money if you hadn't found another use for it? At least it could be put into a deposit account where some interest could be earned and there may be even better opportunities for making profits with it which you have to ignore because the money has now been used. If you have made a wise choice this kind of cost won't matter, but if you could have done better the cost is important. That is why we call it **opportunity cost**.

5.17 Conclusion

In this chapter the distinction has been made between internal sources of finance and external ones and profits have been discussed as the main source of funds from inside a business. In the next chapter we look at the way a business manages its finances and records financial information. This will suggest ways in which funds can be found by better management of cash flow and by the decisions about the use of funds which a business makes.

THINGS TO DO

Short answer questions

1 Say what is meant by the word 'capital'.
2 What is a 'limited liability company'?
Why is limited liability important?
3 Give three examples of national businesses which are limited liability companies.
Give three examples of local businesses of the same kind.
Give three examples of local businesses which have unlimited liability.
4 Why does the text say that a 'mortgage' is 'a special form of hire purchase'?
5 How does the idea of 'opportunity cost' apply to (a) using your own money to finance a new venture? (b) using someone else's money to do so?
6 Why is 'interest' sometimes a bigger burden than 'dividend'?
7 Draw a diagram which illustrates the meaning of 'cash flow'.
8 Why is 'retained profit' not a very big source of finance for small businesses?
9 How does the 'rate of turnover' influence profitability?
10 What is a partnership?
11 Think of local businesses. Which kinds of business are most often undertaken by partners?
Find five local businesses which are run as partnerships. Say what business they are in and how many of them there are.
12 What are the main factors which have to be considered by a firm when seeking finance for a project?
13 If you were approached for financial support for a project what things would you give careful consideration to?
14 What do you think might be the important considerations for you as a potential provider of funds in each of the following circumstances:
a A firm wants £3,000 to help them over an immediate cash crisis.
b A firm wants £8,000 to make their own funds up to the £36,000 needed to purchase an additional coach for their transport fleet.
c A firm has offered £3m shares for sale and the prospectus shows that a new chemical plant is to be built in India.
15 'It is better to use our own funds because that costs us nothing.'
Explain why this statement is not true.

Essays and structured questions

1 Why is it easier for registered companies to find finance than it is for one-person businesses?
2 John Smith needs £800 which he can pay back in a year. Explain the difference between a loan and an overdraft and why (a) John might be better off with an overdraft, and (b) his bank manager is only prepared to offer a loan.

3 John wants the £800 to replace his motor bike, offering the old one in part exchange. Explain how he might buy the bike on HP using the value of the old bike as deposit.

Go out into your local town and find out the kinds of terms that are being offered on HP. Use this information to explain why HP is an expensive way of borrowing.

4 How much would John save if he could increase his deposit by (a) £200 or (b) £400?

What does this suggest about other ways of finding the money?

5 In the chapter a distinction is made between 'internal' and 'external' sources of finance. What is the difference? Give three examples of each to illustrate the difference.

Finding finance from outside the business often means giving up some or the ownership of it. What does this mean? Why is it important?

SECTION C

Coursework and assignments

1 Look for an opportunity for the development of a new bus route either within your community (e.g. to serve a new housing estate) or between it and another one where you think there may be a need.

Consider the equipment and resources a firm might need to begin such a service.

Calculate the total and then say with reasons where you think the money might be found.

2 Find an empty shop or the site for one in your community.

Consider what is on offer in the community at the moment and what kind of new shop might be most likely to meet local needs and be profitable. Give reasons for your choice.

Now determine how much money a business person might need to

(a) buy the shop   (b) stock it and prepare it for opening

(c) run it for the first year.

For this exercise use money values which you have discovered from your community and not ones which you think might be right. Determine where the money might be found.

3 Suppose you have £100,000 for which you have no immediate need. Look at the various organisations with which you could save your money in your town or elsewhere locally. Decide which you think would be the best choice, calculate your likely return per year and explain your decision.

4 Go back to your survey of your local community.

a How many and what kinds of business are organised as PLC's?

b How many and what kinds are private limited companies?

c How many and what kinds are partnerships?

d How important are the small businesses in your town?

It is relative numbers rather than exact ones which you need.

Now consider the rest of the activity of your town, how is it organised and financed?

What can you say about the nature and organisation of your town from the survey you have undertaken and the answers you have just given?

Chapter 6

Accounting for business activity

6.1 The business

Whatever the size of a business it is separate from those who own it and there has to be a method of keeping a careful record of everything which happens within it. In this chapter we look at the main ways in which the accounts of a business are kept. The way this is done is less important than the kinds of records which must be kept and the information we can obtain about a business and its activities from reading those records.

6.2 Business transactions

You have all bought things in shops, paid your fare on a bus or train, and bought tickets for a disco or cinema. These are typical business transactions and there are two sides to all of them.

a	You buy a record and take it away with you.	You give some of your cash.
b	You pay your fare at the railway station.	You ride on the train to your destination.
c	You pay for your entrance to the disco.	You have the right to enter and take part in it.

In each case you have given up **money** and received goods or services. The same sort of exchange has happened for each of the business organisations in those examples and if they are to be efficient and know what their financial position is **both** sides of each transaction must be recorded.

a	The **stock** of records has been reduced by one.	The stock of **cash** has been increased by the price of the record.
b	The cash in the booking office till has been increased by the fare.	One of the seats on the train has been taken.
c	The cash in the till has been increased by the admission money.	The number of people in the disco has been increased by one.

6.3 Transactions and the balance sheet

Suppose you have won £300,000 in a competition and have decided to open a shop. This money is your **capital** and you decide you can use your skills in building repairs and maintenance as well as having a small shop which will sell do-it-yourself tools and materials. You call the business The Odd Job Shop and open a bank account in its name.

We are going to follow some of the things you will do and record each side of each transaction as it takes place so that, at any time, the position of the business is clear.

Transaction 1

	£		£
Cash	300,000	Capital	300,000

The statement above records the fact that you have capital of £300,000 and, because you haven't done anything with it yet, it is still available as cash in the bank. The business owes you that money, and is going to use it. It is these two facts of owing and use which are recorded. To show this clearly a statement is drawn up which shows **liabilities** – i.e. what the business owes to its **owners** and to others and **assets** – i.e. what the business is doing with the money. So we can rewrite transaction 1 like this:

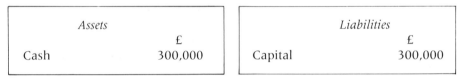

Assets		*Liabilities*	
	£		£
Cash	300,000	Capital	300,000

Transaction 2
Perhaps the first thing you will do is to buy a suitable shop. All sorts of things will be important in making this decision, particularly the **location** of the shop and the **size** you will need for the things you intend to sell. After looking around for some time and considering all the things that matter you buy a shop for £80,000 and pay cash for it. Now your statement will be like this.

Assets		*Liabilities*	
	£		£
Shop	80,000	Capital	300,000
Cash	220,000		

Transaction 3
Suppose your shop and the builders yard which you have next to it need special shelves and equipment which you go out and buy. These kinds of things which make a business capable of doing the things it wants to do and able to display goods for the public are usually called the **fixtures and fittings** of the business. Suppose the cost of all this is £25,000. Your statement will now be:

Assets		*Liabilities*	
	£		£
Shop	80,000	Capital	300,000
Fixtures & fittings	25,000		
Cash	195,000		

Transaction 4

Things are moving quickly now. You need a van, builders tools and equipment, and a range of stock both for your own use and for the shop. You buy all these things in a fortnight and at the end the statement looks much fuller and is:

Assets	£	Liabilities	£
Shop	80,000	Capital	300,000
Fixtures & fittings	25,000		
Equipment	30,000		
Van	11,000		
Stock	75,000		
Cash	79,000		

Transaction 5

The 300,000 you started with has gradually been used and you have not yet earned any money to replace it. You need a lot more stock and the first job you have found needs some equipment you have not got. You work out that another £60,000 must be spent. You do not want to leave yourself short of cash and so try to buy on credit. This is not easy because yours is a new business and other traders are not sure whether they can trust you yet. You have not proved you can run a business successfully. However, you find credit for £25,000 and spend £35,000 for the rest. As a result your statement looks like this:

Assets	£	Liabilities	£
Shop	80,000	Capital	300,000
Fixtures & fittings	25,000	Creditors	25,000
Equipment	55,000		
Van	11,000		
Stock	110,000		
Cash	44,000		

For the first time there is a second entry on the liabilities side. This is because the business still owes the £300,000 to you its owner and it also owes £25,000 to the traders who have allowed equipment to be brought without immediate payment.

The statement now looks much more like a **balance sheet** and, in the next section we learn a number of things about it.

6.4 The balance sheet

The balance sheet is a statement about a business which tells you what the position of the business is at a particular moment in time. Its like stopping everything and adding up all the values which the business has and all that it owes. To actually do that would damage the business so we have to make guesses about some of the values in the business. For example, you couldn't know how much The Odd Job Shop was worth unless you sold it, and the only way to be completely sure of the value of stock is when a customer buys it.

As we saw in the five transactions in 6.3 there are two sides to the balance sheet. The statement of what is owed to the owners, £300,000 of capital in this case, and of what is owed to others, £25,000 to creditors. A business which had been going for some time would have several other entries on this side of the balance sheet. On the other side are the various assets which the business will use to earn money.

We can make this balance sheet a little more useful by organising it into four different parts.

Fixed Assets
Those assets which the business uses for the same purpose all the time, e.g. the shop, the builders yard, the specialist equipment, the shop fittings and the van.

Current assets
All the other assets which are there are changing all the time as they contribute to the success of the business. Cash is used to buy things and then comes back as things are sold and people pay for them. Stock is taken off the shelves and sold, being replaced by more items when the business needs to restock.

Long-term liabilities
Amounts which the business will owe for a long time and which it does not expect to have to pay back yet. The capital which you have put into the business is like that. Sometimes firms borrow for long periods of time and although they know they have to pay back at sometime in the future, it won't be this year.

Current liabilities
Some people will want to be paid quickly, and certainly within the year. The creditors of a firm are like that and bank overdrafts are also changing all the time as money is paid into and taken out of the firm's bank account. *Figure 6.4* shows our statement about The Odd Job Shop organised as a balance sheet in this way.

Figure 6.4 The Odd Job Shop Balance Sheet

The Odd Job Shop Balance Sheet
year ending 31.12.19____

Assets	£		Liabilities	£
Fixed assets			Capital	300,000
Shop and yard	80,000		*Current liabilities*	
Fixtures & fittings	25,000		Creditors	25,000
Equipment	55,000			
Van	11,000			
		171,000		
Current assets				
Stock	110,000			
Cash	44,000			
		154,000		
		£325,000		£325,000

This is the first time we have added the figures up. If you do it for all five of the transactions you will notice that, in every case, the totals on each side are the same – the **balance sheet balances**.

There is nothing special about this; it must happen all the time because each side of the balance sheet is recording the same amounts in different ways. On the left is shown **where the finance has come from** (£300,000 from the owner and £25,000 from creditors), and on the right is shown **how it is being used** (£171,000 in fixed assets and £154,000 in current assets).

6.5 Profits and the balance sheet

The Odd Job Shop is opening for business on January 2nd and the balance sheet written above is the starting position. During the coming year the firm will work and sell, and, at the end of it, will have made a profit. This profit is calculated in a special end-of-year statement called the **Trading, Profit (and) Loss account**. The business will make money both in the shop and as a result of work done on repairs and maintenance, but to keep things simple we will look only at the activity of the shop. The account is in three parts:

The trading account
This looks at the transactions alone and does not take into account the expenses of running the business. In it the cost of goods sold is found and taken away from the sales receipts to give the **gross profit**.

The profit loss account
This account begins with the **gross profit**. To this are added any other income that the business earns from activities other than those of the business, e.g. investments or rent from subletting part of the premises. From this total the expenses of running the business are taken. Examples include telephone bills, advertising costs, and the wages of staff who work in the shop. When these expenses have been taken away the business is left with the **net profit**.

The appropriation account
A business has to show what has been done with the profit and one of three things is likely to happen

a Some must be paid to the **inland revenue** as **tax**. The Chancellor of the Exchequer decides how much will be paid in the **Budget** each year.
b Some will be taken out of the business by the owners. In registered companies this will be in the form of a **dividend** on shares. In other businesses it will be the share of the profits to which the owner, or each one of the partners, is entitled.
c The owners, whether they are sole owners, partners, or shareholders, may agree to leave part of the profits working in the business and this **retained profit** is the main way that most businesses obtain the finance they need. Retained profit appears in the **balance sheet** because it adds to the capital of the business.

A possible profit and loss account with these three parts is shown in *Fig 6.5a*. In *Fig 6.5b* we see the effect of retaining profit in the business on the balance sheet and it is possible to work out, from the changes in the asset side of the balance sheet, how that profit is being used.

The Odd Job Shop
Trading Profit Loss a/c year ending 31.12.19____

Trading account

	£		£
Opening stock	110,000	Sales	178,000
Purchases	58,000		
Total stock	168,000		
Closing stock	69,000		
Cost of goods sold	99,000		
Gross profit	79,000		

Profit/Loss account

	£		£
Wages (shop)	19,000	**Gross profit**	79,000
Advertising	6,000	Net profit (yard)	55,000
Heat and light	2,500	Lease upstairs	2,500
Telephone & stationery	2,300		
Delivery costs	1,400		
Net profit	105,300		
	136,500		136,500
Appropriation			
Tax	52,650	**Net profit**	105,300
Drawings	10,000		
Retained profit	42,650		
	105,300		105,300

Figure 6.5a

Profit loss account:
The Odd Job Shop

This is a simplified version of a profit loss account and, as we shall see later in this chapter, there are some things which have not yet been taken into account. It shows a good trading year in which you have been able to take £10,000 of the profits for your own purposes and yet still leave a healthy sum in the business for growth next year. The £10,000 you have taken out is in addition to any wages which you would have paid yourself from the activities of the yard.

The business started with stock of £110,000. We know this from the opening balance sheet. Not surprisingly the firm has not purchased much stock during the year and now has £11,000 less stock than it had at the beginning. A new business is not quite sure what stock will be necessary and during the year gets more experienced and develops more trading contacts so that the amount of money tied up in stock can be reduced.

The sale of £99,000 worth of goods has produced a **gross profit** of £79,000. You might think this is very high, but remember that all the expenses of running the business still have to be taken away.

Some of the normal expenses of the business have been taken away in the profit loss part of the account, but later we shall want to deduct some **provisions** like those for **depreciation and bad debts**.

The activities of the yard side of the business have not been considered. We have assumed that there would be another set of accounts like this one in which the net profit of the yard side is calculated and this is included as extra income. The new business probably has a larger shop than is needed now but which will be valuable when the business grows. For the moment, part of the premises can earn an income by letting to an outsider.

The sum of £42,650 is retained in the business. Of course, this belongs to you as the owner of the firm and that is why it appears as a liability in the balance sheet. It is being used in the activities of the business. It would be poor business to just leave it in the bank account doing no work.

The Odd Job Shop balance sheet as at 31 December 19____

Liabilities				Assets	
				Fixed assets	
Capital	300,000			Shop and yard	80,000
Retained profit	42,650			Fixtures & fittings	40,000
				Equipment	55,000
				Van	11,000
		342,650			
Current liabilities				*Current assets*	
Provision for tax	52,650			Stock	99,000
Creditors	8,500				
		61,150		Debtors	11,900
				Cash	106,900
		£403,800			£403,800

Figure 6.5b

6.6 An explanation of the changes

By comparing the two balance sheets, *Fig 6.4* which shows the business ready to open on January 2nd, and *Fig 6.5b* which shows the business at the end of its first year of trading, we can see what has happened. *Figure 6.6a* looks at the changes in the liabilities and *Fig 6.6b* at the changes in assets.

	Liabilities January 1st:		
Capital	300,000		(Your original input)
Creditors	25,000		(Part of set-up costs)
		325,000	(Balance *Fig 6.4*)
ADD:			
Retained profit	42,650[1]		
Provision for tax	52,650[2]		
		95,300	
		420,300	
LESS:			
Repaid creditors		16,500[3]	
		403,800[4]	

[1] See appropriation section *Fig 6.5a*
[2] This to be paid by the end of next year
[3] £25,000 was owed at the start, £8,500 is owed now
[4] Balance of *Fig 6.5b*

Figure 6.6a
Change in liabilities
during the year

Assets January 1st: Total fixed	171,000	
Total current	154,000	
		325,000[1]
ADD:		
New fixtures and fittings	15,000	
Debtors	11,900	
Cash	62,900	
Total:		89,800[2]
		414,800
LESS:		
Reduction in stock levels	11,000	11,000[3]
		403,800

[1] The balance sheet total *Fig 6.4*
[2] Some credit sales, greatly increased cash and new fixtures and fittings during the year
[3] Not all the stock has been replaced during the year

Figure 6.6b Changes in assets during the year

The two statements made in *Figs 6.6a* and *6.6b* are usually combined into one and are called a **fund flow statement** because they show the way that funds have flowed into and out of the business producing the changes which occur from one balance sheet position to the next.

6.7 Making provisions

The statements we have made about the business so far have been very simple, concentrating only on the profit the business has made and the uses to which that has been put. One important set of calculations have not been made and that is those which make **provisions**. There are two kinds of provision which are particularly important:

Bad debts
If a business sells on credit, allowing the customer to pay sometime in the future rather than now, there is always the danger that some customers will not pay or will make the collection of debts much more expensive because they have to be chased for the money. A business which does a lot of credit selling will assume that some of the outstanding debts are not going to be collected and will write them off. This is just playing safe and if, in the end, the money does come in, it can always be accounted for. The way that accountants make this provision is shown in *Fig 6.7a*.

Depreciation

Fixed assets have to be replaced either because they have come to the end of their useful life or because the firm considers the risk of failure and the cost of maintenance of old equipment too great, or because improvements in technology have produced much better ways of doing things.

It is sensible to provide for this over the life of the asset and not at the end of it. This provision is called **depreciation** and it sets aside some portion of the value of an asset at the end of each trading year. It is normal to depreciate plant, machinery, and vehicles in this way but not land and buildings because their value tends to stay constant or to increase.

Depreciation keeps part of the gross profit in the business until such time as it is needed to replace an asset. The way in which this appears in the records is shown in *Figs 6.7a* and *6.7b*.

Total expenses		31,200	Gross profit	79,000
			Net profit (yard)	55,000
			Lease (upstairs)	2,500
Depreciation				
Fixtures	4,000			
Equipment	17,600			
Vehicles	7,000			
		28,600		
Provision for bad debts		357		
Net profit		76,343		
		136,500		136,500
Appropriation				
Taxation		38,172	Net Profit	76,343
Drawings		10,000		
Retained		28,171		
		76,343		76,343

Figure 6.7a Profit loss account showing provisions

The effect of provisions is quite clear from these accounts.

a **Reported profit** is reduced – 76,343 instead of 105,300
b **Taxation** is reduced – 38,172 instead of 52,650
c The depreciation deducted remains in the business for the benefit of the firm.

Notice that provisions are taken away from the value of the asset to which they apply and that both the original value and the depreciated value are shown in the balance sheet.

Assets			Liabilities		
Fixed assets			Capital	300,000	
Shop & yard		80,000	Retained profit	28,171	
Fixtures	40,000				328,171
Less depreciation	4,000				
		36,000	*Current liabilities*		
Equipment	55,000		Creditors		8,500
Less depreciation	17,600		Provision for tax		38,172
		37,400			
Van	11,000				
Less depreciation	7,000				
		4,000			
			157,400		
Current assets					
Stock		99,000			
Debtors	11,900				
Less provision	357				
		11,543			
		106,900			
Cash			217,443		
			374,843		£374,843

Figure 6.7b Effect of provisions on the Balance Sheet

6.8 Methods of depreciation

The method which is shown in the *Figs 6.7a* and *6.7b* is sufficient to illustrate the effect, but actual methods will be more sophisticated. We consider the two most frequently used.

The fixed deduction

Every asset has a limited life, some of them much shorter than others and some because of changing technology rather than the use of the asset. Various questions must be asked in calculating depreciation. We will assume that the life of the asset is five years and that its value must be recovered in that time.

a	What is the expected life of the asset?	Assume five years.
b	What was the original cost?	Assume it's the lorry, £24,000.
c	How much can we expect to sell it for at the end of five years?	A guess – say £4,000.
d	How much do we have to recover?	Original cost – scrap value £24,000 – £4,000 = £20,000.
e	How much depreciation each year?	$\dfrac{\text{recovery value}}{\text{expected life}} = \dfrac{20,000}{5}$
		£4,000 per annum

The diminishing balance method

This method takes the same percentage each year but from the book value of the asset and not its original value. Since the book value is falling each year this means that a smaller amount is taken away each time as the asset gets older. To make sure that the value of the asset is depreciated to its expected scrap value in the agreed time a quite large percentage deduction has to be made. From the first example we know that the original cost of the lorry is £24,000 and that this has to be depreciated to £4,000 which is the expected scrap value in five years. A percentage deduction of about 30 per cent will be needed. To keep the numbers simple the calculation is rounded up to the next hundred pounds each time.

		Method
Original cost of lorry:	24,000	
Year 1 30% depreciation	7,200	Each year 30% is taken from the
Book value year 1	16,800	balance sheet value of the asset at the
Year 2 depreciation	5,100	beginning of that year.
Book value year 2	11,700	Rounding up makes the calculation
Year 3 depreciation	3,600	easier.
Book value year 3	8,100	After five years the balance sheet
Year 4 depreciation	2,500	value of the asset is very close to the
Book value year 4	5,600	expected sale value.
Year 5 depreciation	1,700	
Book value at replacement	3,900	

Figure 6.8a Calculation of depreciation: diminishing balance

Fixed deduction	**Diminishing balance**
a is easy to work out	is complex to work out
b reaches the exact expected value	gets close to expected value
c takes the same amount each year taking no account of the age of the asset	takes a decreasing amount each year
d does not take the possibility of earlier replacement into account	if the asset has to be replaced earlier most of its value has been recovered
e takes no account of the profitability of the asset	takes more when the asset is new and likely to be making its greater contribution to profits
f has the same effect on net profits	has a much greater effect on profits and tax liability in the early years of an asset's life
g total costs of holding an asset rise each year since depreciation provision stays constant and repair and maintenance costs rise.	spreads costs over the life of the asset providing more when the repair and maintenance costs are low and less as such costs rise.

Figure 6.8b Comparison of the two methods

The comparison made in *Fig 6.8b* suggests that the only real value of the fixed deduction method is its simplicity, but it is quite useful for long-life assets. The diminishing balance method is the most realistic in modern times since the rate of technological change is so rapid that assets are often out of date in their first or second year. As you can see from the example in *Fig 6.8a* more than half the recoverable cost of the lorry is provided for after two years if the diminishing balance method is used.

6.9 Interpreting final accounts

The trading profit and loss account and the balance sheet are both produced to give information about a business at the end of each year. This is why they are sometimes called the **final accounts**.

When they appear several different groups of people will be interested in them:

Workers
All workers will be interested because the accounts will say something about the profitability and security of the business. They may be able to judge how safe their jobs are and what the prospects are for a pay rise in the coming year.

Trade creditors
These are most interested in the likelihood that they will be paid and in the current assets of the business as compared with their current liabilities. If the business seems insecure they may want to press for payment. What they see may make them more or less willing to give credit to the firm in the future.

Lenders
The firm may have borrowed from banks or from other people with money to spare. Lenders will be interested in the profitability of the business partly to see whether their money is safe and likely to be returned when the time comes and partly because they will want to be sure of their interest payments.

They are interested in present profits and ability to pay but they are also interested in the efficiency and long term prospects of the business.

Shareholders
Registered companies will have shareholders who, like lenders, are interested in today's reward in the form of dividends and in the long-term prospects. If the long-term prospects are poor the value of shares will fall. Ordinary shareholders have a greater interest partly because they take the biggest risks and partly because the reward they can get is much larger if the business is really successful.

Competitors
These are very interested in the trading results and prospects of the business and they may also be looking for opportunities to take over the firm or to co-operate with it.

Trading contacts
Consumers are not always very interested but industrial customers are. Those who are nearer the market want to be sure that their source of supply is secure. Those further away from the market will want to be sure that their own markets with the firm are safe.

Government

It will have a direct interest in the accounts of businesses operating in the public sector and a general interest in others, laying down through legislation such things as the form company accounts must take and some of the things that must be in them.

Figure 6.9a is a simplified set of accounts of a sole trader. Until now we have used the traditional way of setting down accounts and balance sheets but the narrative form which lays everything out in one straight account and deals with the balance sheet in the same way is more and more popular and we are using it in the example.

Figure 6.9a A profit loss account in narrative layout

	£	£
Sales		178,000
Less cost of goods sold		
Opening stock	110,000	
Purchases	58,000	
Total stock	168,000	
Less closing stock	69,000	
		99,000
Gross profit		79,000
Add other incomes:		
Net profit from yard	55,000	
Upstairs lease	2,500	
		57,500
Total		136,500
Less business expenses:		
Shop wages	19,000	
Advertising	6,000	
Heat and light	2,500	
Telephone & stationery	2,300	
Delivery costs	1,400	
		31,200
Total		105,300
Less provisions:		
Bad debts		357
Depreciation:		
Fixtures	4,000	
Equipment	17,600	
Vehicles	7,000	
	28,600	
		28,957
Net profit		76,343
Less taxation		38,172
Net profit after tax		38,171
Less drawings		10,000
Retained profit		28,171

The advantages of this kind of layout are:
a Each step of the calculation can be seen
b The account does not have any balances which have no real meaning
c The important totals at each stage are highlighted
d The final figure clearly shows retained profit.

Figure 6.9b shows the balance sheet set out in a similar fashion.

	£	£
Fixed assets		
Shop and yard		80,000
Fixtures & fittings	40,000	
Less depreciation	4,000	
		36,000
Equipment	55,000	
Less depreciation	17,600	
		37,400
Vehicles	11,000	
Less depreciation	7,000	
		4,000
		157,400
ADD:		
Net current assets		
Stock	99,000	
Debtors	11,900	
Less provision	357	
	11,543	
Cash	106,900	
		217,443
LESS:		
Creditors	8,500	
Provision for tax	38,172	
	46,672	
		170,771
Total assets employed		328,171
Financed by:		
Capital	300,000	
Retained profit	28,171	
		328,171

Figure 6.9b A balance sheet in narrative layout

In presenting the balance sheet in this way the same advantages are gained.
The new thing about it is the calculation of **net current assets** which takes
current liabilities away from **current assets**. A more commonly used term
for this value is **working capital**.

6.10 How well is the business doing?

Any analysis and any rules which are applied, must take into account things
like the kind of business it is, the time of year, the size of the business and so
on. You would expect a firework business to have high stocks in late summer

in preparation for the November demand. You would expect a moneylender or a bookmaker to carry higher cash balances than most. You would expect the stocks of a toymaker to be low at or around Christmas.

We made £800,000 last year – didn't we do well?

This and other comments which talk about success just in terms of the size of the profit are often made. They seem even more impressive when the figure is much larger and refers to a multi-national company. In fact £20,000,000 might be a very small profit and in other circumstances £20,000 might be very good indeed. What we must also know something about if a sensible judgement is to be made include:

a the size of the business
b how long it has been operating
c its recent history.

It is this last point that gives us a clue. We have to **compare** figures with something to make them useful.

In all final accounts there are some figures which are not precise and which involve either an estimate or a choice from a number of different ways of arriving at the value. *Figure 6.10* contains some examples of this.

Figure	*Possible method*
Premises	The original cost of the land and buildings. Sometimes this is revalued upwards to try to keep the value realistic.
Machinery, vehicles fittings	The original cost minus a provision for depreciation which may be calculated by any one of a number of methods which will have different affects on the value shown.
Stock	Can be valued by reference to what was paid for it when it was bought, what was paid for the last addition to it, some average of those two values or by estimating the likely market value. Choosing different methods considerably influences the balance sheet value of stock and therefore the calculation of net profits.
Debtors	Some firms deduct a provision for bad and doubtful debts and some do not.
Profits	The provisions which are made, the method of calculating depreciation, and the method of valuing stock, will all help to determine the stated net profit.

Figure 6.10 How some final accounts figures may be determined

If we are going to compare one firm with another it is important to establish how the way they measure the values in *Fig 6.10* differs, and how this influences the interpretation of the results.

A particular figure in the final accounts can only be thought of as 'good news' or 'bad news' if we compare it in some way with other figures. There are four commonly used sources for such a comparison.

a the same figure for the same firm from one year to another. This will give a **trend**.
b the figure related to one or more figures in the same set of accounts. This will give a **ratio**.
c the figure compared with similar figures for businesses of the same size in the same line. This is called **inter-firm comparison**.
d the figure compared with an objective which was set or a standard which is generally accepted, i.e. a comparision with **budgets**.

6.11 Measuring profitability

This is usually measured by relating profit to the **capital** which is used to produce it expressed as the ratio

$$\frac{\text{Net profit before tax}}{\text{Capital employed}}$$

This ratio may be affected by the factors which determined the calculation of profit. There are also some problems in working out the amount of capital which is employed in a business. The ratio is valuable when measuring change or when comparing the success of businesses known to have used the same conventions and method in calculating profit and capital employed. The intentions of a firm are often expressed in terms of an expected **return on capital employed** and it is always useful to compare the budgeted result with the actual one. In our balance sheet *Fig 6.9b*:

Net profit before tax	76,343
Capital employed	328,171
Percentage ROCE	23.26

This would seem reasonable but not spectacular. Compared with last year it might be anything from bad to excellent and because this comparison is valuable final accounts always show the figure for last year as well as the current year.

Profit may be related to other features of the final accounts to get further evidence. For example sales:

Net profit before tax	76,343
Sales revenue	178,000
Ratio of two as a percentage	42.89

A high profit margin on sales will be expected when the number of units sold is low, e.g. antiques, or where the technology of the industry is expensive so that it takes large amounts of capital to enter the market, e.g. oil refining. In The Odd Job Shop, particularly for the first year, this return would be very pleasing.

Revenue from sales related to capital employed would show how effective capital is in making sales possible. This, too, would vary from industry to industry and in accordance with ways of working in the same industry. In retailing the market barrow will require very much less capital than the specialist shop and the supermarket very much more than the village shop. For The Odd Job Shop this ratio is:

Sales revenue	178,000
Capital employed	328,171
Ratio	54.24

It is possible to be more specific than this and focus attention on any part of the business. The most helpful use of this kind of ratio would be in observing a trend over a number of years within the business. Examples of such ratios would be net profit/operating expenses or sales/fixed assets.

6.12 Measuring liquidity and stability

Survival is one of the main objectives of a business and one of the main interests of those who might be involved with it in any way. We often speak of a business going bankrupt or, if it is a company, having to be wound up, and there are news stories about that almost every day. When this happens it is because the assets of a business are not enough to cover its liabilities, but problems can occur long before this position arises and checking into the **solvency** of a business is one of the main reasons for analysing its accounts.

Solvency is the ability of a business to meet its immediate liabilities. It may be very profitable but not able to do that because its cash management has not been very good. *Figure 6.12* shows the problem by comparing firms A and B:

	Firm A	*Firm B*
Net current assets		
Stock	123,000	86,000
Debtors	86,000	42,500
Cash	1,000	81,500
Current assets	210,000	210,000
Less		
Overdraft	22,000	–
Creditors	86,000	63,000
	108,000	63,000
Net	102,000	147,000

Figure 6.12 A comparison of two firms

Current assets are substantially greater than current liabilities in both cases and it would be reasonable to suggest that Firm B is not taking advantage of opportunities having far too much idle cash. But let's look a little more closely at Firm A. Suppose the trade creditors demand payment within a week, suppose the bank call in the overdraft. Where is the money coming from?

Debtors and creditors are nicely balanced so they ought to take care of each other and there is a lot of stock which could be sold to cover the overdraft. But the firm is short of time – it needs the money now. Debts will take time and money to collect, stock that has to be sold quickly may have to be offered at a reduced price. Perhaps the debts are old and doubtful, perhaps much of the stock is not easily marketable. The firm could be in trouble it is short of **liquid assets**. The working capital policy of the firm is a high risk one which may be very profitable if it comes off.

The policy of Firm B is a very low risk one, it could cover all its liabilities from cash and still have a healthy balance. The price of this degree of safety is that cash which could be working in the business is idle in the bank.

The simplest of the ratios used to check on the solvency of a business is the **current ratio**.

	Firm A	Firm B
Current assets	210,000	210,000
Current liabilities	102,000	63,000
Ratio	2.06	3.33

Money tied up in current assets is wasteful, but you have to be able to meet the needs of the customer for goods (stock) and credit (debtors). A balance has to be found between the two. Anything more than 2 for this ratio is too safe. The ratio suggests that Firm A has maximum safety and Firm B is too cautious.

Again this ratio is of greatest value in pointing out trends. However healthy a current ratio is, a downward trend over a period or a sudden drop are danger signals.

In *Fig 6.12* we saw that Firm A still has difficulties because stock and debtors are not as available as cash and this problem can be highlighted by taking a tougher ratio called the **acid test**.

	Firm A	Firm B
Current assets – stocks	87,000	124,000
Current liabilities	102,000	63,000
Ratio	0.85	1.97

Again this shows the difference in the risk-taking attitudes of the two firms but it now shows that Firm A is in danger of insolvency if their liabilities are called in quickly.

There are several ratios which can be used within these overall figures which are very helpful:

Ratio of debtors to total sales
Back to The Odd Job Shop:

Debtors	11,900
Sales	178,000
Ratio	6.7%

If we assume there are 50 weeks in a trading year, the ratio suggests that nearly seven per cent of sales are outstanding and this represents three and a half weeks. Most businesses send out accounts at the end of the month and expect to be paid within a month, giving an average of six weeks credit overall, so the size of the debtors seems reasonable.

Further analysis would be necessary to really find out, asking questions like:
a How many accounts does this represent?
b How much of the firm's business is with customers who take time to pay?
c Are there any accounts there which are owed?

Ratio of credit to stock
This would give a similar answer for the extent to which The Odd Job Shop is relying on credit. That one can be left to you.

Ratio of stock of goods to sales:

Stock	99,000
Sales	178,000
Ratio	55.61

This suggests a very high investment in stock as compared with sales. Unless there is a considerable increase in sales, more than half of next year's sales would appear to be in stock already. But the picture is a slightly false one when we realise that this is a builders yard as well as a shop and some of that stock will be used in doing work for firms. In our set of accounts we don't have the figures to work this out.

6.13 Financing the business

As we saw in Chapter 5 a business can obtain its funds from internal sources, most likely retained profits, or from a range of sources outside. The possibilities open to a firm will depend on its financial structure and stability and upon judgements made by those who are approached with a request for finance. They will be interested in the ratios we have already discussed, since they give an insight into profitability and liquidity, but there are some others which may be significant.

Finance for The Odd Job Shop comes from the owner as initial capital (£300,000) and retained profits (£28,171) but it is also relying strongly on short-term finance from creditors (£8,500) and money to be paid later in tax (£38,172).

THINGS TO DO

Short answer questions

1 Using examples say what is meant by the term 'double entry'.
2 Explain why it is important for a business to keep 'double entry' accounts.
3 Which of the following do you think is 'capital'. Explain your decision in each case:
   a the money you have to spend each week
   b the house you live in
   c the roads in your town
   d shares bought in British Gas or the Trustee Savings Bank
   e the reserves which a firm shows in its balance sheet.
4 Say what is meant by 'working capital'. Give three examples from any business known to you which will illustrate this idea.
5 Why do you think it is necessary for a business to have a bank account?
6 A business buys £200,000 worth of stock. Half of this is on credit and the other half is paid for at the time. Write down the balance sheet entries which would reflect this transaction and explain why creditors are a liability of a firm.
7 Why doesn't a grocer's shop stock every brand of baked beans?
8 Write down one example of each of the following and distinguish between them:
   a creditors and debtors
   b fixed and current assets
   c owners and lenders.
9 What does the 'appropriation account' tell us?
10 In the appropriation account of The Odd Job Shop £10,000 is shown as 'drawings'.
   What does this mean?
   What entry might be made in this account if The Odd Job Shop was a plc?
11 Why is it good business practice to:
   a make provisions for depreciation?
   b make provisions for bad debts?
12 Which method of depreciation would you choose in each of the following cases?
   Explain your choice.
   a a new lorry
   b a new factory
   c a second-hand coach bought to transport staff.

13 Why should you be careful in using 'ratios' to interpret accounts?

14 Why is a 'trend' more useful than a single set of figures?

15 Why is the 'acid test' sometimes used?

SECTION B

Essays and structured questions

1 Suppose you were asked to advise a new shopkeeper about accounts:

   a Say which books of account you would advise should be kept, indicating the role and importance of each.

   b Explain briefly, drawing a model to illustrate, what a profit and loss account is and what is calculated within it.

   c Explain why the narrative presentation of such an account is the best one.

2 At a meeting with the shopkeeper later in the year you are asked to explain how a balance sheet is drawn up. Provide this explanation using the narrative form of presentation and making sure the meaning of any terms you use is understood.

3 How would you try to discover whether a business has sufficient working capital?

   Use figures of your own to explain.

   If your calculations told you that a firm was very short of working capital how might you try to increase it (a) from internal sources, (b) externally.

4 What are the three main ways in which the value of stock can be calculated? Giving an example explain the circumstances in which each of these methods might be (a) a good way, and (b) a poor way of valuing stock.

5 Hamblewick Cricket Club is a private limited company. Its balance sheet shows £250,000 as reserves. At the annual general meeting someone suggests that these reserves should be used to build the new pavilion the club needs. The cash book shows £23,400 in the bank. Explain why the suggestion cannot be followed up.

6 With the aid of calculations show the difference between the 'straight line' and 'diminishing balance' methods of depreciation. Explain why most assets would be depreciated by the diminishing balance methods.

7 Draw up a model balance sheet for a firm and then analyse it in order to determine:

   a liquidity

   b profitability

   c efficiency.

   Invent any profit and loss account information you need in order to do this.

SECTION C

Coursework and assignments

1 Find an empty shop or other premises in your town.

   Decide a good business use for it explaining your choice.

   Calculate how much initial capital you will need to start your business explaining the amounts you have chosen.

   Undertake each of the transactions you will need to make in getting ready to open for business, making an account of them at each stage in the same way as the models in this chapter.

   Balance your final statement so as to provide an opening balance sheet.

2 Exchange balance sheets with another member of the class.
  Comment upon the balance sheet you now have including anything which surprises you about it.

3 You want to run an event of your choice but your friends think it will make a loss rather than a profit.
  Trying to find actual costs or good estimates for them draw up a possible profit and loss account for the event.
  Who was right – you or your friends?

4 Exchange your model with one of the others. Comment on their calculations and expectations.

5 If there is a tuck shop or some other small business activity in your school or with which you are involved, try to produce final accounts for a trading period of one week or one month and comment upon the profitability of the business, offering advice where you can which might improve it.
  If there is no activity of this kind think of one which might be worth consideration and write a report which includes budgeted profit and loss information recommending the activity.

Chapter 7

The origin and organisation of a business

7.1 Running a business

This chapter and the next are linked. Here we discuss some of the problems of starting a business and in Chapter 8 we look at other aspects of management. The major concern of this chapter is **organisation**, by which is meant two things:

a the need to plan and arrange all the things that are done so as to be as efficient as possible

b the structure that a business develops within which all its activities are arranged.

We saw in Chapter 1 that there was a variety of business activity in Culmford and this will be true of any community. There is also considerable variation in size, a matter which is discussed in more detail in Chapter 13. Some businesses start large because they need to. Examples are oil refining and aircraft production. Others become larger as they achieve success. Many start small and remain that way. In this chapter we take the example of John and Pamela Phillipson who start a cafe and eventually develop the business to include a restaurant as well. At the end of the chapter you will find a number of tasks appropriate to the stages of development which the owners go through as they start and develop their business and which you can undertake within your own communities.

7.2 Where to open the cafe?

Both John and Pamela have some experience of working in a cafe. John had a summer job during his university years and Pamela worked in a local cafe for three years after she left school. Pamela thinks there is room in the town for a cafe which will serve good quick lunches as well as snacks for the rest of the day. They are both keen to run their own business and are lucky enough to be able to find the £350,000 they estimate will be needed. They searched their town for a suitable site.

The discussion about the location of Lovells in Chapter 12 might help you to decide what the main location questions would be for a cafe like this in your area.

7.3 Getting the business ready

The new owners of a small shop just off the market place in their town now have to prepare to open. There are many questions they must answer and some of them are listed in *Fig 7.3*. They are in no particular order. See if you can add to them and then ask the same questions for a cafe in your area.

a How much cash do we need?
b What about the law. What do we have to do?
c What professional help do we need?
d What are the risks? How great are they?
e What can we do to reduce risks or protect ourselves?
f What are we going to call the cafe?
g How and where shall we advertise?
h What hours and days shall we open?

Figure 7.3 Some important questions

Many of the questions they should ask are about the design of the cafe and the things they will need to buy both as furniture and fittings for the cafe and kitchen and also as stock. You can find out these things by asking questions at one or more of your local cafes.

7.4 Organising the work

Organisation makes a contribution to the smallest activity and the tiniest decision. Think of the things you would do to organise yourself and the occasion for each one of the examples given in *Fig 7.4a*.

a You have applied for a job and been asked to come for interview. You must be there by 10.00 a.m. and it is in a town about 25 miles away from where you live.
b You are going on a camping holiday in France with several friends and you have agreed to arrange the trip for everyone.
c You are the chairperson of a committee which is organising a disco to raise money for a local charity.

Figure 7.4a Examples of things which have to be organised

Now that you have thought about these things we can look at some of the questions which John and Pamela might be asking as they get the cafe ready to open.

What work has to be done?

Once they are in business the main worry for a while will be to **survive**, and they will have to be sure they have realistic **objectives**. They might work out that they will have to take £500 each day in order to survive and reaching a target like this will mean **planning**. *Figure 7.4b* shows how the objective of survival can be expressed as a number of steps which must be taken in order to achieve it. Survival obviously depends on enough profit to live on and this in turn means they must do the things they set out to do successfully.

The best way to do this is through targets, and when they arrived at an estimate of £500 a day takings John and Pamela were setting a target. It could have been expressed differently, for example as so many meals each day. If they employ other people in the cafe the targets should be passed on to them in language which they understand because it relates to their part of the job. In *Fig 7.4b* the objective of survival is broken down in this way.

Survival

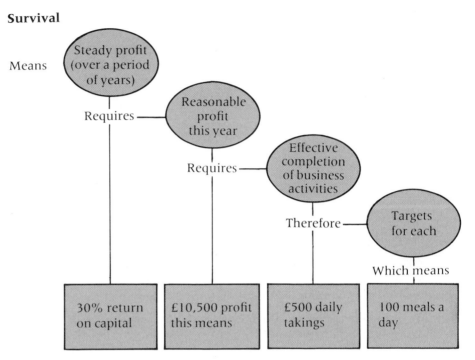

Figure 7.4b What the survival objective means

It is much easier to work out what 100 meals a day means for those who must do the work than it is to simply try to be profitable. It is not likely that they will achieve this objective from the start and they will have to think of ways of attracting people to the cafe as well as of keeping them as regular customers.

Who will do the work?
One person must work alone but there are two of them and this will give some scope for **specialisation**, each hoping to do the things they are good at and like. It will be better to agree certain things which are the special responsibility of one of them so that nothing is left undone and they don't both do the same job. Two orders for fish and none for potatoes would be a recipe for disaster.

When should the work be done?
For most tasks there is a natural or best order and it is sensible to plan to do them that way. Any other way is likely to be expensive in terms of **time** and **money**. Firms often spend money observing how things are done and working out how they should be done in order to be efficient. This is known as **work study** and is discussed again in Chapter 12.

Planning helps to reduce the possibility of mistakes but it cannot take care of everything. There are always things that happen and take us by surprise. The best we can do is to be able to cope when they happen and also to be on the alert since we can often see things coming. *Figure 7.4c* gives examples of some things which can upset the best laid plans.

Changes in prices of raw materials One of the best examples is the price of oil. Big increases put up prices of a wide range of goods and affect the value of the pound abroad and thus import and export prices. In 1986 changes in the price of tin led to unemployment in Cornwall.

Effect of new technology This is discussed in Chapter 12. Few of us would have foreseen the effect of electronic developments. The goods which are now commonly bought and the ways of doing things which are revolutionary have had enormous effects on both production and consumer behaviour.

The effect of severe weather conditions We can anticipate that there will be bad weather and difficulty in movement sometimes in our winter. But we are not used to very low temperatures or to long periods when parts of our country are cut off.

Changes in local or national government policy Sometimes there is warning but not always. In every town you can see the effect on businesses of decisions made by local authorities. It may be a one-way street order or the building of a bypass or the making of a pedestrianised zone, all of which will hit some businesses very hard and be of advantage to others.

Figure 7.4c Changes which affect business plans

Part of good planning is good **timing**. There are certain businesses in which such timing is very important. Shops which sell fashion goods and records are good examples. They must have whatever is popular today in their shops and they must not have high stocks of yesterday's goods.

Part of the planning for John and Pamela will be how they work together successfully and the need to organise will be greater when they employ others to work for them. The basis for good planning is accurate **records**. In a business like a cafe this might be very important because there will be days of the week which are busy and ones which are not. Records help to show a pattern both day by day and week by week.

Suppose they decided what each was going to do but didn't consult each other about things or keep records of what had been done. *Figure 7.4d* gives some examples of the kinds of thing that might happen.

Figure 7.4d Things that happen when people don't work as a team

a   John is cooking and decides to make 100 cakes. Pamela knows that she can't sell more than 60 and she could have told him that. Result – 40 wasted cakes and a loss of time.

b   Pamela does the menu – and John orders the supplies and he does so without consulting Pamela about the things on the menu next week. Result – ingredients are not there when the cooking starts. Maybe the cafe loses custom because one or more of the choices is off the menu.

c   Customers phone to book a table. One of the table staff takes the message, but the book in which these things are kept is locked in the kitchen and the message is forgotten. There is no table when the customers come. Result – loss of business and of goodwill.

How should the business be controlled?

Plans make **control** possible because you can compare what actually happens with what was intended. When it is clear that something has gone wrong, possible actions to put things right are shown in *Fig 7.4e*.

> *a* **Change the objective**. Maybe what you want to do is no longer possible. You can't drive to your destination if the road is blocked or catch the train if it has been cancelled. Pamela could not sell cottage pies if there was no potato available.
>
> *b* **Change the method**. If the road is blocked and the distance short you might walk. If the train is cancelled you might drive to your destination. Pamela might serve minced meat with rice if potatoes are not available.
>
> *c* **Get someone else to do it**. If you cannot meet a friend arriving by train someone else might do it for you. If you need greater strength to loosen a nut either a combined effort or another stronger person might be successful. Pamela might buy cottage pies so she can keep to her menu.
>
> *d* **Use different equipment, resources or materials**. If a car is in the ditch people may not get it out, but a tractor will. Producing a large number of cars requires capital equipment and mass production rather than personal skill and a toolkit.

Figure 7.4e Things to do when something goes wrong

Poor organisation is at the centre of many of the things that go wrong and it is worth taking a lot of time and patience getting the **processes** of business right before rushing into the **tasks**.

Now we look at organisation in the second sense we talked about at the beginning of this chapter, the building of a structure within which the business can operate.

7.5 Formal organisation

In any activity there are obvious divisions of the work. In your school there are departments for most subjects and there are other activities like cleaning and maintaining the school, cooking and serving the midday meals which are left to specialists. The head will spend most of the time managing the school and its work.

In Pamela and John's cafe it is likely that one will do most of the work preparing meals and that they will employ people to serve customers. As the business grows the scope for specialisation will increase. In a large business there are likely to be several departments and further specialisation within them. *Figure 7.5a* shows a likely department structure for Anyfirm plc. It is a public limited company with a board of directors who make the important policy decisions. Leading the team is the managing director who will make sure the board knows about the activities of the firm and that the firm carries out the instructions of the board. Each of the main functions has its head of department and *Fig 7.5b* briefly explains the kinds of things those departments normally do.

Purchasing	The firm will have stocks of raw materials and components. It will also have small tools and other equipment used in production. The purchasing department probably has responsibility for **stock control** and must ensure that things are ready when needed, in the right amounts and in good condition.
Production	A large firm might well divide its producing activities into several divisions either by region, by product, or by process. We discuss production in Chapter 12.
Marketing	Marketing is much more than selling, and includes things like market research, packaging, design, pricing, and advertising. We discuss marketing in Chapter 11.
Finance	We discussed finance in Chapter 5. It is always a part of decisions since every activity involves **costs** or brings in **income**.
Personnel	The personnel department recruits for the firm and looks after the interests of employees. Training is often a separate section of the work. It usually deals with wages and conditions of work and with negotiations between workers and management. We discuss these things in Chapters 9 and 10.

Figure 7.5a Departments of a medium-sized firm

In *Figs 7.5a* and *7.5b* the organisation of Anyfirm is by **function**, but this is not the only way it could be done. Sometimes it is not the most suitable and does not tell you very much about how the firm really works. If a firm is involved in several different kinds of activity, like ICI, Unilever, and Grand Metropolitan, some of the departments will be product based, e.g. ICI's paints division. If a firm is working in several countries there is likely to be a division of the company for each country. Nevertheless the functional approach to organisation is a part of almost all structures and essential services like finance are usually centralised.

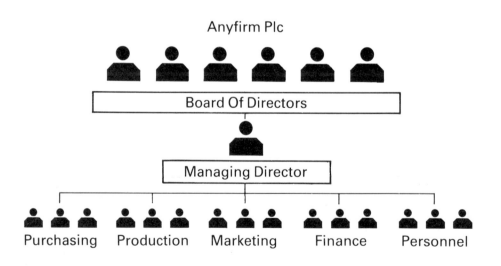

Figure 7.5b Possible departments of Anyfirm plc

7.6 Features of formal organisation

Figure 7.6a shows the organisation as it might be for the marketing department of Anyfirm. Using it we can discuss features which are true of most organisations of this kind.

In any department someone must be in charge. The department begins with that person and is described downwards, each following level being subordinate to the one above and people on the same level having the same **status**.

Figure 7.6a The marketing department of Anyfirm plc

In most organisations you can observe:

Specialisation
To have a marketing department at all is specialisation, but this firm goes much further defining seven subgroups in which people will specialise. Only a small part of the work is in the hands of any one person and only the director has overall responsibility. The department has several experts and in doing so expects to enjoy **economies of scale**. These are discussed further in Chapter 12.

Delegation
The managing director has handed over the day-to-day responsibility for the marketing function of the firm to the head of this department. He or she has delegated it. He or she hasn't abandoned it since the success of the firm will still be his or her responsibility. In their turn heads of department give responsibility to those who are heads of section.

Co-ordination
When work is divided between several people what they do has to be brought together. This will be done by committee work, by various ways of regular communication between the members of the department and as part of the work of the head of department.

Authority
When you are made responsible for part of the work of a business you need to be able to do that work and the business must ensure that you have the authority. In a business authority is usually given by **title** and by **job description**.

Status

Title usually suggests status as well but there are often other indicators which everyone can observe. It is often these additional things which attract people to status positions. Examples would be a company car, a large well-carpeted office, or the right to use certain facilities of the firm. Outside business both status and authority are often indicated by a uniform and symbols.

A chain of command

The chain of command in a business is from the board to the managing director, then to the heads of department and down through those departments to the shop floor and office workers. The number of levels in this chain varies from one business to another. There is no right length but if it is too long decisions often take a long time and information passes slowly through the chain. If it is too short the firm is not taking sufficient advantage of opportunities to delegate and there are likely to be some people who are overworked and therefore inefficient.

A span of control

The managing director is in control of the whole firm but he or she only directly controls the work of the five heads of department shown in *Fig 7.5a*. Similarly the marketing director has overall responsibility for the whole department but only directly controls the six section heads shown in *Fig 7.6a*.

The number of people a person directly controls in this way is the **span of control**. You can check the span of control of all people at each level by counting up the number of people who report directly to them. In some situations where people have to work together all the time it is usually best to have small spans of control but in situations where people work mostly on their own a span of control can be quite large. For example a regional bank manager may be responsible for a large number of branches but a supervisor cannot control too large a group. The kinds of things which influence the number of people it is possible to be responsible for and remain efficient are:

a   the nature of the responsibility. Is it general or must work be closely supervised?
b   how often and for what reasons subordinates have to report or superiors have to check.
c   the way in which communication occurs. Is it face to face by written memo, by telephone, or by electronic means? Some methods are more time-consuming and tiring than others.
d   the nature of the work. Some work is easy to check whilst other work has to be probed in detail and with great care.
e   how well the people concerned get on with each other.
f   the status of the people concerned. Sometimes a worker has to control the work of others who are of the same status; the work of committees is often like this. Sometimes the status of the people present varies and this can cause problems.

Job description

Job description is not obvious from the formal organisation chart but it is the basis of responsibility, authority, and status. It helps people who have to work together to know what their respective positions are and what they are supposed to do. People often leave a job because they find that it isn't what they expected or they are never certain what their job is. Sometimes this happens through misunderstanding but it is often because there was no job description or it was a poor one. *Figure 7.6b* gives some ideas of things that might be in a job description.

Job descriptions vary with the extent to which an employer thinks they are useful and wants to control what staff do or how they do it. For example, one employer might give a van driver a job description which says what has to be done but leaves the route planning to the driver. Another might provide quite specific routes and an order to deliver so that it was fairly certain where that driver was on a given day and a particular time. A post office driver has to be very controlled because collections from boxes are timed, and a bus driver has to keep to a published timetable. If the organisation of work can be left to the employee it gives most people greater **job satisfaction** but there are some who prefer to be told what to do and how to do it.

a It would tell you what qualifications, experience, and abilities you were expected to have.
b It would tell you what you were expected to do.
c In many jobs it would tell you how and when these things should be done, although in other cases you would be expected to work this out for yourself and do it in your own way.
d It would tell you who and what you are responsible for.
e It would give all this information to others, particularly those who work with you, so that you all know where you stand.
f It would be an accurate basis for other decisions which have to be made in the firm, e.g. working out pay and advertising for someone to fill the job.

Figure 7.6b The advantages of a job description

Centralisation

In the organistion chart for Anyfirm all the marketing decisions are centralised in the work of the marketing department and the same is true of the other functions. If the firm had several branches it is likely that some of those functions would remain centralised at head office and some would be decentralised so that the people in charge of the branches made their own decision. If every decision, however small, had to wait for the approval of head office business would be very slow and inefficient but if head office did not retain a large measure of control of things which it thought were matters of **policy** and of the **finances** of the whole business there may well be problems. *Figure 7.6c* suggests some of the things which help a firm to decide how centralised its working should be.

a Major decisions of policy would normally be at head office because these things affect the whole firm and should be dealt with in the same general way all the time. Even in a firm with no branches such decisions would normally be taken by the board and not by the departments.

b Some departmental roles are central to the operation of the whole business and are normally centralised. These might include finance, personnel, training, and the employment of senior staff.

c Some things are centralised because there is a possibility of economies of scale. Purchasing is often done centrally for this reason.

d Some things need to be co-ordinated and decisions about them are made centrally. For example electricity has to be supplied through a national grid and British Rail has to decide the timetable for the whole country nationally.

Figure 7.6c Things which affect decisions about centralisation

7.7 Informal behaviour

The formal organisation chart defines the **rules** and **relationships** which the firm expects and through which it intends to work. But every business also works through a number of informal contacts, some examples of which are given in *Fig 7.7a.*

a In small businesses like the cafe all the workers and the owners will know each other, be working together continually, and be much less formal in the way they work and respond to each other.

b In small communities, even if the business is large, many of the people will meet socially and may come into contact in entirely different roles and relationships. A junior member of the firm may be chairperson of the parish council whilst the manager is a member of it.

c In some organisations people have more than one role and a different status may attach to each. Very often the head of a school also acts as a junior member of one of the subject departments.

d Ties of family relationship or social contacts may mean that the formal relations required in the workplace are difficult to maintain.

Figure 7.7a Informal contacts which may influence working relationships

You will find some links of the kind in *Fig 7.7a* in almost any organisation. They are useful because they help us to learn to react to each other as people and not just as workers or managers. They usually promote co-operation and job satisfaction. But they can be damaging when people who meet informally outside business use those contacts rather than the formal system. Such behaviour leaves some people uninformed when they should know, unconsulted when they should have been part of a decision. When people feel their status is being ignored they become frustrated and annoyed, they often over-react and their job satisfaction is greatly reduced.

Informal influences also develop within a business if it is big enough to have several members of the workforce at or about the same level and associating with each other during the working day. In these conditions people with similar ideas, ambitions or concerns, people with similar interests or intentions will tend to come together and form an **informal group**. Some groups do not always have the interests of the business in mind and what they do is not helpful to the business and may be harmful. Television programmes often show this side of what goes on in organisations like businesses, hospitals, schools, and newspapers, emphasising power struggles and group interests more than the daily work.

Those going into a job for the first time are often particularly suprised by these parts of working life and it is wise to keep an open mind, being observant and waiting to see before deciding how and when to fit into the pattern. *Figure 7.7b* gives some examples of informal behaviour. It must be emphasised that informal behaviour of this kind is a part of job satisfaction and in this way works for the benefit of the organisation. It is more often a positive contribution than it is otherwise.

a a grapevine in the firm which is the source of information, much of which is rumour rather than fact.

b some people are respected more than others and have privileges. These may be simple things like their own seat, coatpeg, tea mug, or car parking space.

c some unwritten rules only to be found out by watching how others behave. These will be part of the tradition of working in the firm and often about how you communicate with other workers, or how and when you use facilities.

d among the workers as a whole there will be friends who see each other as a group, support each other, and do not always welcome approaches from outside the group. Membership of one or more of these groups is often an important part of job satsifaction.

e many firms like to project an image and put pressure on workers to conform to that image. An example is the dairy firm who have insisted that roundspeople should dress to a certain standard which for men means a collar and tie.

Figure 7.7b
Examples of the informal working of a firm

7.8 Conclusion

We began this chapter by looking at the need for organisation as it applied to the starting of a new business. From this we learned that all activities need to be planned and organised if they are to be efficient and if we are to have a way of controlling them and putting things right when they go wrong. From that we moved to the formal organisational structure of a firm concentrating on the functional approach. In fact, people tend to work together in teams with a lot of committee work rather than in the way that an organisation chart suggests. From such a chart we were able to discuss many of the ways in which people work together. We return to several of these themes in the next two chapters. Finally we discussed those ways in which people behave as people rather than as work machines and relate to each other both within an organisation and outside it.

THINGS TO DO

Short answer questions

1 Distinguish between primary, secondary, and tertiary business activity and give one example of each.

2 State three ways of measuring the size of a business and give an example of the kind of business for which each of these may be most suitable.

3 Is the business that John and Pamela have decided to open primary, secondary, or tertiary? Explain your answer.

4 *Figure 7.3* shows some of the important questions that John and Pamela have to ask about their new business.
   a Think of two other important questions they might ask.
   b What hours of the day do cafes normally open in your area?

5 Do you think there is a need for another cafe like this in your area? Explain your decision.

6 What three objectives would you expect all businesses to have?

7 State three types of plan you might expect each of the following to make and use.
   a John and Pamela
   b The Odd Job Shop
   c A bus company near you
   d A local supermarket.

8 What is meant by delegation? Give examples to illustrate your answer.

9 Explain why co-ordination is important in each of the following situations:
   a a relay race
   b a football match
   c when a committee organise a dance
   d the transport system of the UK
   e the work of a marketing department.

10 What is a budget and what things would you expect John and Pamela to budget for?

11 Write down the names of five departments you might expect to see in a medium-sized firm.

12 What is meant by economies of scale?

13 What is status?

14 Define span of control and explain how it is related to chain of command.

15 Why is control of finance usually centralised?

Essays and structured questions

1 Explain why very few small shops can be seen in the main street of most large towns.

2 Explain why it is often difficult to measure the size of firms and illustrate with examples of firms from your area.

3 Take any five of the questions in *Fig 7.3* and show why the answers are important to any business.

4 Draw an organisation chart for your school or for a business you know and from it explain the meaning and importance of:
a delegation
b responsibility
c chain of command
d span of control.

5 Explain why the number of people reporting to a manager may be less important than other things in determining how well he or she does the job of being responsible for them and their work.

6 Using the steps in *Fig 7.4b* explain what objectives you would expect a firm to have and how these must be worked out and communicated to others if the business is to be successful.

7 You have been asked to organise an event, a dance or a football match for example.
a Decide when and where it is to be, explaining your choice.
b Decide how much you will charge, saying why.
c Draw up a budget for the event and work out how many people you think must attend if it is to be worthwhile.
d Decide how you are going to advertise it.

8 Some people have offered to help you with the organisation of your event.
a Do you think you can use help?
b What problems of organisation might occur if you are working with several other people?
c How will you cope with them?

9 What are the arguments for and against centralisation of responsibility? What things do you think ought to be (*a*) centralised and (*b*) decentralised in a firm which has a chain of shoe shops throughout the country?

10 'The organisation chart of a firm may not be a good indicator of the way it really works.' Using the organisation chart you drew in Question 4, or by reference to another one of your choice, explain the different reasons why this statement may be true.

SECTION C   ## Coursework and assignments

1 In your local town
   a What kind of restaurant and cafe do you think might be a worthwhile business?
     Explain why you think this is so.
   b Discover which premises are available at the moment, how much they would cost and then decide which would be the best site.
2 Find a business which has only just started in your town and find out what the main organisation problems were and how they were tackled.
3 Consider the examples given in *Fig 7.4a*. Choose two situations, either from those, or of your own and starting from your home base work out a detailed plan to achieve your objective. Find an appropriate diagrammatic way of expressing your plan (a flow chart or a critical path network might be appropriate).
4 One of the main objectives of a business is to survive. Find a business in your area which as recently closed down and try to discover why it did not survive.
5 Talk to people who work in the offices or on the shop floor of firms in your area. Find out what they think the objectives of the firms they work for are. Comment on your findings.
6 Look at some of the changes which have taken place in your area in recent years and explain why you think they have taken place.
   Does your survey of your area suggest any ways in which it might change in the future?
   Which businesses in your area do you think might need to respond to changes?
   Why do you think this is so?
7 If you were a craftsman made redundant with a substantial sum as redundancy pay, what business opportunities do you think exist in your area which would be a reasonable use of the money?
   Give reasons for your choices.
8 Consider *Figure 7.4c*. Show how each of the changes which are listed in the figure have affected or might affect your locality.
   If there are any other causes of change which have been or you think might be important write about those as well.

Chapter 8

Managing a business

8.1 The need for management

In Chapter 7 we looked at many things which owners or managers must do if they are to make sure that the business survives and is successful. In this chapter we look at some of those things again in more detail and at some others which are part of the work of the manager.

In a sole trader business, in a partnership and often in a private limited company, it is the owners of the business who will also manage it, but in larger businesses management is by employees who specialise in these tasks. When you think of managers it is most likely to be of people who are at the top of the business but in most businesses all those tasks which add together to make up management are done by many different people. The main things that those who manage have to do are shown in *Fig 8.1*. You will recognise some of them as things which were discussed in the last chapter.

Figure 8.1. Management activities

Setting objectives	**Survival** was the objective we discussed in Chapter 7. Making a good **profit** and **growth** are among the other objectives managers might set. Those who set objectives in the **public sector** might be more concerned with providing a **service.**
Organising	In Chapter 7 we looked at organising in two ways. Firstly the kind of ordering of our actions which we all have to do if we want to be efficient, and secondly at the framework within which a business operates.
Planning	Plans help us to work for our objectives. We looked at some in Chapter 7 and we look at others in this chapter.
Motivating	Managers spend much of their time trying to make sure that what workers do helps the business to achieve its objectives. In this chapter we discuss ways of encouraging and rewarding good work – ways of **motivating**.
Communicating	Communication is important in everything we do and in this chapter we look at good and bad methods of communicating. We try to find ways in which communication can be improved.
Controlling	Work will not run smoothly without direction and control. Things often have to be changed and in order to do this what is happening must be observed and interpreted.
Developing	You might recognise this as **training**. It is part of a managers job to learn from things that happen and make sure that others learn as well so that the performance of individuals and of the business as a whole gets better.

8.2 Risk-taking

We all have to make decisions and make a large number of them each day. Most are routine and a bad decision will often be a pity without being a disaster. Managers make decisions many of which could be quite harmful to the success or future of the business if they are not well thought out and put into effect carefully. The effect of a bad management decision could be the end of the firm, the end of some people's jobs, or less profit for the shareholders. The manager takes the personal risk of losing the job or not being promoted but it is the **owners** who take the full risks of the business.

It is necessary, in an economy in which much business activity is in the hands of private enterprise, that some people should be prepared to take the risks of business but they will only do so if they can reasonably hope for a reward in the form of **profit**.

For sole owners the risk is complete and they could lose all they own if a business fails. Someone in a partnership takes the same kind of risks but at least has one or more other owners to share it with. For companies the risk is shared between many people, each risking only the shareholding he or she has in the business.

8.3 The entrepreneur

Think of a house and then of the work of an architect. Architects do not build houses, neither do they provide the materials. They provide the design for the building, they visualise what it will look like when it is finished. They control the things that are used and the work of the builders so as to ensure that the finished house matches the design and is in accordance with the specifications. This is exactly what the **entrepreneur** does. The role is partly creative, partly organising, and partly controlling using the factors of production we discussed in Chapter 2.

In small businesses the entrepreneur, being the owner, is easy to identify, but as a firm gets bigger the role is divided between those who take the business risks, called owners, and those who are responsible for the activities of the firm, called **managers**. In Anyfirm, whose organisation chart we considered in Chapter 7, we saw that the activities of just one department were divided between many people who were doing the things which together we call management. How much more difficult then to identify the entrepreneur in such firms as ICI and General Electric, or in public organisations like British Coal.

Most businesses start small with the creativity of one or two people and their preparedness to back their ideas and take risks. A dynamic economy is one in which new business ventures are being started all the time. Many organisations in this country, and particularly the state, actively encourage new enterprise. If jobs get more difficult to find in large firms, if capital is taking the place of labour in many manufacturing firms, then an important part of job creation is the emergence of new entrepreneurs and of small businesses.

In Chapter 1, particularly in Mill Street, Culmford, we saw several examples of the entrepreneur at work. Small businesses with owners determined to make a living found ways of adding to their main income. One good example was the sweet shop owners who also ran a taxi service.

8.4 Setting objectives

In Chapter 7 we discussed survival as an objective. This is important for all businesses but most of the time, certain of survival, they will be able to turn their attention to other objectives. The message from the two comments in *Fig 8.4a* is that **objectives** have both a starting and a finishing point. They are the purpose of what we do in business, and without which it is not easy either to be efficient or to check whether others are efficient. Many businesses have failed to grow or have gone out of business because their objectives were not well thought out or were not very realistic. We need objectives so that we can:

a explain to others what the business is working to achieve.
b help people decide between alternative courses of action.
c check the present position and decide what must be done next.

There is no business behaviour for which objectives should not be set. A business, as a whole, will have objectives expressed in terms of

a **survival** making sure that they are still in business tomorrow and the day after that.
b **profit** sufficient to provide for a reasonable standard of living or an acceptable dividend as well as the continuation of the business.
c **growth** sufficient profit to plough back into a business so that its future prospects are greater than its present achievements.

The departments of a business will translate these overall objectives into ones which make sense for it and which are likely to promote the overall success of the business, so those of a marketing department might by any of the following:

a **Maximisation of sales** This might be a good obejctive when the product is new or the firm is extending into a new part of the market. It may be a poor one if the productive capacity of the firm is less than its sales capacity.
b **Increased rate of turnover** If the firm empties the shelves quickly it will look good in terms of the **turnover** ratios but it may be at the expense of profits if discounts have to be offered or the expenses of finding the markets are high.
c **Maximisation of net marketing revenue** This does take the expense of marketing into account but may lead the firm into a low-risk marketing policy which leaves the market open to the more aggressive competitor.
d **Market penetration** Here the emphasis is on finding new markets or new parts of the existing market. This could be worthwhile in terms of long-term reputation but poor in terms of present results.

The important thing is that such marketing objectives are in line with the overall objectives of the firm, are realistic in the light of market research, and are attainable, particularly when compared with the capabilities and intentions of the production department. However well objectives are worked out it is pointless to be selling 50 units of a product a day if the production department can only produce 35 units a day.

'Would you please tell me where to go from here?'
'That depends a good deal on where you want to get to,' said the cat.
'I don't much care where,' said Alice.
'Then it doesn't matter which way you go,' said the cat.
(from *Alice's Adventures in Wonderland*)

Traveller to a local resident: 'Can you please tell me how I get to Culmford?' Resident replies; 'If I'd bin you I wouldn't 'ave started from 'ere.'

Figure 8.4a Who needs objectives?

You will remember Pamela and John from the last chapter. Suppose they have been successful and decide to open a restaurant next door. This is a different **segment** of the catering market and, as such, presents different challenges to the entrepreneur. Some of the areas of activity in whcih they might set objectives for the new part of the business might be:

Productivity   Resources will be needed, including food, drink, equipment, items which could be sold over the counter, raw materials, and people. Productivity is about the efficiency with which these resources are combined.

Reputation   The best indicator will be the people who, having been for a meal, want to come back regularly. Managers have to ensure their **market standing** is good and that their **market share** is maintained.

Creativeness   There is scope for creativeness in most businesses. In the new restaurant this might be found in the surroundings or in the menu. It is often seen in the names which are given to businesses or in the way the firm advertises.

Resources   The main obejctive will be to make the best use of resources of time, labour, and equipment. But they may think that there is a need for new resources in the expanded business. Perhaps there is now room to use a computer or greater technology in the kitchens.

Finance   In larger businesses there is a greater financial commitment and it is more likely that cash is borrowed or has been obtained through partnership or becoming a company. The main objective will be to obtain a reasonable **return on capital employed**.

Profit   Survival is the first objective and then a continuing profit. The pursuit of profit will not be the only objective and some of the things they do to maintain reputation, or for their own job satisfaction, or to care for employees may even reduce profit a little.

Employees   Employers know what they want and will want to find a motivated workforce to help their achievement. Employee objectives might include effective training, good conditions of work, promotion of job satisfaction, and welfare services.

Customers   The source of profit. Particularly in the early days they must be persuaded that they like the restaurant and given the opportunity to develop the habit of coming to it. This kind of **promotion** will reduce potential profits in the short run but help to ensure long term profits. Customers who have enjoyed an evening in the restaurant will be the best source of advertising and dissatisfied customers do a lot of damage to trade.

General Public   A source of potential customers and of publicity. Objectives will include keeping up the appearance of the cafe, ensuring no litter around it, and making sure customers don't leave noisily late at night. What the owners want to achieve is a **good image** for the business.

Only the owners of a business can decide what its objectives shall be and which ones are most important at a particular time. The decision is always influenced by employees, customers, those the firm trades with, the general public and, in many instances, the government. Objectives must always be flexible, and the firm ready to change them.

8.5 Working through people

In Chapter 7 we saw how important plans are and how great the need is for people in business to work together as a team. As a business gets larger it employs people and must rely upon them to put plans into effect and achieve the objectives of the business. But workers do not automatically want to achieve other people's objectives. There has to be some stimulus to persuade them to do so. Finding ways of persuading employees to work purposefully for a business is called **motivation** and is one of the important skills of management.

What things do motivate workers?

How many of your class are immediately thinking of words like money, pay, and cash? I suspect most are and, of course, pay is one of the most important motivators for all of us. We need enough of it to satisfy our needs and most of us would like a little extra money to provide for a comfortable standard of living. In Chapter 9 we discuss different ways of paying employees and how pay may be used to motivate. In Chapter 10 we look more closely at the reasons why we go to work and what we hope to get out of it.

8.6 Management planning and development

The importance of good planning was established in the last chapter. In this chapter we look at some important plans which managers produce in order to run the business as well as they can. Some of these plans are part of the daily routine and some are about the long term control and development of the firm. In some cases it is enough to make use of plans which have been made by others but most businesses have their own special needs and must make a lot of their own plans.

Budgets

Budgets are plans which enable managers to see what return on capital employed they are likely to get. They can see whether it wil be worth doing and where the risks are. They may be able to see where the high income points are and perhaps think of ways of protecting those and increasing the others. Once the plan has been put into action they can check progress against the plan and see if action has to be taken. The way a budget works is shown in *Fig 8.6a.*

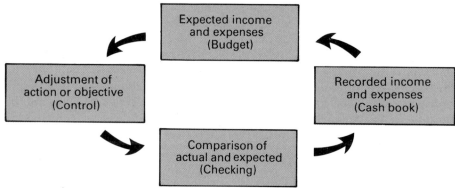

Figure 8.6a The use of budgets

The budget cycle starts with the present position and information which will help in forecasting. With a budget the firm will move towards its objectives. The budget comes from the work of many people. Each head of department will propose things for the coming year and will work out a departmental budget. It will show in money terms, the intentions of the department.

All the requirements of the departments will be much greater than the firm can afford and some of the ideas of each department will clash with those of others. Someone has to make a decision about priorities. Some departments may get all they want, some may get very little, and most departments will have to sacrifice something. The **master budget** is three things:

a a statement in money terms of the objectives of the business
b a compromise between the wishes and needs of departments
c a means of co-ordinating and controlling the work of the departments to meet the firm's objectives.

Budgets are produced by people and they have to be worked by them. Those who prepare budgets commit themselves to the ideas they contain and work hard to make them successful. A budget is more likely to work if the people who have to carry it out have been involved in its development and have some understanding of both its purpose and the reasons behind it. You know from your own experience of situations in which you felt you had a right to be asked about things but were not. How did you feel? How prepared were you to co-operate, particularly if you thought the decision was wrong?

Budgets can motivate if people are involved in them and will not do their job of **controlling** business behaviour if people have no interest in making them work. Examples of control through budgets are given in *Fig 8.6b*. It is important that control is tight enough but not too tight. If sales targets are so high that not even the best salesperson can reach them they will frustrate rather than help. If expense budgets are too small for even the most careful user they will either prevent things happening which should happen or they will be ignored.

Budgets are **forecasts** of likely events during the course of the business year. The actual happenings are rarely identical with the budget and nobody expects them to be. To make sure budgets help rather than hinder, control but do not prevent things that should happen, it is common practice to make them flexible as shown in the sales budget for Anyfirm plc in *Fig 8.6c*.

Figure 8.6b. Ways in which budgets control

Production	There may be a monthly target for say the number of cars which come off the assembly line. This may be broken down into targets for each line of workers or for each shift on a daily basis.
Marketing	Each salesperson may have a personal target based on experience and the area in which sales are made. Such targets are often made competitive with bonuses for the most successful person in a week or month.
Expenses	Budgets often impose authority limits for particular staff. These may be about the total amount which can be spent in a period or it may be a maximum size of cheque which can be signed without higher authority.
Time	A school timetable is a typical budget allowing so much time per week for each subject depending on priority decisions which have been made. It is also a budget for each day and for other resources such as classrooms, gamesfields, and teachers.
Cash	A cash flow statement is a budget showing how the firm expects cash to move in and out of the business and what the balance available is likely to be.

Figure 8.6c Flexible budget: Sales division Anyfirm plc

Figure 8.6c is nothing more than all of us do when thinking about what is going to happen. It shows three sales forecasts with the one in the middle being the budget and the two outside ones likely happenings. The firm can allow actual sales to move around within those two limits without being too bothered about it. The position in *Fig 8.6c* looks to have started poorly but to have picked up during the year with a tremendous surge of sales in the middle. The firm should be happy you might think. But lets look more closely. Apart from a drop from a very high peak in the summer months sales have been rising steadily all year. They are substantially higher in December than they were at the start of the year. *Figure 8.6d* suggests some questions that might arise or have arisen during the year.

a Is there a **trend** of rising sales throughout the year?
b If this trend is going to continue will the firm be able to cope next year? What is the projection for next year likely to be and can the resources be found?
c If the trend isn't to continue can we expect a drop back towards the low sales of last January?
d There was a high peak in the summer months. How did the firm cope? Did they have to work overtime, make customers wait, buy in stock from elsewhere, or use poorer materials?
e This peak was not foreseen. Steady sales increases had been expected. Is it likely to occur again next year and, if we think it is, how can it be planned for?
f Were there any cash flow problems? Sharply rising sales often lead to these because production increases have to be paid for in advance of income.

Figure 8.6d Some questions the chart (*Fig 8.6c*) suggests

Cash flow forecasts

References were made to this in Chapter 5 when we considered sources of finance, in Chapter 7 as one of the plans that John and Pamela might use, and in *Fig 8.6d*. In this chapter when we referred to a possible cash flow problem. A budget of this kind gives managers some idea of the way cash is likely to flow into and out of the business and helps them do two important things:

a take action to prevent a cash flow problem which the forecast suggests might happen. Many firms have seasonal sales patterns and find that there are some months of the year when many of the expenses are met whilst there are others when most of the income is earned. Farming is a good example.
b plan to spend money on things which can wait until when the forecast suggests a cash surplus is likely to be available.

The things to work out in making this forecast are shown in *Fig 8.6e*.

a likely sales income from cash sales

b likely income from debtors who bought things in the previous period

c how these normal figures may be affected by special events or the time of year. What happened last year at the same time might help with this

d normal running costs for the period

e regular payments like rent, rates, and insurance which have to be paid in the period

f special expenses which have to be met

g timing and size of any intended capital expenditure in the period. Examples are new cash register, or new delivery van

h creditors who must be paid during the period. This could include traders, the inland revenue, interest payments, or loans that have to be paid back.

Figure 8.6e Steps in working out cash forecasts

8.7 Measuring and controlling costs

A business has to do better than cover its costs to show a profit. A budget helps to identify the main cost centres and control those costs during the year. In Anyfirm plc, whose marketing department we looked at in *Fig 7.6a*, there were six sections of the department. Each of these would be a cost centre with its own budget for costs and some of the sections might have more than one, for example design and development, and advertising and promotion might be split. Sales might have cost centres for each region or for each product. For each cost centre there will be a number of different kinds of cost:

Direct costs

These are costs which occur within a particular cost centre and which can be related to it. Costs are direct if the expenditure was intended to benefit a particular cost centre or if it was caused by that centre. Paying the expenses of salespersons is a direct cost to **sales**.

Indirect costs

Costs are indirect if they have been met for the work of a particular cost centre and are either shared with other centres or cannot be directly related to the work the centre does. For example each cost centre is likely to use company stationery, telephone time, and the time of certain specialists within the firm but it is not always possible to work these out.

Overhead costs

In addition to the work done in particular departments there will be the general costs of running the firm and these are called **overheads**. Some way must be found of allocating these costs over the business as a whole. A department store is a good example. Each department will have its costs but those of rent for the building, lighting and heating, advertising the business, and so on, will have to be shared.

Figure 8.7a is an example of a possible costing statement for one product produced by a firm

Direct costs:		£	£
	Wages	12,000	
	Materials	5,600	
			17,600
Indirect costs			6,400
Production costs			24,000
Add overheads (allocated by an agreed method)			7,400
Total costs			31,400

Figure 8.7a Example of cost calculation

Suppose the department whose costs are shown in *Fig 8.7a* makes fireside chairs and that those costs are for 1,000 chairs. It is often helpful to work out costs per unit of production (i.e. per chair) and then the statement would be as shown in *Fig 8.7b*:

For 1,000 chairs produced:		
Direct costs:		
	£ per chair	
Wages	12.00	
Materials	5.60	
		17.60
ADD:		
Indirect costs	6.40	
Overheads	7.40	
		13.80
Total Cost		31.40

Figure 8.7b Calculation of unit costs of production

There are some problems with this method of costing. It is sometimes difficult to decide what kind of cost a particular item is and it is difficult to allocate overheads to the various cost centres. The most common method is to link it in some way with the activity of the cost centre and that is why many firms use a proportion of the labour costs.

Because the allocation of some costs is a guess it is often difficult to be certain whether a particular activity is making a loss or a profit. For example: suppose Pamela and John decide to have a bar in their restaurant and suppose it is not staffed but run by the waiters and waitresses who are on duty anyway. What proportion of the wages of the staff should be allocated to running the bar? Some proportion of the cost of goods sold may be as good a method as any of making the decision. If these costs are added in and some part of the overheads of running the firm are also allocated to the bar the costs it is responsible for may be greater than the income it earns. Is it then true to say that the bar makes a loss?

Direct costs:	£
Wages	18
Materials	15
	33
Indirect costs:	
Heat and light	1
Power	2
	3
Overheads	9
Total cost per chair	£45

Figure 8.8a Cost statement for office chairs

8.8 Contribution

Let's work this problem out with another example. Suppose one of the products of a firm is office chairs. Suppose they cost £45 to produce and are sold for £70. Do you think a firm would be interested in an offer to buy 100 chairs at £40 per chair.? On the face of it this is a loss of £5 on each chair and the answer should be no, but lets take a closer look. We have cost information in the form of a statement like that above in *Fig 8.8a*.

Overheads are the kinds of expense which must be incurred anyway regardless of the number of chairs produced. They won't be increased by the order and are already being paid for at the rate of £9 per chair by the other chairs produced. The only costs which the new order will involve are the **production** costs; that is £36 per chair. Since the order is worth £40 per chair it will make a **contribution** of £4 for each one sold and a total contribution of £400, therefore it should be taken.

It is this idea of contribution which tells us the real answer when a decision has to be made about part of a business. It should only be closed down if it is not making a contribution, that is if the production costs are not covered by the sale price. A lot of pricing decisions are made on the basis of contribution and *Fig 8.8b* has some examples.

British Rail	base their standard fares on the full cost of the service but all the other fares are charged to fill up trains and pay for lines and stations that are already there and even a small fare will make a **contribution**.
British Telecom	charge the full price of the system partly by a standing charge and partly by full cost prices at peak times. They encourage use of a service which is already there and under-used at other times by charging cheaper rates for the afternoon and even cheaper ones for the evenings and weekends.
Electricity	The national grid system and the power stations need to be kept going at a steady rate. Those who want to use electricity at off-peak times are encouraged to do so, their payments being sufficient to make a **contribution**.
Cinemas	are already there and their cost will be covered by full-price tickets for performances. They can make more money by offering cut-price tickets to certain groups of people at times when they know the seats would not be needed for customers paying the full price.

Figure 8.8b Contribution costing and everyday prices

To use contribution costing as a basis for a decision a firm must already have its overhead costs covered by other things that it does. It must also make sure that those who are paying full prices can't switch to the cheaper ones. In the examples above British Rail does it by banning the use of cheaper tickets on certain trains, the electricity groups do it by providing different meters for those who want to use off-peak electricity. British Telecom does it by time bands.

8.9 Break-even

This is a term we all use and it means the same in business as it does ordinarily, i.e. being in the position that you earn from what you do exactly as much as it costs you to do it. The break-even point is the minimum position for long-term survival and if a firm can make and sell more units of a product than break-even point at the same or lower costs per unit then it will make a profit. To use this technique we look at costs in the same way but use different words to describe them.

Fixed costs	are really the equivalent of overheads. Those costs which the firm must accept in order to run the business regardless of the number of units produced within a given time and capacity. Such costs are called fixed because, in the short run, they do not change.
Variable costs	are costs which are a result of output and which vary with it.

Figure 8.9a Fixed and variable costs

Break-even analysis can be done using a graph, and this is the first method we choose. *Figure 8.9b* shows how the costs described above might appear on a break-even chart.

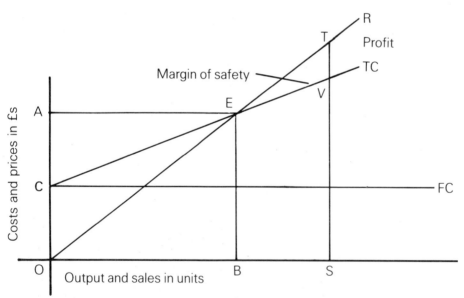

Figure 8.9b Finding the break-even level of output

Fixed costs are shown as a straight line because they have to be paid in order to make output possible and will be the same anywhere between 0 and 20,000 units of output. Variable costs are on top of fixed costs, i.e. beginning at point C they give the total costs at any level of output. As an example at an output of 11,000 units total costs are £19,000. This is fixed costs of £6,000 plus variable costs of £13,000. If we want to find the break-even point we must now add information about revenues to our chart.

Break-even is at E where the total cost and the revenue are equal. At that point the firm will make and sell OB units of output at a cost and revenue of OA. After the point E the distance between the total revenue (R) and the total cost (TC) widens. This is often called the **margin of safety**. The vertical distance at any point represents **profit** so that at output and sales level **S** the profit is the distance **VT**.

The diagram is only a model and that is why we can draw revenue and total cost lines which are straight. In an actual situation neither variable costs per unit nor prices would necessarily be the same at all levels of output and sales. The diagram also assumes that a firm will sell all that it produces which is not always the case. Nevertheless it is a useful way of working out what level of output the firm must aim for if it is to make a particular level of profit.

Suppose typewriters can be sold for £80 and that the fixed cost of producing them is £80,000, with a variable cost per typewriter of £36. Then:

Total cost is £80,000 + £36 × P (where P is the number produced)
Total revenue is £80 × P
Break-even is where total cost = total revenue

i.e. $80,000 + 36P = 80P$
i.e. $80,000 = 44P$
i.e. $P = \dfrac{80,000}{44}$

$\qquad 1819$

Figure 8.9c Numerical Method

8.10 Running the whole business

When people go into business it is mostly to pursue an idea or an interest, to use their skills or talents in some way which will be profitable. Often they do not appreciate the large amount of paperwork which has to be done as part of a successful business. Some have no talent for it and some are defeated by it. The demands which the state makes for returns of one kind and another and for the collection of taxes from both employees (income tax and National Insurance contributions) and from customers (value added tax) contribute to the burden of administration. Larger businesses will employ specialists to do this kind of work but they still have to understand it and be able to do it themselves if they have to. Some of the main areas of administrative work are:

Employees

Staff have holidays, are sometimes ill, and are absent from work for other reasons. The management of the business has to be able to cope with this with as little disruption as possible. It also has to record the facts because they will affect so many things like pay, tax, claims for sickness benefit, and so on.

Many firms have welfare facilities for staff or incur expenses for them for things like meals and uniforms. As employees they will sometimes have things to grumble about or to negotiate for. This may be dealt with through union representatives.

Customers

The lifeblood of the business and given greatest consideration in Chapter 11. Customers have to be attracted and retained. Much business comes from regular customers and from those recommended to come. Administration for customers might include advertising and promotion, dealing with orders, complaints, public relations, providing credit facilities, and chasing debtors.

The product

For manufacturing firms and those working in extractive industries this might be extensive since stock has to be ordered and kept, it has to be valued each year, and distribution may involve a lot of arranging and recording.

Owners

If owners are running their own business they will be in direct touch but in larger firms finding shareholders and keeping them both informed and paid their regular dividend is a big administrative effort. When firms need to raise new share capital they often pass the administration of that on to specialists.

Lenders

Those who have lent money to a firm will want their regular interest payments, information about the firm, and the eventual repayment of the loan.

General public

Public responsibility is very important to some businesses, particularly where there is a danger of pollution. There are many cases where public opinion has to be discovered before a business may do certain things. Most firms will take out insurance to protect them against public liability claims.

The state

Businesses are tax collectors in a big way and a considerable amount of time is given over to this task but in addition all are subject to regulations about different aspects of their activities which often say how things must be done and require permission or licences to be obtained for, e.g., supplying food, postage stamps, alcohol, or for extending premises.

Competitors

A business must know what the opposition is doing and what they are likely to do in response to its own action. One of the objectives that many businesses have is to maintain market share and this needs research to keep informed about the actions of others.

8.11 Management and change

We look at the effects of technological change on production in Chapter 12. Here we are concerned with the more general changes and the role of management in responding to it. History tells of many animals now extinct because they could not change as their world changed. It may be less obvious but history also tells of businesses which have suffered the same fate for the same reason. The last ten years should have taught us all that change is a continuing and speedy fact of modern life. Both managers and workers have to respond in order to survive.

Sometimes it is easy to see why change is resisted. One person buses meant that conductors were not needed, new electric trains can be worked with fewer staff, mass production has taken away the need for some craftspeople – and central heating requires no chimney sweep. These changes can be accepted in time and arguments that there will be other jobs to replace those that are gone seem reasonable unless you have been a chimney sweep all your life or have worked on the buses for many years and have no desire to do anything else. People whose jobs are directly affected find themselves doing what they don't want to do and living in strange places in order to find work. It is not surprising that they resist. *Figure 8.11a* looks at some of the reasons why change is taking place so quickly nowadays and *Fig 8.11b* looks at some of the reasons why it is resisted in more detail.

Figure 8.11a Some of the major causes of change

Education	is a response to change but is also the way it takes place. Modern education concentrates more on developing skills and abilities and less on knowledge.
Innovation	New things are made or the same things are used in different ways. Microchips; space travel; 130mph trains; video-recorders are some examples.
Changes in tastes	New consumer wants from new technology, e.g. dishwashing machines rather than washing-up bowls; television rather than cinema seats; central heating, rather than coal fires; compact discs rather than records; prepacked food rather than personal service.
Communication	News of new things is instant and means of persuasion are more extensive and rapid. Products can come quickly from anywhere in the world.
Competition and choice	The world is one big market place and there are many more competing uses of our money.
Governments	The state and a range of international institutions like the EEC and OPEC have a significant effect on what happens. Dairy farmers cannot produce all the milk they might wish, and lorry drivers must have a tachograph in the cab. Many products must keep to design regulations, firms are not allowed to get together to fix prices, cigarettes must not be advertised on TV.
Social factors	More women now wish to have their own careers and firms must give them equal opportunity. Young people are more important in the market particularly for fashion goods, fast food, pop music and electronic goods. There is high unemployment and this has produced changes in education and training. Many of our communities are international and we make provision for different ethnic and social groups.

Ignorance	Most people resist the unfamiliar because they do not know how to cope with it. Many older people shy away from computers whilst children are using them with ease and enjoyment.
Insecurity	New ways of doing things may mean jobs disappear or become so different that they no longer give satisfaction.
Social barriers	Many changes are about ways of doing things and we put up barriers which protect our own interests, making it difficult to change. Some unions have rules which govern the work to be done by members, some religious organisations have ways of life which they see as threatened by change. A good example is the controversy over the Sunday trading laws.
Status	What a person does, the way it is done, and the payment received all help to determine status and changes which might reduce status are often resisted. Good examples are those which have replaced craft work and skill with a machine.
Power	We all enjoy influence and the opportunity to have some say in what is going on. Changes which might reduce the influence of individuals or groups are often resisted. One of the best examples of this in history is the resistence to votes for everyone over eighteen.
Roots	Much change means moving from one job to another or one place to another. The more we are associated by ties of family, friendship, and social activity to a particular place the more we are likely to resist change.
Fear	comes either from ignorance and uncertainty or from the attitudes and perceptions of people. This is why changes which seem to be good are often resisted.

Figure 8.11b Some reasons why change is resisted

8.12 Responding to change

In every older community there are businesses in which nothing seems to change from year to year. On the other hand some businesses seem so used to change and so ready to make changes that there is always something different about them. Many changes can be foreseen and planned for, and some can be brought about by firms determined to be leaders of change rather than followers.

Innovation

This may lead to new products, new ways of using the same products, new ways of making them, or new components for them. Such innovation may be drastic in that it completely changes the face of an industry, e.g. North Sea Gas, instead of coal gas and compact discs instead of records, or it may be partial and steady so that the change is only noticed when we look back. The firm that is to cope in the modern world has to be concerned with research, has to be looking for new ideas and for ways of putting them into effect, has to welcome and use new technology, has to train and educate its workforce so that changes can be made when necessary and as efficiently as possible, and has to be prepared to take risks. The worker most likely to cope with innovation is the one prepared for change, who is looking for new experience with an open mind.

Demand

Business thrives by providing what the customer wants. What the customer wants changes partly because of innovation and partly because of changing circumstances. The successful business anticipates demand. There are more cafes and restaurants in most towns than there used to be. There are computer software shops and shops which sell and hire video tapes. Staying in line with demand also means selling things in the way the customer wants. There are few larger shops which are not self-service as far as they can be, which do not offer credit facilities for durable consumer goods, and which do not take at least one credit card. Most now stay open in the lunch hour and an increasing number have at least one night of the week when they open late.

Competition

There are many competing uses for our limited spending power and that competition is worldwide. There is still some advantage to being local, particularly for small businesses in rural areas and those where the reputation of the business is an important part of the decision to trade with it. Britain is having to come to terms with the knowledge that 'Made in Britain' does not automatically sell goods; with the fact that there are as many foreign cars on British roads as British-made ones; and with the preparedness of many people to take their holidays abroad rather than in this country. There are two ways to respond to the challenge. One is to make our own goods more attractive to consumers, so that they are likely to buy British. The other is to sell abroad so as to earn the ability to import. There is another way which doesn't cope with change, but rather tries to prevent it happening, and that is to keep foreign competition out. To prevent international exchange is likely to do more harm than good.

Control

Some types of potato have disappeared from our market stalls, some designs of oil heater can no longer be bought, some ways of advertising are no longer allowed, some restrictions like those on the selling of spectacles have been changed or removed. These are just a few examples of the way in which governments bring about changes by the policy decisions they make. It happens at local level too, a one-way order for a particular street, a decision to make a pedestrian precinct, the decision to close (or re-open) a local railway station, planning permission for a new housing estate. A local bus company plans the routes of bus services in the knowledge that some of its buses will no longer be able to go down a particular street or it may persuade the local authority that there should be an exception for buses. Re-opening a railway station is likely to be the result of local pressure and most people will be prepared for it.

Management techniques

When a business is very small, the owner is the centre of activities and is often a practical person who has developed an idea into a source of job satisfaction and profit. As the business gets bigger the organisation must change its structure and do things in different ways using specialist techniques and personnel. In a large business the accountant is important, and increasingly those who develop the systems of a business and operate them are at the centre. A large business may fail to survive or a small one fail to grow because it has not changed the way it does things and has not taken advantage of modern tools and techniques of management. On the other hand some have failed in recent years because they have rushed too rapidly to new ways of doing things without thinking clearly how effective they will be and how they can best be used.

8.13 Making changes

Changes do sometimes happen but they are more often planned and controlled. Suppose that a firm which is a leading producer of typewriters decides that new technology has to be introduced and this will mean significant changes in the way people work and what they do. Some ways in which the change might be made more acceptable are shown in *Fig 8.13*.

Increases in the content of the job Enlarging jobs in this way often increases job satisfaction and gives scope for individual ways of working and initiative. Often it also gives greater status.

Links between activities If people can be trained to work in groups performing tasks in sequence so that they are responsible as a group for the whole activity, communicate with each other, and depend upon each other they are more likely to see job satisfaction in the change and accept it.

Increased responsibility We see the significance of this when we discuss individual needs in the next chapter. Group responsibility not only for doing the work but for its quality control often makes change acceptable.

Work with the employees to decide upon the extent, nature and pace Employees are more likely to accept change if they understand the reason for it and have been involved in discussions as to how it should take place and at what pace. Firms often do this in negotiation with union representatives.

Involve those with experience in its planning At the very least people should be told what is to happen and this is best done with the aid of people who have experienced such changes and are able to discuss what might happen and dispel fears about things that are not likely to happen.

Figure 8.13

THINGS TO DO

SECTION A

Short answer questions

1 What do you think a manager does?

2 State and explain five things which are a part of management.

3 What two things does an **entrepreneur** contribute?

4 Why is it difficult to identify the entrepreneur in ICI or United Biscuits?

5 State three objectives you would expect all businesses to have.

6 Make a list of six things·which might motivate an employee to work well.

7 Why should budgets be flexible?

8 Distinguish between direct and indirect costs, giving examples.

9 What are overheads? Give examples to illustrate.

10 Draw a rough sketch to show what the words 'break-even point' mean.

11 Explain why a firm might be prepared to sell their product at below the total cost of producing it.

12 Give four reasons why a worker might resist changes in the way of working.

SECTION B

Essays and structured questions

1 'Management is the business of everybody in the firm.' Say, with reasons, whether you think this true.

2 Read through the activities of managers as outlined in *Fig 8.1* and show how they might be undertaken by the manager of
   a a supermarket   *d* a bus company
   b a football team   *e* a small shop
   c a library   *f* a manufacturer of telephones

3 Consider each of the following activities and then explain:
   a what plans you might consult when deciding how to do them
   b what use you might make of each of those plans
   c what plans you would make yourself in order to do them.
   (i)   Organising a school disco

(ii) Going on a holiday to Australia
(iii) Applying to university or polytechnic
(iv) Attempting to win a local charity half marathon
(v) Applying for a job.

4 Explain how budgets can be useful in
   a explaining objectives
   b getting departments to think about what they should do
   c helping all the managers of a firm to work together as a team
   d helping a firm to respond to change.

5 What actually happens is never the same as what was planned, so what is the point of budgets anyway?

SECTION C

Coursework and assignments

1 Make a local contact if you can with a small business and discover how much management time is spent on the tasks in *Fig 8.1*. From the information draw your own conclusions about the nature of a manager's job.

2 In a larger firm and using the same list discover how much of the work of a supervisor could really be described as management. From your information draw you own conclusions about the nature of a supervisor's job.

3 Do your discoveries from question 2 tell you why quite a lot of workers do not want promotion to a supervisory job?

4 Set up a business either using your own initiative or using one of the schemes nationally available, such as Young Enterprise. It should be a limited company, should make and sell a product, should be wound up by the end of the year, and should return capital (plus dividend) to shareholders.

5 Plan and run an activity of your choice for a charitable cause you would like to support. Make a careful note of all the management activities in which you engage and particularly:
   a Work out what your objectives are and how they are to be achieved.
   b Draw up a plan of action from beginning to end.
   c Decide who does what.
   d Decide who needs to know about it and plan and effect your advertising/ information campaign.
   e Write a report of your activity at the end commenting upon the management skills which were involved.

6 Using your own locality as an example wherever appropriate explain how each of the following might have had to respond to change in recent years:
   a one or more of the shops in the area
   b the people who live in the area
   c one of the industrial/commercial activities in the area.

Chapter 9

People at work

9.1 So you want a job!

Where do jobs come from? There are several examples in this book of people who have had an idea, taken the **risk**, and become **employers**. Three things make this possible.

a **The opportunity** Sometimes this is obvious but many opportunities are created by people who have ideas and interests they want to make a living from.
b **The finance** Some opportunities need a lot of money in order to get started. Others can be taken with very little. If necessary a determined and enthusiastic **entrepreneur** will work ideas out carefully, draw up plans and find the arguments to convince those who have the money to help – friends, a bank, or a government agency.
c **The 'bottle'** determination to take the **risk**. There will always be risks and they are often quite high for new businesses but they can be measured and either reduced or anticipated.

Employers must decide how many staff they need and what they will expect their employees to do. Employing others adds to both the risks and the responsibilities. They take these and many other risks because they think they will be successful and expect to make a **profit**. There are several stages in finding people to work for you and they are:

a **Recruitment** informing people through advertisements and other means that you have vacancies and inviting them to apply.
b **Application** usually with the aid of information about the job and an application form which the responder must complete and return.
c **Selection** making the choice from those who have applied.
d **Induction** introducing the successful applicants to the firm, to their work-mates, and to their jobs.

9.2 Recruitment

Figures 9.2a and *9.2b* are two examples of advertisements taken from a local newspaper. *Figure 9.2c* is an advert you might see in your local Job Centre. These advertisements are based on **job descriptions** which the employers will have written. It is likely that those same jobs are advertised in several other places chosen because the employer thinks they are likely to lead to applications from people who will be suitable for the jobs. Where, how often, and in what way people advertise will depend on what they are looking for and how much they have decided to spend. Not all ways are appropriate to each case. A television spot is too costly for most firms but Central Television does run a Job

Search programme at night after the entertainment programme transmissions have stopped. They use job cards like that in *Fig 9.2c*. Cards in shop windows are often used for some types of job but most will use Job Centres and newspapers. Some specialist jobs will be advertised in magazines which are likely to be bought by suitable applicants. Recruitment must be done as cheaply as possible but adverts must create a good impression of the business and must appear where they are likely to be read by the kind of applicant a firm wants.

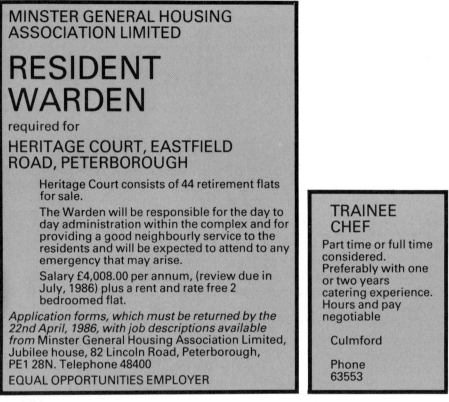

MINSTER GENERAL HOUSING ASSOCIATION LIMITED

RESIDENT WARDEN

required for

HERITAGE COURT, EASTFIELD ROAD, PETERBOROUGH

Heritage Court consists of 44 retirement flats for sale.

The Warden will be responsible for the day to day administration within the complex and for providing a good neighbourly service to the residents and will be expected to attend to any emergency that may arise.

Salary £4,008.00 per annum, (review due in July, 1986) plus a rent and rate free 2 bedroomed flat.

Application forms, which must be returned by the 22nd April, 1986, with job descriptions available from Minster General Housing Association Limited, Jubilee house, 82 Lincoln Road, Peterborough, PE1 28N. Telephone 48400

EQUAL OPPORTUNITIES EMPLOYER

Figure 9.2a

TRAINEE CHEF

Part time or full time considered. Preferably with one or two years catering experience. Hours and pay negotiable

Culmford

Phone 63553

Figure 9.2b

JOBCENTRE

(MAN OR WOMAN)

JOB	WORD PROCESSOR OPERATOR
DISTRICT	CULMFORD
PAY	Salary £6,000 per annum
HOURS	9.00-5.00 Monday to Friday. 1 hour lunch.
DETAILS	Will be operating Wang 6110. Previous experience of this model or similar necessary (2 years preferred). Nice telephone manner essential as there will be some telephone work. There are no formal educational requirements. Good prospects.

ASK FOR JOB No. CULMFORD 93

ES 101 (JC)

Figure 9.2c

9.3 Applications

Figure 9.2a invites applications for the post of resident warden. Notice that it requires an application form to be filled in and offers a job description to help you decide whether it is the kind of job you want to apply for. It gives enough information to attract attention. The advertisement in *Fig 9.2b* is less formal and gives little information. It expects a telephone call giving just enough help to make it possible. However you are asked to apply you have to give enough information about yourself to satisfy the conditions of the job and make the employer think you might be a suitable employee. If you are successful in doing this you wil be involved in the selection stage.

9.4 Selection

The care with which you have made your application will influence the employer. Tidy, readable information, careful explanations, and interesting comments about yourself will help to decide whether your name is on the **short list** and whether you are called for **interview**. Normally employers will want to check what you say about yourself and for this purpose they will consult people you have suggested might be able to help. The supporters you have chosen will write a **reference** about you. The best references come from people who have been your employers previously or who have known you well at school.

An interview is a chat between an employer and an applicant which gives each an opportunity to decide about the job. An employer will respond to what you look like, what you say, and how you respond during the interview. You have to make up your mind too. You should make sure you get all the information you need and be prepared to ask questions yourself. Sometimes the interview will be more structured, with several people either one at a time or in a group. It may be a test of some kind particularly if the employer must make sure you have a particular skill required for the job. The more senior a job is and the more it requires qualifications or skills the more demanding the interview will be. So what do interviewers look for? Some of the main things are listed in *Fig 9.4a*.

Figure 9.4a Some purposes of the interview

Presence	The first impressions come from punctuality, the way you come into the room, look, and respond to a greeting.
Response	An interview is meant to be a conversation and not just questions and answers. The interviewer looks for natural and helpful responses and a preparedness to talk freely.
Thought	Questions can be anticipated and the good interviewer will ask some which you should be prepared for. The interest will be as much in whether you have prepared as it will be in the answers. Some questions will be asked to see if you can think about questions you didn't expect before answering.

continued

Prospects	The interviewer wants to find out whether it will be a good idea to employ you and what your future with the business might be. If you have any ideas of a career or of progress in the firm you will have an opportunity to talk about this.
Compatability	You will have to work with others. Someone who might not find this easy or who might be a source of problems in this respect is less likely to be successful.
Suitability	Do you have the qualifications, experience, skills, abilities, and interests that you have claimed on the application form? How do you compare with the other candidates in this respect. In short – are you the best person for the job?

In most cases you will get the chance to ask questions and it is a good idea to have one or two prepared. In large organisations the people who are going to interview are trained. You may find *Fig 9.4b* useful in thinking about any interviews you attend.

Figure 9.4b What to do or avoid doing when interviewing

You should	**You should not**
Plan the interview including questions and the time to be taken.	Go in **unprepared**. Documents should be read and notes taken.
Be **informal**. Put the applicant at ease quickly.	Ask difficult questions too soon. First questions should be ones you know the applicant can answer easily.
Encourage full answers and give plenty of time to answer.	Ask questions which imply an answer. Where you want a particular answer it should come freely.
Cover all the things you planned but be informal and, as far as possible, led by the applicant's responses.	Cut applicants off in mid-answer or draw conclusions from what they say without sufficient evidence.
Ask difficult questions and probe thoroughly in a way likely to get a considered response.	Pay too much attention to characteristics which are not important to the job or the applicant's ability to do it.
Find out how the applicant sees the post both now and in the future.	Allow the applicant to dodge a question or give insufficient answers.

continued

Control the interview and yet allow the applicant room for free response.	Talk too much.
Remember the next applicant and don't delay unnecessarily.	Finish the interview before you are satisfied.
Keep notes or a tape.	Confuse or embarrass the applicant by the way you record the interview.

The final stage is an offer. Sometimes offers are made at interview and this is often difficult if you need to think about it. Ask for that time if you really need it.

9.5 Starting work

Your employment is a **contract** that is an agreement between you and the employer which will have **terms** and **conditions** you have both accepted by signing the contract. There is time for you to settle in with each other before the contract will be signed. The state has set legal minimum requirements in **Contracts of Employment Acts**. These minimum requirements are set out in *Fig 9.5a*.

Figure 9.5a Main terms of a contract of employment

Job title: Waiter

Duties	to serve customers in the restaurant and to do such other tasks as may be required under the direction of the head waiter.
Date	employment from Monday January 1st 19__.
Service	length of service will be taken on a weekly basis from Monday January 1st 19__.
Pay	either a fixed salary e.g. £8,900 per annum or the way in which it is worked out, e.g. £2.35 per hour.
Hours	11:30 a.m.–3:30 p.m. and 6:00 p.m.–12:30 a.m. Break in each duty of 30 minutes. One day and one half day off per week. Roster arranged. Guaranteed minimum week 40 hours
Holidays	how holidays are calculated and what entitlement will be. Rate of pay for holidays, dates when holidays can be taken, policy about public holidays.

continued

Sickness	pay for time lost, how illness should be notified, how long sickness pay will last, National Insurance.
Notice	length of notice to and by employer and arrangements for leaving.

There are other matters which might be important, such as arrangements for union membership, particularly if this is required, rules about the work, and what happens if things go wrong. These do not have to be in the contract but you have to be told where you can find out about them.

9.6 Induction

Can you remember the first day at your present school? Starting work is not unlike that except that there may not be other people who are starting at the same time. Because starting a job is difficult for everybody most firms have a special way of doing it called **induction**. It has three purposes:

a to help you get over the feeling of strangeness and of not knowing anybody or anything about the firm
b to make you feel you want to be there so that you are more likely to stay
c to make it more likely that you will do your job and make a contribution to the work of the firm as quickly as possible.

You will have a lot of things on paper and in some cases a printed handbook. There will be opportunity to meet people you are to work with and some of the senior staff in the firm.

9.7 Training

For many years before your first full-time job you will have been in full-time education at school, at college, or university. Some of this may be of direct use to you but its main purpose was to develop your understanding and general intellectual skills and abilities and not to prepare you for the job. For this and for the jobs you are likely to have during working life you need **training**. This will be a part of work for most of your life and not just a part of starting work. It can be in or outside the company and on or off the job. The diagram in *Fig 9.7a* shows how training has to be planned. It shows the use of a plan outlining what has to be done to make it more likely that it will be done. Anyone in training can see what is supposed to happen and how but cannot see how effective it has been. *Figure 9.7b* completes the cycle.

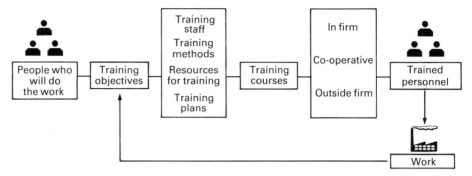

Figure 9.7a A plan of the training process

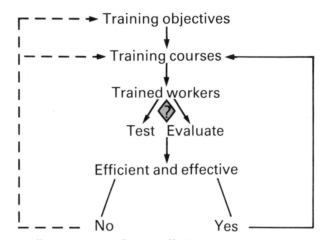

Figure 9.7b Controlling training so that it is effective

If training doesn't work something has to be changed. If the objectives need changing it may be because the work has not been thought about carefully enough in relation to training needs or that people are selected who are not really suitable for the job or whose training needs need more thought. Maybe the objectives are correct but the way they are put into practice is wrong – things like the pace of the course, the quality of the trainers, or the resources which are used. A training programme may be right today but wrong tomorrow, right for one group but not for another. The results should be monitored and reported upon every time.

9.8 Different types of training

On the job
This is the most common kind of training. There is something of this in every job, as we are always learning from experience. It may consist of definite teaching or coaching, e.g. a trainee bus driver or someone learning to operate a lathe. It may be observing others and then trying for yourself. With on-the-job training you work, learn, and respond to learning all the time.

There are disadvantages. Your product may be poor and the wastage rate may be very high. If it is a service, e.g. serving a customer in a shop, the consequence could be a customer lost. The person training you may not be good at it and may not like doing it. Some people asked to train others prefer not to and in most cases a training allowance is paid. The consequence of poor or unmotivated training may be lack of interest in the job or bad habits which the trainer has passed on.

Off the job

The Health and Safety at Work Act requires some training to be given in training areas away from the shop floor until a minimum level of skill and safe use has been learned. It also applies to some administrative jobs and ones where good customer contact is important. Workers who go on to the shop floor or into the office with some competence are usually more confident in working with others. But real life is always different from the training school and some people find it difficult to start work with those who will expect them to be able to do things rather than to need to learn from the beginning.

Outside

This is useful when needs are similar for several firms and when there is a benefit from people with different backgrounds working together and sharing their experiences. It is also of value for promotion. There is added motivation if the course is somewhere else and employees compete with those of other firms. External training can be for large numbers and in specialist surroundings so the quality of training and of resources should be higher than it would be in one firm.

Development

A firm will want to make sure the full potential of its employees is developed. Good firms watch the progress of workers with care and give opportunities for development and promotion. This kind of training should be a continuous part of working life and fit the needs, abilities, motivations, and interests of individual workers.

9.9 How well are you doing?

Much of the time, discussion, and analysis will be necessary for your first report. There are good reasons to work out how well you are doing, apart from the satisfaction of a pat on the back. These are:

a   to check the usefulness and quality of training
b   to decide whether further training is needed
c   to give you an idea of how well you are doing
d   to help the firm decide how much you are contributing to the success of the business
e   as a basis for promotion
f   to help make decisions about your future payments and conditions of work. This is important during the first months of a job when you may be on probation, and having to reach and maintain certain standards before the firm will agree to make your job permanent.

There are several ways of deciding how well you are doing and a business might use any or all of them.

General assessment

This is rather like the comments on a school report. It includes comments which your superior wants to make about your work, general attitude, and major qualities. This kind of report depends a lot on how well you and your superior get on with each other.

Guided report

Experienced employers will know exactly what they want to know and what sort of comment is most useful. A guided report is often in the form of a questionnaire which the superior has to fill in.

It requires the reporter to think about the same things for everybody. Often the guidelines are vague and can be interpreted in different ways. For example how do you assess 'application to work' and 'enthusiasm', particularly if you have little day-to-day contact with the person?

Graded reports

This is the equivalent of percentage marks or letter grades on most school reports. A job report may not ask for a numerical assessment but may make a number of statements and ask the reporter to say which one is most apt, e.g.

Outstanding
Excellent
Above average
Adequate
Poor
Very poor

This is still not very helpful since they are so general and there is the danger that a particular incident may be uppermost in the reporter's mind.

Rating

This uses positions or numerical values. They are similar to form positions on school reports. Many judgements are not easy to make and this method of assessment is no more reliable than the others. Unfortunately people think numbers are exact and tend to attach more importance to this way of assessing and to be more prepared to believe it.

Continuous

This is based upon the belief that, particularly at work, it is what you do or don't do that matters most. It keeps a record of all the important things that happen, both good and bad, and then allows that record to speak for itself. It has the advantage of being unique to you. You can check because it is your actions which are recorded. One of the disadvantages is the time and effort required to keep the record, another is that things which happened long ago and are best forgotten are still on file and may play a part in decisions about you.

Results

This is appropriate when the worker works towards targets. Many things are assessed in this way. The sports pages of newspapers have league tables based on this type of information and you have certificates which record subject results at different levels. In some jobs workers are paid by results, e.g. piece rate wages.

The target the worker has to meet must be realistic. Failing A-levels means nothing if it is generally agreed that you were unlikely to pass them. Always winning a race is of little consequence if you are known to be the best runner in the district.

Counselling

This can be based on any one of the methods above or may be a method in itself. This is an agreed assessment in which you and your superior discuss performance and come to an open judgement. The method is common in business, particularly at managerial level.

9.10 What is your attitude to your job?

'Can do better' can be equally true of someone who is top of the class or someone at the bottom and 'makes the effort' suggests hard work rather than reward. What they have in common is a report on **motivation** and **effort**. Those responsible for the success of a business must pay attention to motivation and try and discover what motivates people to work well. We look at motivation theory in the next chapter. Now we are concerned with things firms do which are likely to influence motivation. We begin with their own attitude to workers which shapes the way the work situation is organised and controlled.

9.11 How can workers be expected to respond?

The most famous answer to this question is provided by Douglas McGregor in *The Human Side of Enterprise*. He distinguishes two types of approach to workers. In one workers are thought of as needing direction and control, disliking work and shying away from responsibility. This attitude McGregor calls **Theory X**. **Theory Y** is his name for the approach which sees workers as responding positively to work, seeking responsibility and wanting the chance to be creative and show initiative.

Figure 9.11 Summary of McGregor's Theory X and Theory Y

Theory X	Theory Y
People are lazy.	People look forward to work.
People dislike and avoid work.	People want to work and will look for it.
People need to be forced or persuaded to work.	People find their own satisfaction in work and respond to encouragement.
Most people do not like responsibility and are not very good at it.	Most people can take responsibility and look for opportunities to do so.

The evidence supports Theory Y. Most people prefer working and look for different kinds of satisfaction from it. In most jobs workers find something which is interesting and they like doing. All jobs have boring bits and some have more than their share. Most people could find ways in which their jobs would be more to their liking. If a management incline more to Theory X than Theory Y the firm is likely to have a rigid organisation and people will be expected to work in accordance with the firm's systems and methods. Every job will be defined and work will be monitored and supervised to make sure it is being done exactly as it should be done. There will be little opportunity for initiative and individual ways of doing things.

There are tasks for which this approach is appropriate, particularly where workers depend upon the work of others in order to do their own or where an immediate and disciplined reaction is required. Some people respond to strict control, like to know exactly what they have to do, when and how to do it, do not want to be responsible for their own work or that of others, are lazy, and need to be pushed and threatened in order to get things done.

In a firm organised along the lines of Theory Y the individual will have a feeling of being in control of the work rather than controlled by it. The firm will think of control as co-operation with the worker rather than supervision or inspection of what is done. Relations between workers will be informal and people will be encouraged to take responsibility.

9.12 Job design

Someone has to decide what jobs are to be done and who will do them. In making this decision the need to motivate the worker may play an important part. The job must be done well and contribute to the objectives of the firm but if, at the same time, it can satisfy a worker's needs, can interest and challenge, and can give scope for development then it is likely to be well done.

Job design will begin with **work study** which may lead to a job which gives little scope for the needs of the worker to be satisfied, e.g. assembly line working. There are two approaches to job design which might make it more likely that a worker is motivated. These are shown in *Fig 9.12*:

Figure 9.12

Job enlargement	making the job as big as possible. A worker assembling a component may also be given the task of testing it rather than have the work inspected by a supervisor. A bus driver may have total responsibility for a bus being expected to look after it, and see that it is clean, and always driving that same bus.
Job enrichment	Jobs may be enriched by being enlarged but job enrichment also goes further, building in scope for the worker's own way of doing things, his or her own pace, own ideas, and own assessment. It implies the worker will take responsibility for work done. For example the packaging of toothpaste from raw material to final outer package might be the responsibility of a team who decide how fast they work, who does what job, and whether they rotate jobs. They might also train new members of the group and be responsible for managing the work if one of the group is absent.

continued

Both techniques	*a* put responsibility in the hands of the workers
	b allow them to decide how things should be done
	c reduce over-specialisation. People are responsible for a complete stage of work and not just one repetitive little bit
	d reduce supervision and substitute self control
	e allow more say in the nature of their work to the workers
	f give workers a change to assess themselves and each other
	g give immediate knowledge to workers of how well they are doing.

9.13 How should you be paid?

If you ask people how their pay is worked out it is unlikely this will be the same way for all of them. It is even more unlikely that they will all be paid the same amount. First we look at different systems of deciding wages.

Time-based systems

This is so much per hour, often fixed by agreement at either firm or national level. It frequently means punching a time clock every time you enter and leave the firm.

A higher than average rate for a job may be a good way of attracting the best workers. Time rates are most likely where effort cannot be measured either because the work is being done by a lot of people working as a team or because the speed of work is determined by a machine or an assembly line rather than the worker. This is the method where the work is irregular depending on things the worker cannot control, for example the number of customers in a shop. Time rates might also be paid where quality and standards are so important that work must not be rushed.

From the worker's point of view the advantage is that you know the minimum wage each week and, if you work overtime, you can work out how much will be in the wage packet. There aren't any arguments about how much work was done or whether something is good enough to be paid for. The disadvantage is that there is no link between effort and reward. This may encourage laziness and discourage those who want to get on with it. The system motivates those who want to do a good job and need the time to do it.

Results-based systems

These link the amount paid with the work done. It may be entirely worked out this way with workers paid for each piece of work or it may apply to part of the work. For example a salesperson may get a basic wage and commission on sales or a worker may get a basic time rate and then a piece rate for all work over an agreed target.

The argument for this system is that there is a link between effort and payment. The system is based on the assumption that people work only or largely for money and will be happy if they are working very fast and taking home large pay packets. The arguments against the system are that it places the emphasis on quantity rather than quality, often wasting a high proportion of the work. Most piece-work systems have an inspection system and payment is only made if a given standard is kept up. People work for many reasons other than money and some would rather work at less pressure, get more satisfaction from what they do and take home less.

Piece-rate systems are more trouble to operate. They often have to be negotiated with the unions and can cause conflict among workers. This is particularly true when things go wrong which are outside the control of the worker and affect the amount of work which can be done.

Incentive schemes

An incentive scheme is a **bonus** paid if a target is exceeded. It may be negotiated for a group of workers or it may apply to the firm as a whole. Everyone gets the bonus and some people may not feel that all are equally entitled to it. Another problem with incentive schemes is that, if regularly earned, they become part of the expected earnings and cause problems when the bonus is not paid. They are probably most effective when people have to work together and the firm wants to encourage team work. Such bonuses may be based on profits and are then called profit-sharing schemes.

Productivity agreements

These are always negotiated and involve a target, or a way of working, or a change expected to improve productivity. The return is a share in the benefits. Most agreements are complex and specially worked out for a particular firm.

Salaries

A salary is a wage paid to someone who has a defined role in a firm but payment is not determined by either work done or hours worked. It is usually fixed annually with provision for increases for experience. Changes in salary are negotiated between the employee and management. This is often by individuals although many employees are members of unions through which national agreements are made.

9.14 Take-home pay

If an employee is paid £3.50 an hour and works a standard week of 40 hours basic pay is 40 × £3.50 = £140 per week. Suppose 49 hours are worked and the agreement is for overtime at time and a half. Pay for the week would be:

Basic wage 40 hours @ £3.50	140
Overtime 9 hours @ £5.25	47.25
Total (gross) pay	187.25

This is likely to be far more than the employee will take home. Things which might be deducted from it include.

a **Tax** We all have to pay income tax unless we earn very low wages. Wage and salary earners pay tax on a **pay as you earn** basis (PAYE). The correct deduction is calculated by the Inland Revenue and then deducted from gross pay each week or month.
b **National Insurance** These are contributions made each week which vary a little with size of earnings. They help to pay for the National Health Service and for retirement pensions. The employer makes a contribution for each employee as well.
c **Other deductions** These might include contributions to a private pension scheme, union dues, a voluntary savings scheme, or sums taken by the employer. Waiters might have to pay for meals eaten or for breakages.

It is rare for things to be added to pay but the usual ones are:

a **Arrears** usually happens when a pay rise has been agreed and back-dated.
b **Holiday pay** usually included in the pay for the last payday before going on holiday.
c **Bonuses** There are some bonus arrangements and profit-sharing schemes. Most often paid at Christmas and holiday time.
d **Tax refund** comes when you have paid too much tax or when the budget has provided for a reduction in tax.

9.15 How do businesses decide how much to pay in wages?

Usually there is a going rate which is what is paid for similar jobs in the area. In many cases there is a national agreement which the firm will follow, particularly if employees are union members. If the wages which are offered are too low people will either not respond to the advertisement for the job or leave as soon as they can find one which they think is better paid. The kinds of things which lead to differences in wages include:

a **Location** The same job might be more highly paid in some parts of the country than it is in others. The best example of this is London.
b **The firm** Large national firms prefer to decide pay by negotiation with the unions and keep to the agreed pay awards and conditions of work. Many small firms employ people who are not members of unions. They make independent arrangements about pay.
c **The job** Some jobs may have attractions and advantages which mean the wage can be lower. For example employees may be able to live in or to have meals without charge. For salespeople a car often goes with the job.
   Other jobs have disadvantages like dirt, danger, or unsocial hours and rates of pay have to be better to attract workers.
d **Experience** Some jobs are specialist or senior ones and require experience. Those who have this would expect to be paid more than a new recruit.
e **Age** Some jobs pay less to younger workers and offer a higher rate of pay when they reach a certain age.
f **Responsibility** There are things in many jobs other than the job itself. Workers are often asked to be responsible for the work of others, e.g. supervisors and senior managers and they may expect to be rewarded for that. Sometimes supervisors get a fixed wage for their jobs and have no opportunity for overtime so that their take-home pay could be less than that of those they supervise.
g **Training** If you have been trained you are of immediate use to the firm and they do not have the expense of training you. This is normally recognised either in the rate of pay or in the starting point on a salary scale.
h **Motivation** This does not often influence the starting pay but someone who is keen and enthusiastic is a better risk. It makes it more likely that workers will be offered promotion or a higher rate of pay.
i **Qualifications** Many jobs ask for formal qualifications, either general education ones like so many grade C or better GCSE or rather more specialist ones appropriate to the job.

j **The market** Sometimes the wages offered depend upon the number of people who are looking for work (**supply of labour**) and the number of employers who are looking for staff (**demand for labour**). When it is difficult to find staff wages may be high. When it is easy to find them wages may be low. In 1986 there was a shortage of skilled workers despite high levels of unemployment in the economy as a whole.

k **The unions** One of the main reasons people join unions is so that their rates of pay and conditions of work may be negotiated for them and kept up to a reasonable level. If a union is strong it is likely to be able to do this. Such negotiations are often long and hard and may involve industrial action by members. People who work on their own, in very small groups, or for very small firms are often not memebrs of unions. Even if they are members they do not use the union in pay negotiations. Sometimes this means that they have lower rates of pay than they might otherwise have.

9.16 Would it be possible to pay everybody the same?

Some have argued that wages should not differ, that the jobs we all do are making their contributions· and we should all have opportunity for the same standard of living. Others have argued there should be a national minimum wage. There are problems with both of these ideas. Those who have long periods of training or spend a long time gaining qualifications would be reluctant to bother if there was no reward, those with experience would not like inexperienced people being rewarded to the same extent. If a minimum wage was fixed and this was the same as employers were prepared to offer it would be a waste of time. If it were less it would not be in the interest of the lower-paid workers because employers would tend to offer what the state required. If it were more then this would make employers less prepared to employ people because the wages bill would be higher than they wished. Those in work would work harder, the tendency to replace people by machines would be increased, and some people would find it even more difficult to get a job at all.

Wages differ because labour is not one single resource but a range of different resources, because that resource is more valuable at one time than at another, in one place rather than another, and to one employer rather than another. They also differ because some groups of employees, working together, have more opportunity to influence wage levels than other groups and more success in doing so. A further source of difference, which is gradually being taken away, is that women are paid less than men. The law requires women to be paid the same as men where they are doing the same job but that is not easy to define and there are still many instances where women's wages are lower than they should be.

9.17 Your wage

Figure 9.17 shows two pie charts representing the whole wage and showing the kinds of deduction which may be made from **gross pay** to arrive at **take-home pay**. All the deductions from your pay and other information which helps to identify you as an employee and a taxpayer is included in the wage slip which accompanies the wage you receive. Many people receive only the wage slip because the payments are made directly into a bank account.

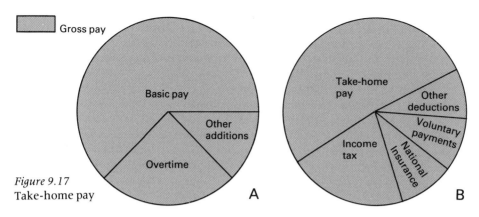

Figure 9.17
Take-home pay

Pie chart A shows how gross pay is made up, the major part being basic pay. Pie chart B shows reductions from that gross pay. All these things often make the payslip difficult to read, particularly if it is small and code numbers are used instead of words to explain the deductions. It is wise to keep pay slips because the information may be needed to fill in tax returns.

9.18 Your health and safety at work

The state intervenes in health and safety at work. This goes back a long time to the Factory Acts of the early nineteenth century. Some jobs, like those of a coalminer, a sewage disposal worker, or someone working with chemicals have a high risk of ill health or injury. You will have seen safety clothing worn by workers on building sites. Managers should:

a analyse the work so that things that might be dangerous to health or likely to cause injury can be spotted.
b remove as many of the problems as possible.
c provide safety equipment and training for the remaining problems.
d inform workers of possible dangers, safety precautions and equipment.
e try to ensure safety precautions are taken, equipment is used properly, and methods of work likely to cause danger to others are discouraged.
f be observant so that new hazards are spotted and anybody not working safely can be warned.
g have a system of dealing with accidents which is efficient, well communicated, and brought into use quickly. A good example is fire precautions which should include regular practices.
h keep accurate records so that action can be taken if a trend is spotted or particular accidents happen more often than they should.

A firm may do all of these things and still have a poor health and safety record if it cannot persuade its workers to be safety conscious. It is often easier and faster not to use guards on machines, and there are often quicker ways round a shop floor than that which you are advised to take. Safety usually means time and trouble and without a positive attitude to it places of work will be unsafe. Some accidents are caused because people drop things and don't pick them up, leave things in the wrong place, don't bother to switch lights on, and put things down in a place where others will not expect them to be.

9.19 Welfare

Employees are not just resources. Much as they might try they cannot leave things in their lives outside work at home and forget about them. Problems away from work will affect quality of work, frequency of absence, punctuality, response to workmates, and the chance of accidents.

There are those who say 'It's none of the manager's business' or 'What I do in my own time is my affair' and this is true most of the time and for most of the things we are involved in away from work. Others will say there are professional welfare workers who have facilities to help with problems and that this should be left to them.

The argument for welfare services is that people are entitled to more than a pay packet and a safe or reasonable working environment. A lot of problems arise from work or are closely related to it and are better solved there by fellow workmates. Problems make the worker inefficient, make communication less effective, and may lead to accidents. The firm is responsible to itself and to other workers and must try to ensure that a worker's problems do not cause further difficulties at work.

9.20 Out of work

The number of people who would like jobs but are not able to find them is very high. The real solution to **unemployment** is **employment** in a worthwhile and full-time job. Anything the state does to help those unemployed rather than to employ them may take some of the sting out of unemployment but it does not solve the problem.

Ways in which the state can help include:

a **Protect employment** There is a system of appeals if you think you have been unfairly dismissed, a set of terms which should be a part of a worker's **contract**, and rights which protect people in special circumstances. For example the right of a woman to have her job held open whilst she is on maternity leave.

b **Redundancy pay** Those dismissed because the job isn't there anymore can get redundancy payments related to length of service with the firm.

c **Reduce discrimination** Some people find it more difficult to get a job than others. The state has made it illegal to discriminate between applicants because of differences which are nothing to do with the job or the ability to do it. For example discrimination on grounds of race, colour, religion, or sex is illegal.

d **Provide education** Education makes us more employable and improves an individual's chances in the job market.

e **Provide training** The extent to which the state does this has been increased in recent years particularly through the **Youth Training Scheme** (YTS) and **retraining schemes** for people made redundant.

f **Reduce working life** By lowering the retirement age or raising the school-leaving age.

g **Encourage job-sharing schemes** Although the working week has been reduced by stages from 48 to 35 hours the idea that we work the whole week is still the usual one. If those of us in work were less fully employed it might reduce unemployment.

h **Encourage firms** perhaps by special payments or tax relief if they employ more people or if they move the business to an area of high unemployment.

i **Unemployment benefit** should be the last resort. People must be able to enjoy a minimum standard of living either through unemployment benefit or through social security payments.

j **Job centres** inform those seeking work which employers want workers. They can only be successful if jobs are advertised through them and if those unemployed regularly go to them to find the jobs.

k **Employ** The state is a major employer both in its own activities like the civil service and local government and for a large number of other firms and activities like education, hospitals, and the public corporations. Policies which encourage or require employment of more staff will help the un-employment problem and those which encourage or require staff reductions will make the problem worse.

9.21 Conclusion

We have been concerned with the actions of the firm in making and carrying out decisions about employment. We have looked at ways you might be paid and at how pay is calculated and accounted for. Welfare and safety at work have been discussed a little and the difficult problem of unemployment completes the chapter. That is one side of the contract. In the next chapter we look at the needs of individuals and groups and what we expect from the jobs we do.

THINGS TO DO

Short answer questions

1 What is an entrepreneur and what contribution does he or she make to the success of a firm?

2 What is recruitment?

3 What six purposes is the interview designed to achieve?

4 Explain what is meant by induction and why you think it is necessary.

5 What sort of training would you think most appropriate for
   a a doctor?
   b a lorry driver?
   c a salesperson?
   d a shopkeeper?

6 What are the main things about McGregor's Theory Y approach to management?

7 Say, with reasons, whether you would prefer to work for a Theory Y manager or a Theory X one.

8 Distinguish between job enlargement and job enrichment.

9 If you were now working would you prefer to be paid piece rates or time rates?

10 Suppose a worker is paid £2.10 per hour and works 53 hours in one week. The normal week is 35 hours and overtime is paid at one and a half times the normal rate for the first 10 hours of overtime and double time after that. Calculate the gross pay.

11 Give three different reasons why take-home pay may be less than gross pay.

12 Give two reasons why take-home pay may be more than gross pay.

13 Why is a solicitor paid more than a solicitor's clerk?

14 State six things that you would expect managers to do to maintain a high standard of health and safety at work.

15 What is redundancy? Why does it happen?

SECTION B

Essays and structured questions

1 Design a job description for any job about which you have information. On the basis of this job description write an advertisement. Explain where it would be put and why you have chosen those places.

2 Design an application form for either the job in Question 1 or another job known to you. Work in groups of six to eight for this and agree a final version.

3 Exchange application forms with one of the other groups and have it photocopied. Fill in the application form you now have as if you were applying for the job. Write a letter to support the application.

4 Take the applications which have come in from the group you exchanged with and read them, making a short list of no more than four of those you wish to interview. Write to those selected inviting them for interview. Write to those rejected explaining why.

5 Sit down and work out the questions you wish to ask each applicant at the interview and make brief notes of what you consider their strengths and weaknesses to be.

6 Take any job you consider boring. Explain why it is boring. Using the ideas of job enrichment, job satisfaction, and job enlargement discuss ways in which the job might be improved to make it less boring.

7 What would be the best way to pay each of the following jobs? Give reasons for your answer.
   a a salesperson
   b a fruit picker
   c a solicitor
   d a supply teacher
   e a shopworker
   f a travel courier

8 Explain why people are paid different wages for different jobs.

9 Write a letter to a friend explaining why you think it would be a good idea to join the union at the firm where he or she works. Explain that if people join unions, they benefit, the firm finds it easier, and other workers have advantages. Give reasons in each case.

SECTION C

Coursework and assignments

1 Visit any firm of your choice. Whilst you are there you need as much information as you can about one of the jobs. On the basis of that information draw up a programme of induction for a new employee.

2 From your visit what sort of training do you think is best for the job? Draw up a week's training programme that you think might work.

3 Take your short list from the job you worked on for earlier questions. Interview the candidates and make a selection using the interview notes and job notes you made. You should do this as a group activity.

4 Once you have both interviewed and been interviewed discuss the strengths and weaknesses of the various interviews from the point of view of both the interviewing panel and the candidates.

5 Go to a firm. Study one worker or group of workers. Do you think the management attitude is McGregor's Theory X or Theory Y? Write a job description for the job. If you can, get the firm to comment on your job description.

6 Obtain a blank pay slip from a firm. Explain what each of the sections on the pay slip means. Complete it for an imaginary worker.

7 Go down to the Job Centre. Choose any three different jobs that are advertised where wages are very different. Explain the wage that is offered and comment on the method of payment. Explain why you think the wages are so different.

8 There is to be a meeting of your union one evening next week and each of you is expected to go. Work in groups of four on this.
   a One is to be chairperson and to conduct a meeting which is on safety on the shop floor. Must be prepared to open the meeting introducing the speakers and to sum up what they have said.
   b One is to speak emphasising the need for safety gear and why it should be worn.
   c One is to speak giving the views of a group of workers who do not want to wear the safety gear.
   d One is to listen carefully in the role of a newspaper reporter, ask questions of both speakers, and write a newspaper report on the meeting.

Chapter 10

The workers and their business

10.1 Starting work

The interview went well. There is an offer in the post. You have thought about the job, the prospects for the future, and whether you are going to settle down. You accept. You will be with the firm to do a job. They may have some idea of your likely future but now you have to prove you can do the job. If things go well you will sign a contract. What does this job really mean? What do you expect to gain from the satisfaction of being employed, apart from the wage?

10.2 Individual needs

Suppose someone was unkind enough to put you in a very cold spot, with very little clothing, no food, and no shelter. You are isolated, what are you likely to need first?

FOOD   DRINK   CLOTHING   SHELTER   WARMTH

Because needs like this come first and must be satisfied regularly they are called **basic** or **primary needs**. If they remain unsatisfied for long they become the most important things in our lives. In the desert? Little matters except **water** and **shade**. **Hungry**? Everything is forgotten except food. **Freezing**? An overcoat or a fire would be more welcome than food.

What happens when these needs are satisfied? Suppose you find a hut with some warm clothes and food and drink to keep you going. What now? Some different needs become important. You are lonely. You would love someone to talk to, to be with. There are some people who can be alone for long periods of time, but in most of us there is an urge to be with other people, to have friends, to have family, to join groups – to **belong**. We call this group our **social needs**. Such needs are unimportant when we are hungry, thirsty, cold, wet, or feel unsafe. They become important when our basic needs are regularly met.

Suppose you have friends, have a good family life, have people you like and who like you in return. You are lucky – no basic needs to worry about and lots of social and family relationships. Being secure you have further needs to satisfy. They are called **higher needs** because they emerge when you have satisfied the lower ones. All of them are concerned with personal development and how other people react to you. They will be different for each person. One may seek **responsibility** or **status**, whilst another is more interested in **self-fulfilment**. A third person may have **creative** abilities.

New needs emerge as old ones are satisfied, rather like a pyramid. The basic needs take much thought and time and, unsatisfied, become important – they are the base of the pyramid. Personal needs emerge in an otherwise satisfied person – they are the top and we don't always reach them. This model was developed by Maslow and is shown in *Fig 10.2b*. *Figure 10.2a* is a list of different types of needs:

Type of need

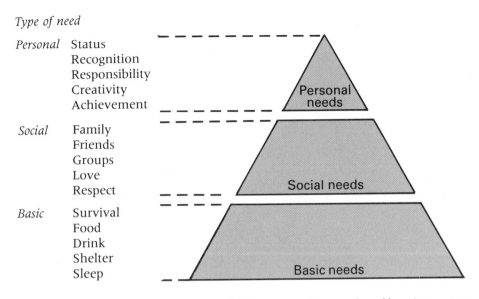

Personal Status
Recognition
Responsibility
Creativity
Achievement

Social Family
Friends
Groups
Love
Respect

Basic Survival
Food
Drink
Shelter
Sleep

Figure 10.2a Human needs   *Figure 10.2b* The pattern of our needs and how it emerges

10.3 Why do people go to work?

Many people have attempted to answer this question based on their own experience or on studies of people at work. *Figure 10.3* shows some of these.

Figure 10.3

Taylor	looked at the economic needs which work satisfies through wages. He argued that people work largely for money. He did not think people enjoy work or come to work because they want to. His approach to recruitment and control of employees was Theory X. He is remembered rather unkindly by workers because they see his work study methods and his insistence on productivity as trying to exploit them. Money is an important incentive and there are workers who find their job so boring that they work only for the money. There are workers who respond to tight control and supervision but this is not the whole story.
Mayo	His most-well known work was the Hawthorne experiments. Out of them Mayo developed the idea that treating workers as people and responding to their needs is the best way to motivate. Mayo also argued that, whilst the individual is important, so also is the group. People work in groups, developing their own ways of working and objectives. Later work suggests that these experiments were not as important as was at first thought.

continued

Maslow and McGregor	The whole person goes to work and not just the resource. The needs of the individual are important and to be satisfied through the job.
McClelland	concentrated on crucial needs particularly achievement. We all need success and will seek opportunities and experiences in the search to be successful. This affects the way we work and what we are prepared to do. McLelland thought the higher achiever will: *a* seek responsibility *b* enjoy solving problems *c* make decisions rather than pass them on *d* accept moderate tasks because of the challenge but not high risks because of the danger of failing *e* want to be informed of progress and development *f* want promotion.
Hertzberg	There are factors in work that are essential, like safety, cleanliness, heating, lighting, proper breaks, and a reasonable minimum wage. These do not motivate workers but they provide the foundation for motivation. If they are taken away workers will fight to have them restored. Factors which motivate are ones like achievement, recognition, responsibility, status, and the opportunity for creativity or individuality.

What happens if you are unemployed? You receive enough money to satisfy basic needs from the state. You satisfy many or all social needs in private life and the social groups of which you are a member. If you ask someone who is unemployed what the worst thing about it is, the money may be mentioned but high on the list of problems will be:

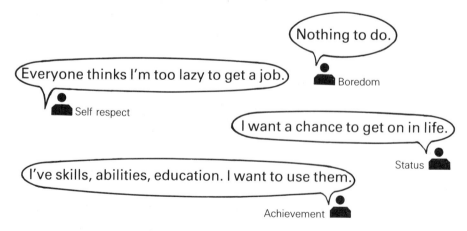

At work we satisfy our basic and social needs but get real motivation from the extent to which higher needs can be satisfied.

10.4 Objectives?

The objectives of a business always include:
    Survival Make sure that the business does not fail, or that it remains independent, not taken over by another concern.
b **Growth** Many businesses want to grow, see opportunities and want to take them. Often survival is only possible by growing.
c **Profit** Not all firms can, or want to, maximise profit but they must make enough to ensure the first two objectives. A profit objective is likely to be expressed as a **return on capital employed**. It may be expressed in terms which are easy to measure and achieve i.e. **targets** for each part of the business and maybe for each worker.

The objectives of the individual at work are partly money but also a range of **personal needs** clearly not the same as those of employers. How do we bring the two together since each can only achieve their objectives through the other?

10.5 Leadership

Leadership involves:
a **An objective** Sometimes this is clear. For example, a **task** to be performed – climbing a mountain, solving a problem, or making something. At other times objectives are less clear or changing – committee meetings and team games.
b **A group** may have been chosen specially, and been told exactly what to do and how to go about it. In this case the group is a **formal** one. They may have come together voluntarily and as long as they have an objective they will be a group, this time an **informal** one.
c **Individuals** Even though you are a member of a group some of the time you will behave as an individual and your needs rather than those of the group may be important. Sometimes the needs of individuals and the group as a whole conflict.
d **The leader** Leaders of formal groups are appointed by the person who called the group together or by the group itself in a formal manner, e.g. by electing a chairperson, or a captain. Sometimes the leader is generally acknowledged without any attempt to appoint or elect one. This often happens in informal groups.

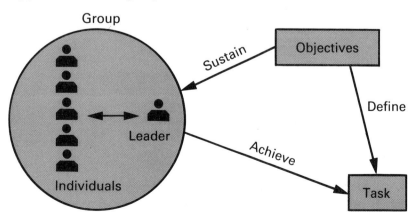

Figure 10.5

Figure 10.5 shows the role of the leader in bringing individuals together as a team in the completion of a task. Objectives will keep the group together and give it identity and will also define the tasks. The way a task is approached and the success the group has with it will affect **morale** and **attitudes** to both membership of the group and the **leader**. This will also determine individual satisfaction.

10.6 The leader and the group

Objectives

In a formal group it is likely that objectives wil come from **terms of reference** given to the group when it was formed. The leader will translate objectives into ways of working and purposes which the group understand and accept. In informal groups the objectives often are decided by the leader or by some circumstance which has brought the group together. For example, they want to play cards during a lunch break, or they want to complain about working conditions. The purpose which brings an informal group together may be outside work, e.g. they travel on the same train, they are friends of someone who is ill or needs help, or they all support the same cause.

It is from objectives that **tasks** will be decided and **methods** agreed. The leader will have a role in this but the main job will be to compare action and achievement with the intention and to ensure success – the managerial tasks of **monitoring** and **controlling**.

Tasks

They may be specified by the objectives. Both long- and short-term planning will be required and some parts of the task may be undertaken by the leader. Other parts will be **delegated** and a leader will show skill by the ease and effectiveness with which this is done.

The group

In groups there are responsibilities, a definite **hierarchy** and accepted ways of communicating. This is what we mean by the **organisation** of the group. Much may be decided by the leader although the things that have to be done, the people who are members of the group, and the working methods of the firm all play a part.

The leader may have power to reward or punish, and to bring people into the group or to dismiss them. The prime minister is a good example of all of these powers. The leader must resolve problems between members of the group which affect its working. The leader may be strong enough to influence the **norms** of the group. Some will have to be accepted, some the leader will formally change and others will change gradually as the group responds to the leader.

The individuals

The main task of the leader is to make sure the group works effectively and tasks are completed. Needs of individuals might make this difficult and the leader has to act where necessary. In many formal groups it is part of the leader's role to observe individual behaviour, assist development, and make recommendations to superiors. In informal groups the attachment to the leader has been the reason why some members have joined the group. There may also be hostility because some individuals see themselves as alternative leaders. One of the greatest problems arises when the appointed leader of a group is not the natural leader.

10.7 Who shall be your leader?

Many writers have suggested that we can determine qualities of leadership and assess the extent to which a person possesses them using the results to decide who shall lead. That is not very realistic but it is useful to watch how successful leaders actually behave and see if a pattern emerges. This has often been done and the things which seem to be characteristic of leadership are:

a   Leaders have abilities which others have acknowledged and have either appointed the person or behaved in a way which showed they wished to follow.
b   They seem to be bright in the down-to-earth sense of seeing what needs to be done.
c   They are enthusiastic, alert, and energetic. They enjoy what they do and this shows in their approach.
d   They are self-confident and prepared to make decisions.
e   They communicate well and persuade others to get things done.

Leadership is an interacting role which some people do well. It is also a matter of **style**. How people are led is more important than who is leading them.

10.8 Styles of leadership

Autocratic

This is the Theory X approach. The leader makes all the decisions and insists on obedience from the rest of the group. He or she rarely discusses anything but gives orders and supervises work. Such a leader normally has a method of communcication which is centralised, i.e. it must go through the leader and is more one-way than two-way. Followers should be asking questions only where they need to know what to do or how to do it. *Figure 10.8a* is a **communication net** which shows how this type of leader normally works.

There is little or no communication back to the leader except the odd question and what may be demanded as feedback. The members will not communicate with each other except informally or as part of a task.

A group led in this way tends to rely on the leader and to do very little alone. In many ways it will not be a group but just individuals working for the same person. Most, if not all, of the ideas come from the leader and if others do comment it will be to grumble among themselves and not to make constructive comments. Output is often large because it is supervised but may be of poor quality. Members get little job satisfaction and are often inclined to argue.

Democratic

The leader considers the group as a whole. Some tasks will be defined in advance but there will be discussion and frequently the way things are done will be changed. The group will be encouraged to determine its own ways of working and often the pace at which it works. They may determine who does what and who works with whom.

Again a communication net can be used to describe the way the group works and this is shown in *Fig 10.8b*.

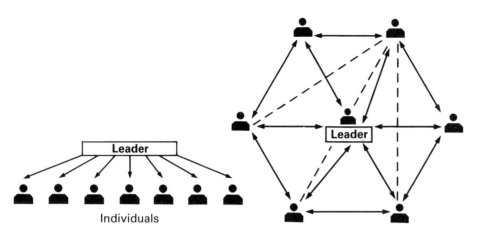

Figure 10.8a Autocratic leadership

Figure 10.8b Democratic leadership

There should be two-way arrows between each individual and the other members of the group. These have been left out because it would make the diagram too complicated. The leader is in the middle of the group to suggest **participation** which is the point of democratic leadership. There is a ring around the whole to show it is working as a group and not as a collection of individuals.

The leader is less important and the group will often work effectively on its own. There is a greater feeling of being a group, of team spirit, and of a task to achieve together. Everybody's ideas may be accepted and the group will produce good work. On the other hand, the discussion, the lack of detailed supervision, and the greater concern for people often means that less work is done. Most people get job satisfaction and there is reluctance to leave the group. There may also be pressure to get into it.

Leave them alone (*Laissez faire*)

This amounts to almost no leadership at all, with a leader there but refusing to take any part. It is just a case of doing nothing unless forced to act. Members do not get to know the leader and rarely rely on anyone but themselves. Communication is high but not necessarily organised and often gets nowhere. The only time successful work is done is when an individual works alone or emerges as a substitute leader. Very often a group which has been led in this way can only achieve if led autocratically because the situation needs to be tightened up and controlled for a while before people settle down and are ready to participate.

Although three styles of leadership have been outlined and although a particular leader may normally lead in one of those ways, the good leader will be flexible, varying styles to suit the needs of the group.

10.9 People in groups

Most of our lives are spent in or responding to groups. Very little of what we do is truly individual. Think of a typical day and work out for how much of it you were on your own without being influenced by groups in some way. There are two main types of group:

a **Formal** are deliberately created with a known purpose. Examples are families, classes of students, a team, a marketing department, or a committee.

b **Informal** just happen because members recognise something in common. It may be the same objective, e.g. football supporters or workmates. It may be living in the same area, friendship, a hobby, skill, or even the same dislikes. There has to be something to hold the group together and make it act together. Otherwise it is just a crowd of unrelated people.

Two things hold groups together:

a **Objectives** Many formal groups have a limited purpose and will break up once the purpose is completed, e.g. a village fete committee or a working party. Some will have a purpose which goes on all the time but a changing membership, e.g. the Cabinet and committees. Many informal groups will have informal objectives like being friends or playing cards or squash.

b **Norms** We have a way of doing most things which tends to be the same each time, and standards which we try to keep. This is what is meant by norms which help to define the nature and membership of a group. For example, some schools still require the wearing of uniform. Some informal groups don't require a uniform but everybody tends to dress similarly.

These things help to explain the groups we join. Some we have little choice about. We are born into our family, one of the most important groups influencing our lives, and often have little choice over the schools we go to. In school some class groups will be decided for us and some, particularly later on, will be our aided choice. Even at work, although the choice of applying for and accepting a job is ours, many of the groups are part of the job. Most of our informal groups and social groups we join because they have objectives we want to follow and norms we approve of or accept.

10.10 Motivation

The clue seems to be in **goals** or **targets** since the achievement of these can give workers the satisfaction they seek. Goals have to be realistic but not too easy and it is **success** in reaching them that seems to be important rather than the reward. This approach is likely to be most effective if workers help set goals and have a clearer idea of their nature. How do workers react to a target?

a **Reward** The most obvious reward is pay, including **bonuses** or **productivity agreements**. But rewards can be anything which relates to the job – promotion, a company car, a status label of some kind, or public acknowledgement of achievement. The worker must see the reward as worth having if it is to motivate. If your name on a board as worker of the week is embarrassing you won't work for it. If you decide a pass in business studies is of no value to you the fact that people think you could get an A won't make you work.

b **Perception** A boss may think a target is difficult whilst a worker thinks it is easy, or the other way round. This difference in perception will mean the target has a different effect on behaviour than was intended. People who think they can't do something often don't try. If they think something is easy they leave it too late to start – remember the story of the tortoise and the hare.

c **Effort** There is no direct relationship between effort and achievement. Some people find a task easy, some find it difficult, and some find it impossible. Even if hard work is needed it has to be directed – if you are running in the wrong direction it won't matter how fast you run.

d **Abilities** The more able, skilled, experienced, and qualified you are, the easier a target is likely to be. Targets should be hard enough to be an effective challenge. This means something different for each individual and that often makes it hard to use this approach.

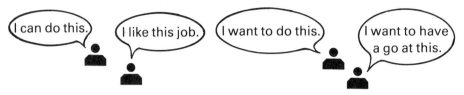

You are more likely to try hard to keep at it and to succeed.

You are more likely to be put off and fail.

Attitudes unconnected with what you are doing like disliking the supervisor, wishing you worked with someone else, or being envious of the success of someone can influence the way you do the job.

Roles

Roles are what we are expected to do and if this has been badly worked out – perhaps the job description is vague or was never written – or if we do not understand what we are supposed to do and how it fits with other people's work we often work badly or in the wrong way. This often leads to misunderstanding.

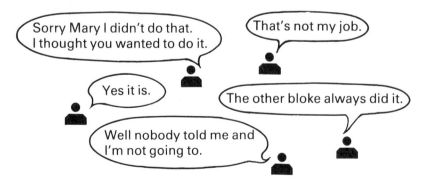

Fairness

Target setting will not work if either the targets or the rewards do not seem fair. This is a problem when individual targets are set and one of the objections workers have to the idea of payment by results.

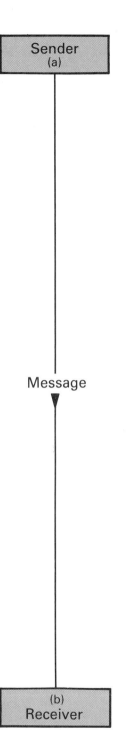

Figure 10.11a Basic model
of communication
down route (a) – (b)

10.11 Communication

We communicate all the time and this produces a response from others. It may not be the response we want but if a message is received something always happens. Communication is important both in the work situation and our daily lives.

In *Fig 10.11a* there are two people – the person sending the message and the one receiving it. In some situations many people are involved as when a leader talks to a group, a teacher to a class, or a Minister to the House of Commons, but each individual receives the message, understands it in his or her own way and responds differently. *Figure 10.11b* gives an example.

Teacher	'What is the square root of 25?'
Fred	doesn't hear the question. He wasn't paying attention.
John	doesn't remember what a square root is.
Bill	doesn't know what a square root is but thinks he does so works it out as 12.5 and puts his hand up.
Jane	knows the answer is 5 but doesn't like answering questions.
Judy	has a calculator so quickly works out the answer and puts her hand up.
Mary	is writing something. Hears the question, knows the answer, but ignores the situation and carries on with her work.
Sydney	doesn't know the answer but puts his hand up anyway because he thinks that is the best thing to do and there isn't much chance of being asked.
Sue	Knows the answer. Is good at maths and is going to say plus or minus 5 and not just 5.

Figure 10.11b Responses to a message

We can use each of these responses to find out something more about communication.

a **Fred's response** The most important thing is to make contact with the receiver. Fred wasn't listening so for him the message doesn't exist. What can the communicator do about this sort of problem? Turn up the volume – shout at Fred. Name him – most people respond then, and there is only one Fred in the class.

b **John's response** Sometimes the question is not understood, sometimes the person doesn't know the answer and never has done. If you ask people things in a way they don't understand that's your fault. It often happens between people, one of whom is an expert and the other an amateur. Think of the technical language of computing, the special language of CB radio, and foreign languages of which we have no knowledge. Sometimes people understand the words but give them a different meaning. If the other person doesn't know it might be your fault because you have not gone to the best source.

c **Bill's response** In schools this doesn't matter very much since mistakes are the things we learn from but in a job we have to get it right – wrong answers are costly. Wrong answers of the kind that Bill gave – dividing by 2 instead of taking the square root are usually avoided by careful selection and training.

d **Jane's response** The message gets across, it is understood, the receiver can respond in the way you want, but nothing happens. If communication is to be successful you have to have the **co-operation** of the receiver.

e **Judy's response** She doesn't know the answer but knows how to find it. This kind of response is valuable. Knowing where information can be found is enough most of the time but it does rely on **assistance**. You have to have the right technique, technology, or reference book handy. You have to be **organised**.

f **Mary's response** Jane wouldn't respond. Mary might have done at another time. Both the teacher, who has asked Mary when she was occupied, and Mary, who was writing when she should have been paying attention, got their **timing** wrong. This is often a problem. People are too busy to see us when we call, too busy to answer the phone, or preoccupied with a problem. The more you know people, the more you can organise things. The easier it is to contact people the better timing is likely to be. Sometimes it requires a change of method. For example someone we need to communicate with may not have time to see us but will answer the telephone or read a letter.

g **Sydney's response** He is the risk taker. Better to appear to know the answer than to be assumed ignorant. If people are misdirected by what is said, or make decisions based on wrong information, they will not trust your advice.

h **Sue's response** How **precise** do you have to be? Sue's answer is quite correct but in many situations it would confuse rather than help. We have to learn to be as **accurate** as necessary and to tell people what they can understand and need to know.

Good communication would appear to depend upon:

Knowledge
Use language people will understand and ask those likely to know. Make sure you know the things you should to do your job.

Ability
Appoint people who have the necessary abilities and give them the training they need. Don't try things you can't do.

Experience
Ask people who have experience. Give people the experience they need. Get the experience which is likely to help you.

Perception
How do you see the people you are communciating with? How do you see yourself? How do they react to you? Are there things about people and their roles to which you attach a lot of importance? How about the receiver?

Attitudes

Communication will be influenced by your attitude to the message, its urgency or importance, the method to use, and the person to be contacted. The receiver will have a similar set of attitudes which will have similar effects.

Expectations

What we expect others to do, will want to do, or will have the opportunity to do, will influence who we contact, how we do it, the nature of the message, and the kind of response. Our expectation of people influences the response. For example you try extra hard not to be late if you are meeting someone who dislikes unpunctuality or won't wait. You do an extra special job if promotion might depend on it.

Timing

What's the best time to approach mum or dad if you want a favour? When's the best time to apologise for something that you have done wrong? There are many situations like this. Getting the timing right can be the difference between success and failure.

Method

There are many methods of communicating and you have to choose the best. Telephone conversations are quick, interactive, flexible, and personal but they can't often be proved and it is easy to forget some of the things which are said. Responses in a conversation are not necessarily the ones we would make later after careful thought. All methods are better for some people and some purposes than they are for others. Choosing the right method is a skill which comes with experience. We all develop habits of communicating and have a tendency to use the methods we like rather than those which are best.

Message

The message must be **understood, accepted**, and **responded to** in the way the sender wants. This means it has to be right for the receiver. A formal message to a friend or member of the family often implies or is taken to mean annoyance or disapproval but is usual in an office where many people like to avoid familiarity. Technical language often shows knowledge but is a waste of time if the other person doesn't understand. There is a rule in big block capitals in one office which reads:

> **KEEP IT SIMPLE: GET IT RIGHT.**

Purpose

Why are you communicating? Advertising is a good example. Some adverts, those for new products, those developing new markets, and technical and industrial advertising, are intended to **inform** and will be full of facts which can be checked. Other advertising is concerned to **persuade**. In training there wil be a need to **encourage** or **discourage**; to **instruct** and **explain**. The receiver will have a purpose as well and this will influence responsiveness.

Process

How a message is communicated will often be as important as all the other things. We often refer to the tone of a letter or to body language.

Often the **context** carries the message. If things are said or written by a judge they seem more believable, if a product is endorsed by a famous person it seems to carry more weight. If things are said by someone we trust we are more ready to accept them, and if you are called to the boss's office greater importance is often attached to what is said than if the message were passed down to you.

Feedback

The purpose of communication is to **influence behaviour**. To check on that, in order to stop us communicating further or to change what we do we need to know what has happened – we need **feedback**.

Feedback is the way communication is modified or continued, e.g. a conversation or a negotiation. Good feedback depends on our ability to **perceive** and **interpret**, which when the spoken word is used is sometimes called **live listening**. This means understanding the full message. Our hearing will pick up the words, the emphasis, the tone of voice, the degree of confidence, and how determined someone is. Our eyes will observe the body language and the visual context in which things are said or written. We can use feeling to interpret a handshake.

10.12 'When two or three are gathered together'

Communication to a group or crowd is still personal and individual response may vary. But the involvement of more than two people in communciation can change what happens. Sometimes the presence of another can be enough to change things. Some examples:

a You don't like strangers listening in on conversations and if they do you will turn away, change the subject, whisper, say outrageous things to persuade them to go, move yourself, or ask them to go.

b Private behaviour is often different from public behaviour.

c Three or more people in a situation may change the status, e.g. the presence of a parent, teacher, or manager.

d Three or more changes the responses because it makes interaction possible on an increasing number of routes.

Two people   One route between them

Three people   Six routes between them

A⟷B   A⟷C   B⟷C

AB⟷C   AC⟷B   BC⟷A

Four people: Six paired conversations
                    Six with a pair addressing an individual
                    Six with a pair addressing a pair
                    Four with three addressing one

In addition, whenever two people are not directly involved they may communicate with each other.

The number of possible combinations increases rapidly even if there are only five or six people present. Try working it out for five people.

e It is much more difficult to give feedback because attention is not necessarily on you. To receive and interpret is difficult because it will be different from each participant.

f Interaction can be used to provoke a stronger reaction and a different kind of response than would be given by the individuals alone. Good examples include the behaviour of a class, and the way a skilled communicator, a politician, or a preacher can rouse a crowd.

g Within a group of people a **leader** often emerges through whom the most effective communication can take place or whose response may determine or influence that of others.

h Unless an individual response is demanded some members of the group will not participate, e.g. Fred, Jane, and Mary in *Fig 10.11b*.

10.13 Ways of communicating in groups

We discussed two of them when dealing with leadership style. *Figures 10.13a* to *10.13e* show them all.

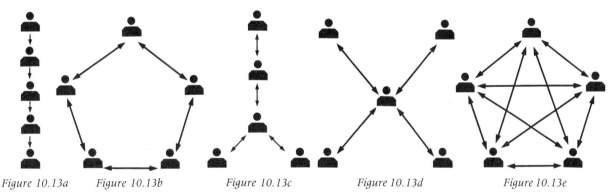

Figure 10.13a   Figure 10.13b   Figure 10.13c   Figure 10.13d   Figure 10.13e

In *Fig 10.13a* messages are passed down or up the line with little check. They may be distorted or misinterpreted with each exchange. This tends to happen in grapevine situations. E gets a message which bears no relationship to the one originally passed by A.

In *Fig 10.13b* communication is a little better. All the communicators can see each other and communicate although the main information will be on either side.

In *Fig 10.13c* E, the leader, occupies a central position able to communicate with each of two subgroups but making complete communication difficult. Each of the subroutes is short so there may be little distortion but control and effectiveness may be poor.

In *Fig 10.13d* C is the leader and members are isolated with everything happening through the leader. Communication is often quick and effective but inflexible and controlled, imposing a Theory X leadership.

In *Fig 10.13e* Complete two-way and multiple communication. Everyone has a chance to participate and anyone can take the lead. Decision making is slow but satisfaction is high and commitment to the decision is strong.

No firm has a single pattern of communciation and we might see all five of these communication nets in the same firm. For example:

Figure 10.13a is the flow suggested by the vertical lines of Anyfirm's organisation chart from managing director down to a shopfloor workers or from them to the top. Chains should not be too long and upward flow is often very difficult since superiors can often stop it if they judge that a message should go no further.

Figure 10.13b Some formal groups and some parts of the vertical flow in Anyfirm may be like this. Much of the communciation is between a subordinate and superior alone, i.e. one way in each direction from a particular point. Large meetings in which most of the people are an audience tend to be like it, talk being with the neighbour rather than general.

Figure 10.13c shows meetings or working groups in which the behaviour is autocratic. Communication is through the leader.

Figure 10.13d could be an autocratic group or a training session where there is the need for a trainer – C – to communicate mostly with individuals perhaps standing at a machine or operating an independent unit. Training may convert to a participative group for some sessions.

Figure 10.13e is a fully interacting group. Many committees, particularly those where the members are of roughly equal status, will operate in this way. Most informal groups will be of this kind. '

10.14 Bargaining and negotiation

The main purpose of communication is to bring about change. In **bargaining** both parties bring something. In **negotiation** each is fighting for advantage. Some examples of bargaining and negotiation are shown in *Fig 10.14*.

Games	Chess or draughts are negotiation where the object is to get the opponent into a losing position or yourself into one where you cannot lose. All games have this kind of element. There are many more obvious negotiation games on the market in which decisions are made and interaction with the other players is essential.
Fight	Sometimes you know the outcome but it is important to continue the fight because it might influence the next time. In an argument you don't give in too easily, you take positions you know are not defendable and from which you will have to move.
Co-operation	Many committees are like this. There is agreement about the goal and often about the method.
Representation	The people are not working on their own behalf and may have different views from those they have to put forward. They often work with rules they would like to break and without other rules they would like. Collective bargaining and committee work where you represent another organisation are of this kind.

Figure 10.14

Negotiation is easier if the people have the same status. It plays an important part in **motivation** and **job satisfaction** because it gives the worker the opportunity to have some say in the definition of work, the way it should be done, the conditions, or the reward. It appeals to **higher needs** like achievement, power, influence, status.

10.15 Worker participation

Worker participation is workers taking a positive part in decisions which affect their work. It involves the opportunity to influence decisions and not simply presence during the process. The highest level would be when workers and managers have equal influence on decisions. It is common for firms to have provision for some sort of worker participation and for that participation to be effective in motivating both managers and workers. There are many reasons why it happens:

a The increased size of firms creates problems of communication and working together for which a solution is needed.

b The technological changes are often seen as a threat to jobs.

c Managers often have no idea of local needs and conditions because they work in head offices, often in another country. Things which may be important locally are of little significance nationally or internationally.

d Rising standards of education and the greater availability of education, e.g. evening classes, education through trade union activity, and the Open University have reduced the status gap between management and staff.

e The separation of ownership and control which comes when firms are public limited companies narrows the status gap. Everybody works for the firm.

f Rising standards of living have reduced the status gap. They make it more likely that workers will seek to satisfy higher needs by being involved in the decision making of their firm.

g The objectives of trade unions now include greater participation in decision making.

h Recent legislation has provided a role for the unions in activities of business which would previously have been left to management, e.g. health and safety, dismissal of employees, and equal opportunities.

i Worker participation is further forward in some European countries and membership of the EEC has influenced the nature and speed of change in this country.

The advantages of worker participation are:

a Workers can contribute creatively to the business but ideas need to be sought and developed in a participative way. A suggestion box on the wall doesn't work.

b If people participate in making decisions that concern them they will better understand what is wanted and why and be more able to do the job.

c They will be more willing to do the job in the agreed way.

d Conflicts are often due to ignorance or because workers do not get a chance of putting their point of view. Participation may reduce this conflict.

e If managers have to work out the implications of decisions and justify them the standard of decision making may well improve.

10.16 Collective bargaining

A case made by one person, particularly to a strong organisation, is not likely to be effective, especially when it is about relationships between the two, e.g. money or conditions of work. There is also the fear that pushing your own case might cause problems for you. So strength through numbers and individual protection through numbers are the main reasons for collective bargaining. *Figure 10.16a* gives some examples of types of issue which are settled with trade union involvement, usually through shop stewards.

Wage Matters	*Conditions*	*Hours*
Basic pay	Allocation of work	Overtime
Piece work rates	Pace	Shifts
Bonus payments	Quality	Breaks
Productivity agreements	Safety	Holidays
Employment	*Others*	*Discipline*
Staffing levels	Pensions	Suspensions
Training	Promotions or gradings	Grievance procedures
Short time	Technological changes	Dismissals
Redundancy		

Figure 10.16a Issues in which unions are commonly involved

Figure 10.16b shows some of the findings of a survey about the extent to which workplace bargaining is important in decisions. The left-hand side shows things normally settled by consultation and the right-hand side some which are usually settled by management alone.

Shop stewards normally involved in		*Not normally involved in*	
Decision about	Percentage of occasions stewards are involved	Decision about	Percentage of occasions stewards are involved
Overtime	72	Output	20
Discipline	62	Pace	13
Transfers	62	Promotion	11
Dismissal	61	Product	9
Redundancy	60	Prices	8
Staffing levels	57	Investment	1
Shifts	56	Ownership	1
Rest periods	53		

Figure 10.16b Shop stewards involvement in decisions

10.17 Being a member of a union

From *Fig 10.16b* you could make a list of the sorts of things with which a union could help you. These include:

a   deciding how much you should be paid or at least the **basic rate** for the job
b   making sure that you get your share of **overtime** if you want it and that there is an agreed extra payment for it

c if things go wrong with those you work with, particularly if you think you have been treated unfairly
d if you are sacked unfairly
e if things go wrong and you need support or legal advice
f if you are to be made redundant
g making sure you get good training
h improving the conditions in which you work.

A union might do some things for you away from work. These include:

a special schemes for some of your normal expenses like travel, insurance, mortgages, and legal advice
b arrangements through which you can get a better bargain. Discounts in shops and for some services, cheap holidays, education, and medical help
c facilities for social activities, clubs, and sports facilities.

To gain these benefits you have to be a member. In some firms you are expected to join a union and this is called a **closed shop**. In others they try to persuade you to but do not insist. In some firms there are no union members. This is particularly true in small firms where there are few employees. When you start work someone, probably the shop steward, will ask you if you would like to join the union and normally this is quite easy with a reduced membership fee for young people. Once you have joined you can choose to do nothing but accept the decisions made by your fellow members, or you can take an active part going to meetings and expressing your point of view. It is a pity that, rather like with other organisations, only a few members are really active.

10.18 When things go wrong

The headlines in *Fig 10.18* all carry the same message; something has gone wrong and a union is going to take action. Such things are always reported in a way which we are bound to see or hear about. Perhaps you think things always go wrong. This is not true.

Figure 10.18 What the papers say

The number of working days lost through industrial disputes in 1981 and 1983 was well below five million and in 1984 it was only just over five million. This is small compared with some countries in Europe and very small as compared with absences through illness or injury. The purpose of action like this is to show solidarity and strength and make management aware that people are prepared to withdraw their labour or to take other action where they think it is necessary. The kinds of action that might be taken are:

A strike

A withdrawal of labour may be complete or selective. In the second case workers hope to make their point at minimum inconvenience to themselves. During a strike workers receive no pay although some money might be available from union funds. Even when on strike workers usually work in an emergency. Every member is expected to strike and a **picket** is usually set up outside a workplace to persuade those who don't want to strike, and others who may have business with firm, that they should support the cause.

Strikes are usually about issues in the workplace but sometimes the cause is a national one, e.g. a wage claim for all in an industry. Some are **sympathy** strikes supporting the cause of fellow workers. Most are **official**, that is called or supported by the union but some are **unofficial**, called by the shop steward but not yet supported by the union. Most unofficial strikes are about local issues.

A work to rule

Many rules are there more to solve problems when they occur than to be obeyed. Observing all of them all the time would slow most work down very considerably. This is what makes it a good tactic to use. It has the advantage of making a point without depriving the workers of their wages.

An overtime ban

In many businesses there are busy times of the year and slack ones. Overtime bans are a good way of making a point when a firm is busy but they do cost workers the money they might have earned or at least put off the chance of earning it until the dispute is over.

Blacking

This is refusing to work with materials which come from a source of which the workers disapprove, and sometimes refusing to work with people of whom they disapprove.

Most disputes are about wage settlements but some are about conditions of work or work sharing arrangements. Disputes usually arise when workers are uncertain and feel their jobs or their potential earnings are threatened. The more this feeling of insecurity can be removed by worker participation the less frequent this kind of dispute will be. Fortunately nearly all disagreements and issues for negotiation are settled peacefully and quickly and it is only a very small number that make the headlines.

10.19 The structure of unions in Britain

There are three kinds of union.

a **Craft or specialist** Among the oldest of the unions, the members must be qualified or skilled in the particular craft or work. Some of them are very small. Examples are the Amalgamated Union of Asphalt Workers and the National Union of Journalists.

b **Industry wide** This does not necessarily cover the whole of an industry but is the main union within the industry. Examples are the Iron and Steel Trades Confederation, the National Union of Mineworkers, and the National Union of Agricultural and Allied Workers.

c **General** Unions for members from all walks of economic life, and often those without a specific trade or skill. Examples are the Transport and General Workers' Union, the General and Municipal Workers' Union, and the National Union of Public Employees. These are the very big unions.

The number of unions has declined recently, largely due to amalgamations. There are now fewer than 400 unions, over half of which are small with less than 1,000 members. The 22 big unions account for about 80 per cent of trade union membership. In the eighties trade union membership was falling and now less than half of all employees are members (48%) although about 58% of male employees are members.

Shop stewards

If a union is to work well in each firm it must have a representative of the workers on the spot. That is the role of the shop steward. All the things you can think of that would be in your interest as a member will be taken care of by or through the shop steward. Managers find the shop steward useful because they need someone through whom to work. For their own purposes they use **supervisors**, but for matters which relate to workers and conditions of work they are glad to have a shop steward. In many firms the shop steward has paid time off to do his or her job as a steward.

The union officials

Sometimes a firm has enough workers who are members to make the firm a branch of the union but more often than not branches involve workers from different kinds of jobs in firms over a wide geographical area. This is one of the things which makes union meetings poorly attended. The branch will have an organisation with the usual officials and members of the committee. These may not be shop stewards.

The regional organiser

The union has business throughout the country and is far too big to run on part-time labour by members in a full-time job. Some people work full time for the union and one of these will be a regional organiser who keeps an eye on union activity and union membership in the region.

The head office and general secretary

All unions have national offices and sometimes these are very big, employing a large staff. The head of the union is probably a **president** who may be the chief national figure but often the most well-known member of any union is the **general secretary** who acts as the spokesperson for the union.

The Trades Union Congress

Just as workers band together in the workplace so unions band together in order to have a national voice. This is the Trades Union Congress (TUC) to which most unions and all the large ones are affiliated. The general secretary of the TUC is the figurehead of the whole union movement.

THINGS TO DO

Short answer questions

1 Draw Maslow's pyramid of needs showing the different needs at each level with three examples of each.

2 Write down the four main features of McGregor's Theory X.

3 Write down the four main features of McGregor's Theory Y.

4 What are the three main objectives of any business?

5 Distinguish between autocratic and democratic leadership.

6 Which kind of leadership would workers find most satisfying? Explain your choice.

7 What is the difference between a formal and an informal group? Give two examples of each (a) from your own experience and (b) which might exist in a business.

8 Draw a diagram which might help to explain communication in a group being led democratically.

9 What are norms?

10 Choose any one group of which you are a member and say what you think are (a) its norms and (b) its objectives.

11 Draw a diagram to show how communication works. Label and explain it.

12 Write down four different responses to each of the following and say what you think might happen then.
   a 'I have lost my pen. Has anyone found it?'
   b 'What time does the match start?'
   c 'Where can I get information about part-time jobs in this town?'

13 By means of an example which you explain show how each of the following is important to good communication.
   a knowledge
   b experience
   c attitudes
   d expectations
   e timing
   f process

14 What is live listening? Why is it important?

15 What is feedback? Why is it important?

16 Draw a communication net to explain the way you think communication works in each of the following cases.
  a in meetings of your form or tutor group
  b round the table for Sunday lunch.

17 State three different negotiation situations which occur when you are playing Monopoly.

18 Look in your local newspapers. Find three different examples of worker participation.

19 From those same newspapers find three different examples of negotiation of issues in which unions have been involved.

SECTION B
Essays and structured questions

1 Write a letter to a firm accepting a job you have just been offered putting in anything you think you need to say or ask questions about.

2 Think of three different ways in which you might respond to each of the following and explain why.
  a the smell of a fish and chip shop
  b a bus coming down the road
  c the sound of the alarm clock in the morning
  d a dog barking

3 'In the work situation it is satisfaction of the higher needs which is most important.' Explain what higher needs are, give examples to illustrate, and say why you think the statement is either (a) true or (b) false.

4 Mayo argued that workers seek to satisfy their needs in the work situation. Hertzberg said that only the higher needs motivate. Taylor said that people work largely for money. Say, with reasons, who you think was right.

5 Choose any three people known to you, or whom you have read about, who led in different ways. Say why you think of each of those persons was a good or a bad leader.

6 Explain the three different approaches to leadership and say which one you would prefer if (a) you were being led or (b) you were leading. Give reasons.

7 Choose any target which you have set for yourself or which others have set for you and comment on it using the headings given in this chapter.

8 Draw the model which explains how communication works. Take each part of the model and give three examples of ways in which things can go wrong. Say what you could to (a) prevent things going wrong in each of these cases and (b) put things right when they have gone wrong.

9 Show how each of the following can make it easy for a good speaker to rouse the feelings of a large audience.
a the words used
b the examples given
c body language
d expression and tone of voice.

10 Jean has just started a new job. The shop steward has invited her to join the union but she knows nothing about it. The shop steward says that everybody will benefit if Jean does join. Show how each of the following will benefit if Jean agrees:
a Jean herself
b her workmates
c the union
d the management.

11 Take any dispute which has just made the headlines. Read several different newspaper reports about it and listen to the news if it is being reported. If it is being discussed on a television programme watch that. As a result of all your research try to write an objective report on the dispute.

12 Compare the role of the shop steward with that of the supervisor.

SECTION C

Coursework and assignments

1 Find out how many people are unemployed in your area. Go down to the Job Centre and discover what vacancies there are. Explain why some of the vacancies are not filled. Talk to some people who are unemployed and find out why they want a job.

2 Observe any group(s) known to you and try to discover:
a what their norms are
b what their objectives are
c what the leadership style is and what its effect is on the working of the group
d how good morale is in the group and what the explanation is.
Then draw a communication net to show how the group normally works. What have you learned from your observation of the group?

3 *a* Draw any irregular shape on a piece of paper. With your back to the rest of the group so that they cannot see your drawing and you cannot see them, tell them to draw the shape and give them the necessary instructions. You must not ask questions and neither must they.
b Check the quality of their results against your drawing and explain your findings.
c Draw another, very different, irregular shape. This time you may face the group. If you think they don't understand you may repeat your instructions or say them again in a different way. Neither you nor they may ask questions.
d Check the results and explain your findings.
e Repeat the exercise with an entirely different diagram but with complete two-way communication.
f What does this exercise and its results tell you about good communication?

4 Form groups of five. Take a message or task which will be given to the leader of your group and using a different one of the five communication nets outlined in the chapter complete it. Report your findings at the end.

5 Break up into groups of five or six (whichever is convenient). You have 10 minutes. At the end of that time the average height of each of the groups should be the same.

RULES: You may join other groups but the number of people in your group must never be more than one bigger or one smaller than it was at the start.

Any negotiation must take place within a group.

The size of each group at the end must be no more than one bigger or one smaller than at the start.

Nobody may be excluded from their original group but may join another group by mutual agreement.

6 Pick out three examples from newspapers or magazines (they can be adverts if you wish) which you think are poor examples of communication.

7 *a* Explain what you think they are trying to do.

  b Explain why you think they are poor.

  c Improve them.

8 You are stranded on a bleak, uninhabited island.

  a Agree between you a list of 20 things which will be essential to survival.

  b Check your list with those of other groups. Note the differences.

  c Now decide whether you want to change your list.

  d Agree a common list for the whole class.

  e You decide you have to go to the other side of the island where there is a better chance of being rescued. There is no chance of replacing any of your items on the way and it will take 10 days to get there. Six of your items have to be left behind. Agree which six it shall be.

9 Work in groups of eight. Four of you are representatives of the staff and four are representatives of management and you have a problem: Bill has been working for the firm for 25 years and is now a senior laboratory worker with seven years to retirement. He has a very good record but was recently caught smoking in the lab. For safety reasons there is an absolute ban on this. It could have been disastrous but wasn't. Last week a young apprentice was sacked for the same offence. Bill has three children and there are few job opportunities for a man of his age in the town. What do you do?

10 *a* List ten (or more) things which you think are your good points and would be valued by an employer.

  b List ten (or fewer) weaknesses which might make it difficult for you to get some jobs.

  c Look at the job vacancies in your area (a) at the Job Centre (b) on cards in windows (c) in the local newspaper.

  d Now decide on three jobs you could do and say why you think you might get them.

Chapter 11
Marketing

11.1 What is marketing

Those words and many others like them tell a story of businesses which make things and then just hope to sell them. In the past many firms were able to work like that but nowadays selling what has been produced is not enough. Firms must **market**. This means that they must go out and find customers and that they must find out what the customers want.

Marketing is concerned with identifying customers needs and satisfying those needs at a profit in such a way that the customers come back again and recommend the firm to their friends. To do this most firms, except for small ones, have marketing departments which do a number of different things as part of their marketing effort. In this chapter we look at each of those things in turn and we begin by drawing again the organisation chart of that department in Anyfirm plc.

Figure 11.1a Marketing department of Anyfirm plc

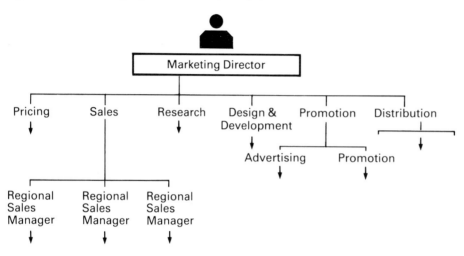

One definition of marketing which is useful for our purpose is:

'The identification of a need, its satisfaction (at a profit), and its regeneration.'

The phrase 'at a profit' is in brackets because many organisations have to be good at marketing but they are not out to make a profit. *Figure 11.1b* gives some examples.

Social service departments like the Department of Health and Social Security have to tell people about the benefits they can claim.

The Inland Revenue has to tell people about the allowances to which they are entitled.

Churches advertise the services they hold and the things they do. They also seek to persuade people to go to church and believe in the things preached.

Figure 11.1b Some non-profit making marketing activities

11.2 The need for marketing

Before the war, when this country was an important industrial one and when there was less money for most people to spend, there was little need for marketing. Most people believed the words of Emerson:

'If a man write a better book, preach a better sermon, make a better mousetrap, the world will beat a path to his door.'

and thought that the words 'Made in Britain' was all the marketing that needed to be done. In recent years the world has become a single market place with such a choice that producers must compete for the custom they want.

11.3 The marketing mix

This is a term used to describe all the different parts of marketing activity. All of those sections of the marketing department in *Fig 11.1a* added together make up the marketing mix. It is a good term to describe what happens because, when anything is marketed, activities from all those sections from pricing through to distribution are mixed together, rather like the ingredients of a cake, to make up the marketing programme. Nearly every product is in some way different, requiring a slightly changed mix to market it successfully.

11.4 Market research

Although it is not the first of the sections listed in *Figure 11.1a*, we begin with it because its main role is to identify customers and their needs. Not all businesses have market research departments. This is not because it is unimportant but because it is a specialist activity which can be given to other firms who make their living by doing it. The kinds of questions which market research might answer are shown in *Fig 11.4a*.

a If a firm wants to produce a new product what would be the important features of it that consumers would want?

b How big is the market for the product and where is it?

c What is the best way of reaching consumers with a product? What outlets would they expect to find it in?

d What price would consumers expect to pay?

e What would be the most attractive way of packaging the product so as to persuade the consumer to buy?

f Is the demand for the product likely to rise or fall?

Figure 11.4a Market research questions

In order to answer these questions a market researcher would collect two different kinds of data:

Primary data obtained by direct investigation, e.g. questionnaire or interview, and specially collected to answer the question. If you stand at a bus stop counting the number of people using the bus; if you ask customers of a shop about their purchases, these are examples of primary data.

Secondary data information which has been collected by someone else which may be of general use. Statistics of the number of people who use buses or of the goods which people most often buy are secondary data.

Primary data is collected by designing your own questions and going out to those who you think can answer them. This is why such research is often called **field research**. Secondary data comes from books, reports, and articles and getting it is often called **desk research**. Secondary data has to be used carefully because it wasn't collected to answer your questions and you cannot be sure of the care with which it was collected or of the conditions which applied. This is why the **source** should always be quoted. *Figure 11.4b* lists some of the most common sources of secondary data.

Figure 11.4b Sources of secondary data

Records of a firm	The ones you know are the final accounts but there will be many others – correspondence, minutes of board meetings, minutes of meetings of committees within the firm, and reports by salespersons and others.
Trade association records	These could be associations of the industry like the National Farmers Union, or professional associations like the British Medical Association. It could be national groups like the Trades Union Congress, the Confederation of British Industry or it could be local groups like a chamber of commerce.

continued

Reports of research activities	The problem may have been researched before and the work of previous groups may be very helpful.
Government reports and statistics	The standard works are ones like the *Annual Abstract of Statistics* and *Social Trends*, but there are masses of reports and other forms of data produced by Her Majesty's Stationery Office.
Media reports	Newspapers and television, magazines and other reporting organisations often research into activities.
Research organisations	Examples are the Consumers' Association, university and polytechnic departments, and other organisations which have been set up in order to research.
Audit firms	make a living by collecting data for others. Examples are firms who do audits for retailers, for the television companies to determine the most popular programmes, for the music business – the record charts, and for others providing political information – opinion polls.

There are three common methods of gathering primary data:

Observation The advantage of this is that it records actual behaviour. The disadvantage is that it tells you nothing about the reasons for it. It is used regularly for road use surveys. It is good when the most important thing you want to know is how often something happens or which choice is made from a number of alternatives.

Experiment The commonest form is for new products or for changes in existing ones. Often a large firm will appoint consumer panels to test products and comment. Tastings are often held in department stores and supermarkets.

Survey This consists of asking people questions. This is the most useful but also the most time consuming and needs care and skill in both designing the questions and conducting interviews if they are used. It does give a chance to ask about motives and attitudes.

11.5 Survey work

You will use this approach in assignments about many things but one of the most likely is in asking about marketing. *Figure 11.5* gets out the stages of survey work. Notice how much time, care, and planning go into stages which go before and after the field work. When you do your assignments these are the stages you should go through, each of them being important if the answers you get are going to be useful. Opposite we list some comments on the method described in *Fig 11.5*.

Figure 11.5 Carrying out an investigation

Aim	Every survey has a purpose. It may be a question to be asked or a decision to be made. This purpose will help you decide what questions you must ask, the best way of asking, and who is likely to know the answers.
Design	At the same time you should work out the questions you are going to ask and the way you are going to use the answers. There are many different ways of allowing people to answer, you want the one most useful to you.
Pilot	Get a few people to answer your questions, just to check that they mean what you intend them to and people can give the kinds of answer you need.
Redesign	Some of the questions will need to be changed, some of the answer forms may need changing. You may realise that some questions can be taken out and others have to be added.
Plan sample	You can't ask everybody so you have to select some. You will need to decide how many and where.
Sample	There are several different ways of sampling, you have to choose the one that will suit your needs and give usable results.
Collate	This just means put everything together using the framework for analysing your answers which you worked out at the beginning.
Analyse	What do your findings tell you. You will have to go back to your aims and answer in terms of those. You may need to use appropriate techniques to sort things out.
Recommend	This is what it was all about from the beginning. Make your decision and suggest what should be done.

Aims Example: Suppose a firm wishes to find out what proportion of those who live in Birmingham own hover-type lawn-mowers. Then your aim is a simple one – to answer this question. You may want to go a little further and find out what proportion own any kind of lawn-mower and then the proportion of those who have a hover. This will tell you something about **market share**. Some people may own more than one so you should make provision for that.

Questions You can see how your aims have helped to determine your questions. They might be:
a Do you own a lawnmower? (if 'no' – end interview)
b How many do you own?
c Is your mower – ? (list types, ask for a 'yes' or 'no')
The last question is the difficult one. People may not understand what you mean by types and may confuse it with makes – hence the list.

Sampling You will need some facts to sample. Half of Birmingham is urban. There won't be many lawnmowers in the office and shop areas of the Bullring and New Street. The other half is suburban. If you ask people who live in the centre or just people who live in suburbs you may get a completely false picture. There are three types of sample you might consider.

a **Random** This doesn't mean as you like but rather that anyone who could be asked has exactly the same chance of actually being asked as everyone else. Most people use a table of random numbers to do it. Finding a list which is usable is the problem. Ones which are sometimes used are not very good, for example the *Telephone Directory* – not everybody has a telephone; the electoral register – only those over 18 who remembered to register are on it, there will be some who have moved in and some who are no longer there. But for the lawnmower problem the register may be all right because it gives addresses.
b **Stratified random** If your survey was about something such that some people were more likely to be involved than others then you would use this kind of sample. It is a random one in which you deliberately attach more importance to one kind of person than another. For example, if you were asking about teenage fashion views you would only talk to teenagers. If you wanted to know what young children thought of a particular TV programme you would ask only them.
c **Quota** This is based on random sampling. You work out how many of each kind of person ought to be asked e.g.

  25 women under 30
  20 men under 30
  15 women over 30
  12 men over 30
   8 children.

This might make up a sample of 80 for a survey. The method is particularly useful when you are going to ask someone else to do the work and you want to have some control over who they ask. The example is based on age and sex. Sometimes quotas are based on other things like:

Income
Type of house
Where people live
What people do.

Collecting At last you have got there. You will have to decide how you are going to ask the questions. You could pop a questionnaire through the letter-box but few of those get answered. You could stop people in the street but some people are impatient. Whatever method you choose will have problems. If you decide to ask the questions yourself you must make sure you ask in the same way all the time so that you can be certain different answers are not a result of the way you asked the questions.

Working it out This is the purpose of your hard work. If your preparation was good it will be easy to put all the data together and much of the time the answer will be clear. You must be careful not to claim more than your data tells you, remembering that the way you had to collect it will limit the value of many answers. For example, if your survey on lawn-mowers showed that out of 200 people asked 140 had lawnmowers and 80 of these had hover-types this would not really say very much because the sample is small and the figure is close to half of them, sufficiently close for it to be possible that from another sample of 200 the answers would be different.

It is important to remember that the purpose of an investigation is to find an **answer** and at the end you should go back to your aims and make sure that you have answered the question you set out to tackle and made recommendations which are in line with your aims.

11.6 The market

Although the word 'market' is used to mean many different things and often a particular place, for us it means the **process of exchange**, normally of goods for money. In the process buyer and seller normally meet either directly or through agents but that is not necessary. Many things are bought and sold through catalogues and adverts and it is now common to buy things over the telephone, quoting a credit card number.

It is common practice to talk about the market for cars and the market for butter but in practice there are many different markets for the same good. There are vey few things which are sold in only one way and at only one price. Working out all the possible markets for a good is called **segmentation** and each part of the market a **segment**. *Figure 11.6* tries this process for the market in watches. It isn't complete but it makes the point.

Figure 11.6 Market segments for watches

Pop	These are cheap replaceable watches which can be bought all over the place for small amounts of money.
Sturdy	The obvious market for these is children and people at work in conditions where they are not going to be treated well.

continued

Presentation	These are often given as presents when leaving a job, achieving a particular goal, or at Christmas. What they look like is very important and so is the packaging.
Pocket	These used to be very popular and there is still a small market for them. They are particularly useful to people who work at jobs where it is better to have nothing on the wrist.
Dress	It is more important that these fit the clothes and look decorative than it is that they tell the right time.
Digital	These now have a large part of the market and there is a wide range even within this segment.
Speciality	Examples are nurses' fob watches, divers' watches, and those used for athletics, work study, and so on.
Combination	This is a watch linked in with something else. It may be at the end of a pen or part of a calculator. It may be a watch which also provides a range of other data – the most common is date and day.

The market for most products can be broken down into segments in the way described in *Fig 11.6* and the importance of doing it is:

a   A firm may identify a segment of the market which is not being catered for. This is what new firms often do.
b   Few firms can attempt to be in all segments and they need to decide which ones their resources, expertise, and marketing skills are most suitable for.
c   Each segment needs a different marketing mix.

11.7 Things which decide the nature of the market

One of the important questions answered by research is about the nature of the market. Of course there is not a once-and-for-all answer and firms must be on the look-out for changes in the market and be ready to respond to them. The important things which might change are:

Population
The total is important and so is its regional distribution but firms are usually more interested in the pattern of the population from the following points of view:

a **Number and size of families** Many products are bought by families for general family use, particularly those which are used to clean, protect, or maintain a house or flat and those like fridges, freezers, televisions, and washing machines which are used in households. The size of families often effects the size ranges which manufacturers put on the market.

b **Age** The age of consumers is the vital factor in the sale of many products. One of the changes of recent years has been in the relative importance of young consumers. A good example is in clothes shops where the image used to be that expected by people of 25 and over and is now more in tune with the needs of much younger people. Many products are obviously for a particular age group, e.g. nappies, primary education, pop music, or retirement homes.

c **Ethnic, cultural, and religious groups** The fact that a firm can make a living out of communion wafers and wines depends entirely on the existence of churches and there are many other examples of this kind. But the real impact of these groups is at the point of sale because they often tend to group together and this makes shops and leisure activities which cater for their special needs a commercial possibility.

d **Income** People have money to spend but it is not easy to discover how much this is. Two things make it difficult:

1 Much of the money we earn each week is committed to fixed expenditures or to known variable ones like rent or a mortgage, electricity and gas bills or standard goods which we must buy each week.

2 Some of it may be committed by intentions for the future (savings) or the behaviour of the past (credit payments).

Disposable income which can be spent on the wide range of goods and services on offer may be very small. It is for the ways in which you may use this income that a great many businesses are competing. This is why competition isn't just about firms producing the same goods it is about all those uses of money which are approximately the same commitment. For example a restaurant, a cinema, a disco, a public house, a theatre, and a bingo hall all compete with each other just as buying a new car might compete with taking on a mortgage for a house or having an extension built. Competition is about the amount of disposable income we have and the wide range of ways we may choose to spend it.

How we spend our money

A lot of research has been done into this question and there is a surprising similarity about the way we spend. The figures shown below are taken from a family income survey and even though we would expect families to behave in the same way more than we would single people, the figures are very close.

Type of spending	Percentage of Income From % To %
Food, drink, tobacco	30–32
Housing	22–28
Clothing	8–12
Transport	8–15
Houshold	7– 9
Personal care	7–11
Recreation	2– 5

Figure 11.7a
How we spend our money

With these bands there is scope for very different behaviour, particularly with things like transport and tobacco, and one of the things that will produce really different behaviour is the structure and age of the family. A couple without children may spend very differently from a family with four children all going to school. In fact couples who have reached the stage of a grown-up family, with a mortgage paid, and with much greater disposable income are particularly appealing to the marketing person. That same family survey found that the recent changes in use of income have been as shown in *Figure 11.7b*

Figure 11.7b Changes in our buying habits

Why we buy the things we do

Concentrating only on our disposable income and not on the larger part which is spent to satisfy known and regular needs, market research has shown that the important influences on our behaviour include:

Impulse Shops have known about this for years and adapt their selling techniques to make it happen more often. Greengrocers allow people to select their own fruit and vegetables and many shops allow pick and mix for sweets. They know customers will buy more often that way and probably buy a larger quantity. In a supermarket products which might be bought on impulse are placed at eye level or near the check-out where people have to wait.

Time Products which claim to save us time and shopping methods which do the same are popular. Prepacked foods, fast foods, self-service, shops with car parks, and one-stop shopping are all examples of situations in which time saving attracts customers.

Conformity Sometimes we wish to conform, or it is required, for example school uniforms and kit, our own leisure purchases when taking part in a sport, and fashion. Many youth groups tend to specify at least one item of clothing which marks them off as a group.

Leisure This ranges from labour-saving devices in the home to the amount we spend on things like garden furniture, accessories for car or bike, and leisure activities in the community.

Convenience Time is one important convenience but there are others. For example:

a Goods must be offered in a range of sizes and forms. Medical products are sold as a liquid, paste, syrup, powder, pill, inhalant, or capsule and in a range of sizes.

b Goods must be available when the consumer wants them and this has led to Sunday opening and markets, late-night shopping, vending machines, and mail order.

c Packages are popular. The best examples are one-stop shopping, package holidays, insurance policies for everything, and British Rail's theatre trips.

Credit All kinds of products and services are now available on credit, either through credit arrangements or through the use of credit cards. Most businesses have found that they have to cater for this if they want to maintain custom and its use has extended into fields where it was not common and into medium-sized and small shops.

Selection Few shops can afford to keep only one brand of good because the consumer likes to choose between an assortment of brands and prices for many goods. On the other hand few can afford to stock them all. The brand leader, the next best, and an own label is common policy.

Tastes Obviously we won't buy the things we don't like, but people's tastes do change. There are several things which lead most consumers to be more selective in what they buy. This has happened partly because:
a Many people have increased disposable income.
b Credit enables people to buy now and to pay more.
c Modern education and increased travel habits widen choice.
d Many people have more time for leisure.
e People are influenced by the groups to which they belong.
f Past experience. A good buy tends to be repeated.

Market research clearly makes a major contribution to what a business produces and to the way that the product is promoted and sold to the customer but the product itself is also very important.

11.8 The product

It is what we as buyers think a product is and the reasons why we buy it that matters, and not the view of those who make it. If most customers are buying a dustbin because they find it very useful for making beer or wine at home then that's what it is and perhaps it should be modified and sold through different outlets. It is because consumers think in this way that **brand labels** work. The products may be the same but if consumers think they are different they will buy one rather than another.

The other thing which makes the same products different from each other is the way they are sold to the customer. For example the same make and type of television set may be sold in several different ways:
a for cash alone
b for cash and with a maintenance agreement
c for cash and with a maintenance agreement and insurance
d for cash and including an aerial and installation
e for cash including a licence
f any combination of the above
g on credit with any of the above added
h not sold at all but rented to the customer
i any of the above in a range of different cabinets.

Another way of looking at products is that people do not buy the products themselves but as the satisfaction of a need. This is very evident in the way many goods are advertised and promoted. *Figure 11.8* shows some examples.

Meals out	We don't buy a particular meal in most cases. It is either the satisfaction of hunger or a leisure activity we enjoy. What is on the menu may be less important than quality, surroundings, and good service.
Motor oil	Most brands of oil are sold as good car care, or economy, or performance.
Holidays	don't sell the place as much as the needs involved like, new experiences, glamour, rest, meeting people, and sunshine.

Figure 11.8 Selling products through needs

Most products are not on their own but are part of a product range, e.g. the sizes of shoes and saucepans, the colours of most products, the screen sizes of television sets, lengths and destination of holidays, and the prices of tickets in a theatre or for a football match. The larger firms will have a product mix which consists of several different products each with its own range, and there are several ways of improving market share by changes in the product mix.

a **Expansion of the mix** It could be a wider choice of fittings in shoes. Clarks made an impact on the market by doing this and making an advertising point of the care with which they measure feet. Expansion may be by new lines, either related to present products or arising from a different use of the same resources. A firm may hire out all kinds of vehicles and also extend into trailers and into holiday provision. Woolworths have substantially increased the range of goods they sell.

b **Contraction of the mix** This may be done when there are products which are not making a contribution, but it may be part of deliberate policy if the firm think they can do better by concentrating more on fewer segments of the market.

c **Changing existing products** This happens all the time to familiar products, especially in the detergent industry in which products are always 'new', 'fresher', 'bluer', 'with new additives', and so on. The motor industry does this every year with model changes which don't alter the car much but make it unmistakably this year's model. Packaging is also another very popular way to present products in a new light.

d **Finding new uses** Many of the new uses come from consumers but firms should be aware of them through salesforce reports and consumer enquiries and should be thinking creatively about this themselves.

e **Up-market and down-market** Many firms project an image for their products, and this sells them to a particular range of customers. It is possible to extend this range although it may be wise to use a different brand name and make some modifications in order to do this. Many shops have attempted to move up-market in this way, e.g. Marks and Spencer and Boots. Recently the Co-op has made enormous attempts to extend its market.

f **Creating and emphasising differences** Basically the same product can be marketed under different brand labels and again the soap products industry is a good example. When a customer transfers from one brand label to another there is some possibility that it will be to a product of the same firm. For example many high street shoe shops are part of the British Shoe Corporation even though they have different names.

11.9 The product life cycle

Products are being introduced all the time, and never more rapidly than at the present time. Many products never get off the ground, others flourish briefly and then depart, and some seem to have been around for ever. All this is summed up in *Fig 11.9*, called a **product life cycle** because of its shape and the fact that it outlines the life of all products. The only difference is in the time it takes to get from one stage to the next. For products like fashion goods, pop music, craze toys, and equipment like hula hoops and so on the cycle is very short and difficult to extend. For products like salt it seems to go on and on. The stages of the cycle are shown in *Fig 11.9*.

Figure 11.9 Product life cycle

a **Development** Often a long stage taking place before the product is on the market. It is the stage at which a firm will satisfy itself that the product has a worthwhile future.

b **Launch** Often accompanied and preceded by high advertising both to convince the consumer to buy and the retailer to stock the product. Advertising may have to be very informative at this stage, particularly if the product is an innovation.

c **Growth** Sales and profits are rising steadily. The emphasis of advertising tends to shift to persuasion and there is a search for product extensions, new segments of the market, and new outlets.

d **Maturity** The product has reached its peak. The effort will be to sustain this as long as possible, perhaps by advertising or by product extension and modification. The product has already achieved its ceiling and the real effort will probably be to find new products.

e **Decline** Efforts may be made to put this off or slow it down or the firm may have anticipated it and let it happen. If there is another product already on the way up nothing will be done to support the declining product. It may even be taken off the market if it is now having a bad effect on the image of the firm or of newer products.

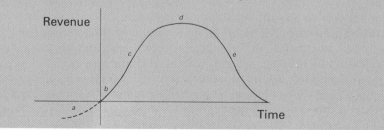

11.10 Product branding and trade marks

This has not always been a part of selling. At the turn of the century products tended to be sold loose and packaged from bulk by the shopkeeper. Now branding is an important part of the marketing process. Brand is a general word which covers names, designs, symbols, words, and packaging to distinguish one product from another and by which it is recognised. It is of great help to customers who have found particular things either good or bad and can therefore either buy or avoid them. Branding is used to achieve a number of marketing objectives including:

a to support advertising and promotion. The brand is the centre of an advert because it is the point of identification with the customer.
b to maintain or increase market share. With firms like the main petrol and soap products firms it is more to maintain share than in any hope of increasing it.
c to make the product a little less price sensitive because users develop brand loyalty. With most products brand loyalty will not go beyond quite small price changes.
d to make it easier to extend the product mix. Once the consumer has identified with a label resistence to new products is less. Heinz is a good example.

Products cannot always be branded. For example:

a If a product is likely to vary branding might imply a standard which doesn't exist and cause consumers to be wary.
b Sometimes the consumer will not accept that there is a difference and then there is no point in a brand, e.g. nails and screws. But even here the increased tendency to prepack goods has led to brand names.
c Where goods are substandard. If goods have been branded and they are sold as seconds, e.g. clothes, it is normal practice to take the brand label out.

What makes a good brand? The short answer is one that the consumer remembers and uses although some brand names like Hoover become **generic** – that is they stay in people's minds as describing the range of products and not the brand. This is not good for the firm because the brand has lost its meaning. Biro is another example, most of us use it to describe any ball-point pen. A brand may be good for any one of the following reasons:

a It suggests the benefits which the product offers, e.g. Inter-City, and Frigidaire.
b It is not confused with other brands and doesn't infringe the rights of another firm. There have been many arguments about the right of other firms to use words like 'sherry' and 'champagne'.
c It suggests product action or a special feature of the product e.g. Instant Whip.
d It is easy to recognise and say. This is why one-word labels are often thought to be best, e.g. Pledge, Mum, Brillo, and Pepsi.
e It is distinctive. This is why using the name of the firm for a brand is not often very effective. If a product is on the national market and television is used distinction can be found by humour, association of ideas, and the use of situations. Examples are the advertising of milk, Coke, and banks.
f It is adaptable. It should be usable for the whole range of products. Here the name of the firm often does win over the brand, e.g. Wilkinson Sword.

11.11 Packaging

Packaging is an important part of the marketing mix, it doesn't just wrap things up. The package usually contains the trade mark and information about the product and is often eye-catching in its own right. Sometimes the packages are designed to be useful after the product has been used, e.g. coffee packed in drinking glasses or storage jars, and brandy sold in decanters. Changing a packet is an inexpensive way of giving the impression that the product itself has been changed. Sometimes the package itself is a selling point as when flip top packets were introduced for many products, and the ring-top can.

Packages are sometimes used to give a false impression of the amount that is being bought. It's true that weights or quantities are often stated but consumers are not always that careful in their buying and packets are often far from full. Biscuits are often sold in odd weights. Packaging is often important for the retailer because it makes storage and shelf stacking very much easier. It can also be used as a promotion activity as when two dissimilar goods are sold together perhaps as an introductory offer. Some products are sold in units of more than one within packaging which it is not easy to break and which retailers may be reluctant to split. For example beer is often sold in packs of four.

An increasing use of packaging which is attractive to the consumer is the complete kit, e.g. screws with a screwdriver, or razor blades with a razor. Retailers like this method because it promotes the gift market. Consumers often like it because one or more of the items in the packet might have required a visit to another shop or a purchase of a larger quantity. Presumably if screws come with a product to be assembled they are of the best type and quality and this is also attractive to a buyer.

11.12 Product design

The marketing importance of design has long been recognised in such areas as furniture, wallpaper, and cars. Some things are bought because of their design, e.g. jewellery. Some products are too design conscious, making design more important than such things as use and users. Some buildings have been well designed as buildings but insufficient attention has been paid to their use as homes, e.g. high rise flats. Some children's toys do not take into account that they are going to get rough treatment and ought to be designed for it. How many toys are useless by Boxing Day for this reason?

A lot of research has been done about the importance of **colour**. What colours in packages and products are most likely to persuade the consumer to buy? In part this is a matter of fashion. Two years ago red was the most popular car colour and in general red and yellow are most noticeable. In supermarkets attracting the customers attention is very important.

Size is also important. Obviously clothes and shoes must fit but in general a shop cannot afford to get a reputation as one in which the full range of sizes is not stocked. Some shops find it possible to specialise successfully in the extremes of size.

11.13 Price strategies

Hilary and Jill both bought office desks. Hilary paid £350 and Jill paid £200. Hilary's desk was delivered to her office, put in place and invoiced to her. She had about six weeks to pay for it and could probably stretch that to two months. It was a beautifully finished desk.

Jill bought hers at a cash and carry, it came in bits and she had to collect it and assemble it herself. It took her about three hours to put together. Who paid the higher price?

Figure 11.13 What is the price of the desk?

Price is just one part of the marketing mix and cannot be considered on its own. For example if a firm decides that it is going for the quality segment of the market it must price high, advertise accordingly, package in a quality fashion, and sell through the right outlets. Deciding to go for the lower segment would have similar consequences for the mix. In general consumers do have some idea of the kind of price they would pay for things, a sort of **price plateau**, and if a firm prices outside this there have to be good reasons. The strategies which a firm might adopt when pricing include:

a **Creaming** This is most likely with new products for which a price plateau has not been established. There is always a group of consumers who like to take advantage of new products whilst they are new and are prepared to pay the higher price for this. In recent years this has happened with computers, computer games, and videos.

b **Penetrating** A low initial price is set to obtain as large a segment of the market as possible. This is particularly common where it is known that competitors are or will soon be in the field. It is also common with products where the expected life is long and consumers are likely to buy regularly.

c **Maximising** It is common to try to maximise profits when the product life cycle is short and demand is likely to be high, e.g. pop records, fashions, and seats for Wimbledon.

d **Capturing** Firms will price hardware low expecting to make high profits from software once their equipment has been bought, e.g. duplicators are cheap but the paper, etc. is not. Computers are cheap relative to the price of the software. Original buys which have a holder or container are cheap but the refills are relatively expensive.

e **Discriminating** This involves dividing the market into segments and pricing differently in each segment. British Rail do this by charging at different rates for routes. Many firms do it by selling the same product under different labels at a range of prices.

f **Range pricing** This means selecting one price at which the whole of the range will be sold. Bus companies with fixed prices for a whole route are an example. Some publishers do it with titles within the same range.

g **Cost leading** This is common among retailers. It consists of reducing the prices on certain goods to the bare minimum in the expectation that customers will be attracted and will buy other things once inside the shop.

11.14 Setting the price

If you ask most people what they think is the most important feature of a product they are likely to say 'price' or things which imply price like 'value for money'. The things which influence a firm's pricing decisions are

a **Practice** What the firm and other firms in the industry have been doing. There is a tradition about pricing in many industries.
b **Costs** In the long run the firm has to make a profit so it can't afford to sell below the cost of production.
c **Purpose** Particularly when trying to attract new customers or launch a new product a firm is likely to make an 'offer'. There is always something in every shop which is either a 'special attraction' or an 'introductory offer'.
d **Competition** Most products are price sensitive within narrow limits and a firm has to be aware of what competitors are doing and change prices if necessary.
e **Market** In different market conditions a firm will charge varied prices. Strawberries or mushrooms bought fresh in the morning are at the highest price of the day. At the same stall in late afternoon prices will be much lower. On and just before Mothers' Day flowers tend to be more expensive just as they are on railway stations or outside hospitals.
f **Customer** A valued customer or a new one likely to be regular may be offered a discount, as might one who is going to place a large order, or a customer whose business might add to the reputation of the firm.
g **Service** What is offered with the good? As we saw earlier a television set, even the same model, is not one product but many depending on the additional services which go with it.

What does price mean anyway?
The case in *Fig 11.13* makes the important point that there is a sense in which price is not just what you pay for something but many other features of the value of the good to you in one condition rather than another. It is all a matter of what you are buying – Jill was buying something she needed at a price she could afford and which relied on her having the time, skill, and patience to put the desk together. Hilary was buying something which was well designed, immediately ready for use, and which she could pay for at her leisure. Although what they bought was called an office desk, in fact they were two different things.

11.15 Promotion

In many ways we have discussed promotion already because it is closely related to pricing and to product policy. Most businesses advertise, some of them regularly spending a substantial amount of money in doing so. There are two general reasons for it:

a **Information** New products, changes in products, movement into new markets, and a range of products where technical factors are important. All of these need an informative approach.
b **Persuasion** Products competing either with others in the same field or in general for the disposable income of customers normally rely on persuasion.

There are a number of other things which will influence the way this is done and they are shown in *Fig 11.15a*. Much advertising is carried out in order to increase market share, particularly when the product is new or a new development, but there is also a lot of advertising by big companies for products like petrol and soaps which is just to keep the product in the mind of the consumer. It is easy to lose business if other firms are advertising but you are not.

One of the main problems is to identify the market. Advertisements need to have a particular group of customers at whom they are aimed. It would be pointless advertising a Mini to someone who is in the market for a Rolls Royce and vice-versa. On the other hand it is possible to move into what appears to be unlikely segments of the market, and *Fig 11.15b* gives some examples of that.

The advantages of a product must be stressed in the right way. For example people are often wary of **cheapness** because they think of poor quality goods and the waste of money when that is emphasised. Yet there are goods that are cheap and designed for the mass-market. This is best advertised as **value for money**.

Figure 11.15a Things which influence the advertising decision

Budget	This is the amount of money the firm has available to promote. Many of the media are expensive to use.
Buyers	The fewer the number of buyers the more likely personal methods of working are. The fewer the types of customer the more effective a single campaign is likely to be.
Extent	A national market will need an entirely different product from a regional one. Regions will require a different approach from a local market. International marketing provides a further challenge.
Nature	Is the market for an industrial product or a consumer one? Is it for a new product or an existing one? Is the product one which will be bought regularly and frequently or just a once-off purchase?
Product	Many goods are commonly purchased and most of us spend the larger part of our income on them. For these shops often rely on national manufacturers' advertising and they also supply display materials which the shops may use at the point of sale.
Cycle	This is the stage the product is in. At launch the advertising will be informative but will become increasingly persuasive in most cases. It will do little more than support sales at maturity and there will be little or no advertising at the later stage.

Mini	Selling a Mini to a Rolls-Royce owner? Second car ideal as a runabout and for short trips into town for shopping. The advert would concentrate on the adaptability, easy parking, and other convenience features of the Mini for short journeys.
Fridges	Selling fridges to people in very cold climates? Sounds unlikely until you think about the use of fridges. We think they keep food cold but they don't; they keep it at a medium temperature. Things taken from the freezer and put in the fridge thaw a little. For such people the fridge would keep things from freezing.

Figure 11.15b Extending the market to unlikely places

Apart from discussions about the morality of advertising there is also the problem of its cost. On the face of it, advertising costs have to be added to the costs of producing and selling goods and therefore makes them more expensive. Where the advertising is not successful that is true, but it is a different matter if it is successful and significantly increases sales.

a Without advertising, sales staff would have to maintain a much more regular contact with retailers wholesalers and individual large customers. Many of the small potential outlets may never get to know about a product. In other words, if money wasn't spent on advertising it would be spent on some other way of contacting the consumer.
b If there was no advertising it is likely that firms would be smaller and local or that the total volume of business would fall. Either way this would reduce scope for economies of scale (discussed in Chapter 12) and increase unit costs.

11.16 Advertising media

'Advertising media' is now a popular term for all those ways in which firms may reach stockists and consumers with news and persuasive material about their products. The list is endless and varies from local window cards to national television and from leaflets through the door to national newspapers. Commercial television is the most expensive but it reaches more people than anything else. Poster sites are quite cheap and the best ones reach a lot of passing motorists and passengers but can only contain fleeting and obvious messages. They are very good for reminding people of messages which they have seen elsewhere. The range of specialist, hobby, and leisure magazines is now so great that there is almost always one which will reach particular segments of the market. This makes them very good for those markets.

When should advertising be used?

Figure 11.16 suggests some of the more usual situations.

Need	When there is a consumer need which the product is likely to satisfy. Advertising cannot sell products which people do not want. This is why when products have reached the decline stage of the cycle firms do not advertise. They don't expect to be able to reverse the trend.
Recognition	There should be some basis on which consumers can recognise the product and see it as different from others. Things like cars, cosmetics, dresses, and machines are easier to sell then salt and sugar.
Feature	There should be a strong point of the product upon which the advertisement can be based. Soap powders, engine oil, and others find this in performance terms, cosmetics look for it in social terms but all these products are easier to advertise than greetings cards and eggs.
Motive	The advertisement should focus on needs or wants which can be associated with the product and can form a basis for a consumer's buying decision. On this basis it is easier to build up a demand for health foods than it is for everyday foods.
Funds	The campaign has to be completed. Persuasion is not a quick or single process and advertising will not work unless sufficient is spent on doing it properly.
Information	When there is something really new to say about a product, when there is an extension of the product range, when the product is moving into new segments of the market, when the product or the firm producing it is new. In all these cases there is a need for informative advertising. Such informative approaches are also the normal way to tackle the trade and industrial market.

Figure 11.16 When is advertising necessary?

11.17 The objectives of promotion

The obvious purpose of advertising is to sell something to a customer who would not otherwise have bought it. But particular advertisements may have more specific objectives than that. Some common objectives are considered in *Fig 11.17*.

Figure 11.17 Objectives of advertising

Personal	A lot of selling contact, particularly between manufacturer and outlet is personal. The purpose of some advertising is to support the personal contact, either to make it more likely that the potential customer will see the sales staff or that they will be kept interested between calls.
Contact	To reach people who can't be reached personally. Many people who make buying decisions are not directly reachable by sales staff. In industrial selling the decision may be made by top management. With consumer decisions consumers can persuade retailers to stock a particular good.
Relations	As a public relations exercise to keep the relationship with the potential buyer a good one and to improve it if possible. This is often done with such additional rewards as gifts or exclusive agencies as in the sale of cars. It is also done by supplying promotional material.
Segments	To enter or develop a new segment of the market. Initial adverts will be informative and later ones persuasive.
New products	Again informative to start with and then persuasive. The extent of the campaign and its nature will depend on whether the product is a minor addition to range, new product available elsewhere, or new development with the firm first in the market.
Penetrate	A firm may identify one or more segments in which it can obtain and hold a larger market share. Such advertising will be persuasive, often with a consumer offer of some kind and prizes for the sales staff and outlets who sell most.
Co-operate	Sometimes the industry as a whole thinks the market can be increased to everyone's benefit and they advertise together. Milk is usually advertised in this way and in the past insurance and pubs have used the technique. Sometimes producers of two different but jointly used products get together and thus share the costs. Washing powders and washing machines is a common example.
Attack	To counteract the advertising of others, particularly if it indirectly attacks your product. This sort of advertising is often necessary in non-business advertising, e.g. the DHSS wanting people to claim the benefits they are entitled to.
Counteract	Some products are thought of as substitutes for others and much advertising is to try and overcome preference for one rather than the other. The never-ending battle between butter, margarine, and other fats is the best example.
Firm	Adverts which advertise the business rather than a product because general goodwill promotes all sales. Multi-product firms like Cadburys and Heinz do this a lot. BP and ICI also have adverts like this.

11.18 Distribution

Figure 11.18 shows all the standard channels of distribution which a firm might use. Any route through the diagram is possible, including some which have not been drawn in. A firm tends to use channels which it thinks serve it well, but few firms of any size use only one route.

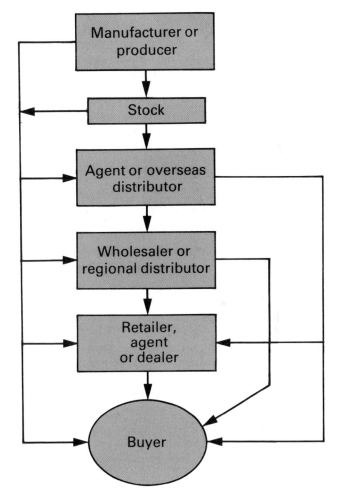

Figure 11.18 Channels of distribution

11.19 The channel decision

The first question for the manufacturer and for those further down the chain of distribution is: Who is my customer? From the answer to this question it is possible to work backwards to the most effective channel for that customer. This is why businesses regularly have a multi-channel approach. They have a range of customers for each group of whom there is a best channel. It is the buying habits of the customer and the outlet in direct contact with the customer that matter most. There are three sets of factors which have to be considered in making the decision.

a those which concern the **product**
b those which relate to the **nature** and **extent** of the **market**
c **organisational** factors for the firm.

Product

a **What is the value of each unit of the product?** The less valuable each unit is the quicker the producer wants to get rid of it and preferably in large batches. This would normally mean a long chain using wholesalers and distributors who can take large amounts. The exception is large retailing chains like Tesco and Gateway who will themselves take large orders.

b **How heavy is each unit?** It may not be heaviness. It may be odd shapes which make the product difficult to handle. The producer is not likely to use routes which will be expensive if handling is difficult. Often they have their own adaptable transport facilities to deliver to the next stage in the chain.

c **How fragile or perishable is the product?** Perishable products, and that includes ones with very short product life cycles like pop records have to get to the consumer very quickly, so short routes are best.

d **How important is technical advice, installation, servicing and after-sales support?** This will depend upon the stage at which the trained staff are to be found. For some products, particularly ones sold to industrial and commercial users, the manufacturers keep their own staff and the direct route is used. For other products, like television sets or washing machines which have to be plumbed in, the support is usually at the retailing stage.

e **Customer requirements** Some goods are made to order and to the specifications of the customer. The route is usually direct in these cases, e.g. garden sheds and prefabricated extensions to houses. Services are always direct but that is the nature of a service. Even there a choice is possible between home-based services and ones where the customer must go to a shop or office.

f **The product line** Many products are sold in ranges, like shoes and saucepans, and manufacturers who do not supply the whole of what is regarded as the normal range often have to find different routes because wholesalers and retailers are not very interested in stocking them.

Market

a **Consumer or industrial market?** Industrial consumers more often expect a direct service except for those things they buy which are small consumables like paper clips and screws.

b **The size of the total market** Small and local markets may be served directly whilst scattered and large markets will need the service of an agent.

c **Market share** If the firm is a market leader it is likely that it can decide its own policy, but firms with small shares need to ensure that they either find outlets through which competitors can be avoided or receive the same kind of support as other firms through the normal channels for the product. Larger firms will, of course, be fighting for special deals all the time.

d **Order sizes** Large orders can be supplied directly or to regional distributors, whilst for very small orders there is unlikely to be any contact between the manufacturer and the buyer.

e **Customer buying habits** Important factors here might be the extent to which the customer will want credit or other services like advice or maintenance associated with the product.

Organisation

a **Finance** A company in a strong financial position needs agents less than others do since it can warehouse its own products and give credit if necessary. Some firms avoid many financial problems by producing all or most of their product for one firm but they are very much at the mercy of the market if they do that.

b **Management experience and expertise** Many companies, particularly small ones or ones selling abroad, lack marketing expertise and prefer to leave the job to experts.

c **Control** The shorter the channel of distribution the more control a firm has. Some companies buy into the distribution chain in order to establish this control and have more certainty of a market. Doing this is called **integration** and because it is the producer gaining control of stages closer to the market it is called **forward integration**.

d **Services** An important point will be the extent to which a firm is able and willing to help the agent. This will also depend on the product since there are many where a joint effort and or technical asistance is worthwhile. Garages are a good example. The leading producers do much to assist those garages which sell their petroleum products exclusively. Some retail changes will not accept a line which does not come without promotional support from the manufacturer.

e **Agent services** Some manufacturers will select the agent who can supply the product services which are needed. If a product requires promotion which the manufacturer cannot provide an agent may do a better job than a wholesaler. If goods require storing, blending, or packaging a wholesaler may be the best route.

f **Appropriateness of agent** Agents may not wish to carry competing lines particularly if they are giving special promotion support to one already.

g **Costs** Where the choice is not made on other grounds the relative cost of one channel rather than another will be important.

11.20 The special problem of new products

Whenever either the product or the firm is new there will be special problems to overcome.

a The demand for some new products may not be very great and is often 'created' rather than real. Much of the marketing mix for the product must be concerned with building up and maintaining a demand and making provision to 'educate' the consumer in the uses of the product.

b Promotion requirements are very high.

c Decision makers in all stages of the channel of distribution may be very wary and producers may have restricted choice.

11.21 Some modern marketing methods

In recent years firms have become more conscious of the importance of the consumer and of the pace of change and have developed more direct techniques to ensure success. Among the most effective of these has been:

a **Value analysis** is a team effort by everybody involved to examine in every detail the nature of a product, the materials it is made of, the uses to which it may be put, its costs, its value to the customer, and its profitability. It is a creative process in which everybody is encouraged to voice ideas. It often produces new uses, new outlets, new designs, and new materials from which things can be made. Originally common in engineering firms now many firms conduct value analysis sessions for all products.

b **Selling systems** Many firms sell a range of products which are part of a total system and they sell the system rather than the product. Examples are systems for wage and salary payments, for keeping records, or for using computers. It saves bargaining over prices of particular elements and tends to secure custom thereafter.

c **Commando marketing** An active and rather dramatic phrase for something which has gone on in some form or other for centuries. In its modern form it usually means special local displays and exhibitions sometimes linked with an event staged at the time. Examples of it include show houses on building sites often lived in by people who are paid to receive and entertain visitors, and the selling of microwave ovens by demonstration.

d **Telephone selling** Knocks on the door don't have to be answered if you see the salesperson coming but most people will not ignore a ringing phone and an increasing number of us are on the phone. Salespeople have long kept in contact with their outlets by phone but the extension of its use into direct consumer marketing is modern. It is common in the sale of home .improvements, books, and some religious beliefs.

11.22 Organising the marketing effort

The same basic principles apply to organising a marketing department as we discussed in Chapters 7 and 8. *Figure 11.1a* has shown the main sections of the marketing departments of Anyfirm plc. The things we have discussed within the chapter may have convinced you that all the sections have to work together to get the mix right and work it well. Perhaps it would have been better if we had shown the various section heads working together around a table with the Marketing Director at the head. This is shown in *Fig 11.22*.

Figure 11.22 Co-operative view of the marketing department

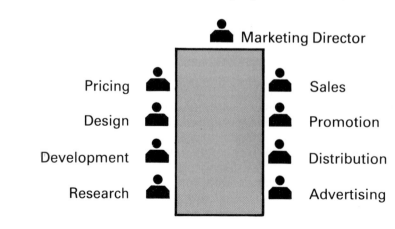

THINGS TO DO

Short answer questions

1 What is meant when a firm is described as 'market orientated'?

2 What is meant by the term 'marketing mix'?

3 Explain why the marketing mix will not be the same for
   a all the products
   b the same product in different markets.

4 With the aid of examples distinguish between primary and secondary sources of information.

5 Name four different sources of secondary information.

6 Name three ways in which primary data may be collected.

7 Write down as many different segments as you can think of for each of the following products:
   a peas
   b computers
   c novels
   d spectacles.

8 Give an example of the kind of product which might be bought on impulse from a supermarket.

9 What is meant by the term 'convenience goods'? Give three examples.

10 What is a product? Use examples to explain.

11 Draw a product life cycle and explain the shape for each of the following:
   a a pop record   *b* salt   *c* potatoes.

12 State the seven factors which a firm might take into account when pricing a product. Give one example not mentioned in the text, to illustrate each.

13 What are the two kinds of advertising?

14 Give two reasons why spending money on advertising is not necessarily adding to costs.

15 What is 'value analysis'?

SECTION B **Essays and structured questions**

1 You have produced a new type of electric screwdriver. It will retail at £6.50. To what groups of customers do you expect to sell this product? Design an advertisment. What channels of distribution would you use and why?

2 Decide between surveys, observation, and experiment as the best method of obtaining primary data in each of the following circumstances. Give reasons for your choice.
a A sports shop manager wants to know which type of tennis racket is most likely to be bought by 16- to 25-year-old customers.
b One of your local grocers is changing to self-service and wants to know what sort of shop layout customers would prefer.
c A manufacturer of conveyor belts wants to know who makes the decision to buy their product.

3 Why is the answer to question 2c important?

4 What kind of sample would you want to take to answer the following questions?
a What brand of dog food is most popular?
b Should a local shop open on Sundays (or one late night)?
c How effective is one of the advertisements you have seen on television?
d Should there be a bus service for a local housing estate?

5 How many segments of the market can you identify for air conditioners? What advertising techniques and media would you use for each? What channels of distribution would you use? Design an advertisement to appeal to one of the segments. State which one it is.

6 Give two examples of products where you think the demand would be significantly affected by each of the following factors:
a Regional distribution of the population
b The size of families
c Occupations which people have
d The availability of credit
e The amount of disposable income people have.

7 Choose an advertisement which you don't like. Say why it doesn't appeal to you. Say what you think the firm's objectives are. Redesign the advertisement in a way which you think might meet the objectives.

8 There is often resistance to the use of safety gear in shops, offices, and factories. Choose a particular item of safety wear. Outline the arguments for wearing it. Design a poster which you think might get the message across.

9 Choose any product new on the market and outline all aspects of what you think would be a good marketing mix for it. You might do this as a group activity with one person responsible for each element of the mix.

10 List five brand names which you think are good ones and five which you think are poor. Give reasons for your answer. Take any one of the poor brand names and replace it by one of your own saying why you think it's better.

11 Say what you think each of the following terms means, giving examples to illustrate. Provide a calculation where you think that helps.
   a mark-up
   b up-market
   c cash discount
   d value analysis.

12 What channels of distribution would you use for the following products? Which of the factors discussed in the chapter have been most important in your decision?
   a life insurance
   b farm implements
   c office furniture
   d toothpaste
   e cosmetics
   f motorcycle accessories.

SECTION C

Coursework and assignments

1 Visit your local supermarket and decide:
   a what that shop does to encourage impulse buying
   b what it does to tempt people into the shop
   c what commodities it doesn't make available to self-service and why.

2 On a second visit to your supermarket or to another large store look around the store and write down:
   a the names of the products which first come to your attention
   b any particular features of the store which you notice more than others
   c the positive things about the store you notice
   d the negative things you notice.
From all your observations what have you learnt about this store?

3 Bring any small item of household equipment to school. Working in groups of about 4–6 do a value analysis of it thinking particularly of
   a alternative materials it could have been made of
   b a possible better design for it
   c improvements in any aspect of its production
   d alternative uses.

   When you have completed these discussions.
   e Write a report of your findings as if for the managing director of the firm producing it.
   f Select one of the alternative uses and for that use consider
      1 what changes you would make in the design/appearance of the product
      2 who would buy it
      3 what the marketing mix for the product should be.

g Design promotional material for the product suitable for
  1 distribution to individuals
  2 use inside a shop selling the item.

4 Organise an event for a charity. Make and comment upon all the marketing decisions. After the event:
  a decide which of your decisions were right and contributed to the success of the event. Explain why.
  b decide which of your decisions were not good and explain why.

5 Undertake a market survey on any question of your choice. Some ideas might be:
  a Should there be a chocolate vending machine in the school?
  b Should the local railway station be closed/re-opened/have an improved service?
  c What is the most important local issue about which the council ought to take some action?
  d Should the High Street be made into a pedestrian precinct, or, if it already is do people think it was better before it happened?
  e What is the most important kind of shop that the town/community needs?

Chapter 12
Producing the goods

12.1 What is production?

At the beginning of the book we said that production was carried out to satisfy our needs. For the economy as a whole, without production there would be no consumer goods, no luxuries, and no machinery to produce these goods. Production helps to turn resources like raw materials into useful goods and services which satisfy the needs of the consumer.

Three stages in the production process were outlined – the **primary** stage when the raw materials are extracted from the ground or grown in the ground as in agriculture, the **secondary** stage when the materials are processed into semi-finished or finished goods, and the **tertiary** stage which provides services to production and which helps to get the finished goods to the final consumer. Each of these stages adds **value** to the product and therefore forms part of production. *Figure 12.1* gives an example of production going on:

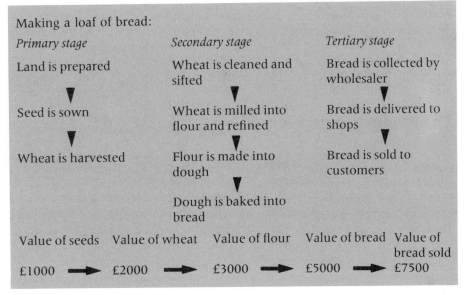

Figure 12.1 Production stage by stage

Each stage of production has added some value to the inputs that went into that stage until the finished good is sold.

12.2 Production in the business

Traditionally production has been the centre of a manufacturing business. Take carpet making as an example. Twenty-five years ago carpet makers, thinking of bringing out a new line would go through the following stages:

DESIGN A NEW CARPET►CALCULATE THE COSTS OF PRODUCTION ►
MAKE THE CARPET (USUALLY TO A HIGH QUALITY) ► SELL THE CARPET.

The reputation of the company and the quality of the product would make it
likely that the carpet would 'sell itself'. But as was shown in the last chapter,
changes in the market, especially through increased competition, have meant
that many manufacturers have moved from being **product orientated** to
being **market orientated**. For carpet makers, this would mean introducing a
new stage:

IDENTIFY THE CUSTOMERS►DESIGN NEW CARPET►CALCULATE THE
COSTS►MAKE THE CARPET►SELL THE CARPET TO THE CUSTOMERS.

As an example, many carpet firms recognised that housebuilders could be
important customers. They could include carpets in new houses they build.
This meant that wall-to-wall carpets were developed for builders to fit when a
house was complete. Production therefore became part of the marketing
process, producing goods which the customer wanted rather than goods which
were technically sound, but too expensive for the customer to afford, or
without the features that the customer demanded. *Figure 12.2* illustrates the
three elements which any business has to combine when deciding which goods
to produce.

Production, as shown in *Fig 12.2*, is pushed three ways. The engineers and
designers would like a product that is technically perfect. The accountants
would like a product that is cheap to make. The marketing people would like
one which includes all the features the customer likes. The final decision about
the product will probably be a compromise, each department giving way a little
for the sake of the other.

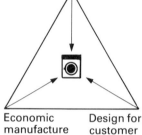

Technical qualities

Economic   Design for
manufacture   customer

Figure 12.2 Three influences
on a product

12.3 Production decisions

The decision about what to produce is taken as a result of research into the
market. There will be a number of problems that the manager or owner of a
small business or the production manager of a large business has to face. Let us
look at the problems from the point of view of a small family business. Lovells
Ltd manufactures diaries for a large chain of stores. It is located in Watford.
There is a fairly constant demand for their diaries year by year, but sales are
very seasonal, nearly all occurring in the last three months of the year. The firm
is a private limited company, and employs about 50 production staff and ten
office staff. *Figure 12.3* shows some of the production decisions that Lovells'
production manager has to take.

Figure 12.3 Production decisions at Lovells

Long-term decisions	Short-term decisions
Where is the best place to locate the factory?	How many workers will be needed? What level of stocks are needed?
What range of products should be made?	How can quality be maintained? How can efficiency be improved?

A **long-term decision** is one which will affect the whole nature of the firm, while a **short-term decision** is a day-to-day one which is needed to keep the operation going. The long-term decisions are likely to be taken by the directors of Lovells, while the short-term ones will be taken by those directly in charge of production.

The most important information which the production staff will have to help them with their decisions will be about costs and the way they affect the profitability of the business.

12.4 Locating the enterprise

For Lovells this decision has already been made, but let us look at some of the factors which will have influenced their decision to set up in Watford. A business will aim to find a location which will keep transport costs as low as possible. Lovells buy in their material and supplies from many places, but wanted to locate quite close to a large market and this made Watford, on the edge of London by the M1 and M25, a good site. However, diaries are not difficult to transport and so Lovells could think of relocating further from London if they wanted to expand.

Some businesses have to locate close to their raw material supply because the materials are too bulky to transport without high costs, while the finished product is much lighter. Others have to locate close to their market because the finished product is bulky while the materials they use are light. *Figure 12.4* gives some examples. Today, most manufacturing industries are free to choose as the costs of bulk transport have fallen and the content of products has changed. These are known as 'footloose' industries. Lovells is a footloose business.

Figure 12.4 Industries where transport costs are important

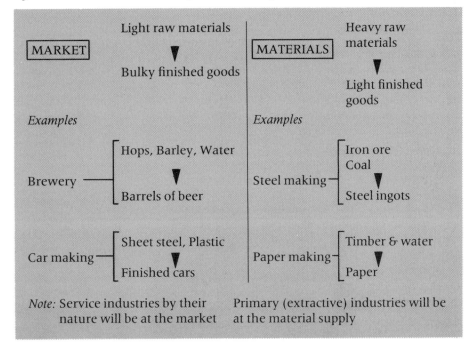

Businesses will also be influenced by the availability and cost of the resources they need for production – land, labour and capital. Lovells found a site at a reasonable rent on a new business park on the edge of Watford. Wages were slightly higher on average in the south east than elsewhere, but Lovells was also wanting to attract skilled labour to run their printing presses, and Watford was an area with a tradition in printing. The initial capital for the company came from the owners but they had links with local banks and were able to borrow at a reasonable interest to tide them over the first period of trading.

Two external factors were also important in their decision as to where to locate. Being close to the M1 gave them the possibility of finding new markets in the Midlands if they wanted to expand in the future. Being close to other printers would help to increase business if the large firms needed to subcontract. A non-economic factor was also present. The Green Belt around London made the location a pleasant one to live in.

This case has suggested some of the factors which can influence a location decision. Lovells were not influenced by government policy which has encouraged firms to move out of the south east, although if a decision was taken to build a second factory, then government grants might become important (these are considered in the next chapter).

12.5 What should be the level of production?

What size is best for a business? This will really depend on the size of the market that the business is selling to: ICI, the largest manufacturing company in Britain, sells chemicals to a worldwide market; W H Smith sells stationery and books to a national market; a department store sells goods to a town; a village shop attracts customers only from the village and outlying houses. Lovells in our example produces specialist diaries (golfing diaries, scouting diaries, etc.) and therefore will aim at a specialist market. The size of a firm is often related to the size and nature of its market.

Lovells is quite a small firm operating in a market which also contains some very large diary manufacturers who aim at the general consumer and office market. In *Fig 12.5a* some of the reasons why small production units can be an advantage are shown.

Figure 12.5a 'Small is beautiful'

This will be true when:
a **The market is limited** A small market needs a low level of production.
b **A flexible or specialist product is needed** to meet the needs of a part of a market, which perhaps has a specialist demand.
c **Subcontracting or making components for large firms** Small firms can live off larger firms by producing for them or supplying them.
d **Personal service is important** This can be more easily supplied by a small firm than a large one.
e **Transport costs are high** This allows local small firms to survive as they are protected from outside competition.
f **Making the product would be unprofitable for a large firm** While for a small business profit might not be the only objective.

As a market grows, it is possible for a business to increase its size. It can buy more machinery and tools, it can move into larger factories, it can employ more workers and managers, it can raise more finance. This is known as increasing the **scale of production**. As the firm grows larger, so its costs per unit of production will fall. *Figure 12.5b* shows how the costs of production at Lovells compares with the costs of two larger diary makers.

Company	Lovells Diaries Ltd.	Miller's Diaries plc	Bailey's Diaries plc
Size of output (per year)	1 million	4 million	10 million
Total costs (per year)	£800,000	£2,400,000	£5,000,000
Cost per diary	£0.80p	£0.60p	£0.50p

Figure 12.5b Costs as size increases

As *Fig 12.5b* shows, the total costs of the two larger firms are greater than at Lovells, but when this is compared with the output of diaries it is clear that the cost per diary at Lovells is higher than at the other companies. There are various factors which cause **unit costs** to fall as the scale of production increases, and these are known as **economies of scale**. They can occur in a number of areas of the business operation and some examples of internal economies of scale are shown in *Fig 12.5c*. Lovells will not be able to enjoy as many of these benefits as the larger firms in the industry. However, we have already shown that Lovells can benefit from its location near to a good road network, and being close to other printing firms. These are examples of **external** economies of scale and both small and large firms can enjoy these. The larger businesses might become too large. Management might find it more difficult to control the business's operations without becoming too bureaucratic. The workforce may feel out of touch with the management, and poor industrial relations might result. The business might not be able to change quickly to meet new needs in the market. These are some of the disadvantages of a business being too big, and they are known as **diseconomies of scale**.

Figure 12.5c Internal economies of scale in a business

PRODUCTION	Greater division of labour increasing workers' skills
	Able to use larger, more efficient, machinery.
	Faster data-processing through use of computers
	Transport materials in bulk, lowering unit costs
	Able to employ mass-production techniques
MARKETING	Able to buy in bulk, therefore benefit from discounts
	Distribution costs are reduced as deliveries can be made in bulk
	Market research made possible, and specialisation in marketing department
	Advertising costs can be spread over a wider range of products

continued

FINANCE
- Easier for large firms to raise capital
- Lenders may ask for a lower rate of interest
- Better access to stock market
- More possibility of finance from retained profits
- Risk is spread over a number of products and projects, therefore less risk of failure

MANAGEMENT
- Greater specialisation possible
- Ability to pay higher salaries to attract best managers
- Use of computers as an aid to decision-making

12.6 Measuring the size of firms

Discussions about the economies and diseconomies which are associated with the size of firms raises the problem of what we mean by 'large firm' and 'small firm' and how we measure size. At home and every day we measure things all the time using specialist tools such as measuring jugs, rulers, tapes, and timers. We know the best or least suitable way to measure most things and, provided we are not careless, the measurement will be the same whoever is doing it and whenever it is done. This is because most measuring is done in terms of standard units – inches, metres, seconds – and we all have a similar understanding of the answer. How can we say what is small or large in business? What tools of measurement are there for us to use? What do they tell us? *Figure 12.6* shows some ideas.

Figure 12.6 Alternative ways of measuring size

The **number of people employed** by a firm used to be an excellent way of measuring its size and is still very useful. A firm employing many people is large, but it is possible to employ very few people and still be a big firm. A traditional brewery employs a large staff in the various stages of making beer, but a modern one works under computer control employing few people making a much larger quantity of beer.

The **profits** of a firm may help since small firms cannot make very large profits. But large firms can make very small profits or even larger losses.

The **number of places of business** a firm has will help. A firm which has a branch in every large town and several overseas will obviously be large but so also are some with a few workplaces each of which produces a lot.

The **value of the product** is a very useful indicator except where things are very valuable, e.g. precious metals and minerals, and are produced by small firms.

continued

Capital employed is a good measure of size, since it is through the capital employed that a business makes its profits. The efficiency of a firm is often judged by the efficiency with which it uses its employed capital. Even here there are problems because the value of assets is often determined by where they are as well as by their extent. For example, premises in the centre of large cities are worth much more than ones of a similar size in a small rural community.

As you can see, most ways of measuring size either mean counting the number of people who work for the firm or measuring what it is and what it does in terms of money. The disadvantage of counting heads is that modern ways of working involve fewer and fewer people. The problem with using money values is that the value of something is not necessarily linked with size of activity and the value of money tends to fall from one year to the next.

Research into this problem has led to the conclusion that there have to be several ways of measuring and that they are likely to give significantly different results. In the Companies Act 1981 parliament tried to solve the problem by providing three ways of measuring size

a Turnover per annum
b Balance sheet totals
c Number employed.

A firm may be considered large or small if two of these three measures put it in that category. It seems reasonable to use **turnover** since a firm doing a lot of business is likely, at least in that sense, to be bigger than one which is doing little. Firms with low balance sheet totals are likely to have little by way of fixed assets and working capital and this too would suggest a small business. Either of these together with a small number of employees is probably the best guide we can get.

12.7 How can production be organised?

There are three basic methods.
a **Job production** where a single product is produced from start to finish as a result of an individual order from a customer
b **Batch production** where products are made in sets, with one whole set passing through a stage of production before moving onto the next
c **Flow production** where products pass from one operation to the next without stopping, as on a mass-production line.

The choice will depend on how the business receives orders for its products. Orders which come from individual customers and which are unlikely to be repeated would be met by job; orders for similar products from several customers which may be repeated would be met by making batches; continuous orders which are regularly repeated would need flow production. *Figure 12.7* gives some examples from industry of where you might find job, batch, and flow production.

Industry	Job ■	Types of Production Batch ■■ ■■	Flow ■-■-■-■-■
Extraction	Quarries	Normal mines	Oil wells
Agriculture & Fishing	Normal farm	Special stock & poultry farms	Herring, salmon fishing & canning
Building	Bridges Houses	Housing estates Industrial estates	Road building
Manufacture	Luxury goods Special machines	Most manufactured goods	Paper & flour mills Car making Telephones & electronic equipment
Transport	Charter planes Furniture removal	Most forms of transport	Public (mass) transport Milk deliveries

Figure 12.7 Types of production

Lovells uses a batch method of production. They receive regular orders for different types of diary and organise their production so that they spend a week producing a batch of scouting diaries, then a week producing gardening diaries and so on. Each time more than are wanted are produced so that they have some **stock**.

12.8 Some short-term production decisions

Those involved with the production process at Lovells will be making many day-to-day decisions to make sure that the production line runs smoothly. The most important will include:

a **Decisions about the level of stock** Stock includes raw materials and components, work in progress, and finished goods. For Lovells, as for any business, there are costs and benefits from holding stock. If stock falls too low, then production might be halted, and sales lost. But if stock is too high, then resources which could be used in other parts of the business are being tied up and there is an opportunity lost to the firm. Lovells faces the problem of producing diaries over the whole year, but selling them only in the last quarter of the year. Stock therefore has to be built up over a long period, based on an estimate of the likely level of sales. This would make the job of stock control a difficult one.

b **Decisions about the number of workers needed** This will depend on estimated sales and therefore the output of the business. In a larger firm workers may be shifted from one production line to another to meet a sudden rush, but in a smaller business like Lovells part-time workers would probably be employed. Lovells would want to keep its full-time workforce employed for the whole year, rather than having lay-offs during any slack period, and this might mean taking in work for another company, or producing another product on the same machinery when sales of diaries are low.

c **Decisions about quality** Again there are costs and benefits involved with quality control. A perfect product would never be rejected by customers, but would involve high inspection costs and high standards of work and machinery. If quality control is reduced though, more finished products will be rejected. Lovells are given an indication of the quality that their customers expect, and involve all the workforce in making sure that the quality is achieved. But they accept that a small percentage of the diaries will be returned.

d **Improving efficiency** For a business this involves two elements. First, output per person or output per hour can be improved by introducing more efficient machinery. This will depend on whether the business can raise enough finance for new machinery. Second, it can be improved by changing the way the work is done. Many businesses have used **work study** where jobs are carefully observed, to find out better ways of doing things. It is also useful to ask the workforce through regular meetings about ways of improving efficiency. This is an approach Japanese businesses have used successfully, and which has now been introduced to Britain. It has often been found that the workers who are involved in actually producing the product know much more about what improvements could be made than the managers in their offices.

12.9 Production and technological change

The BBC 'B' microcomputer which was introduced into many schools and colleges from 1981 is a more powerful computer than the one that the lunar landing module had on board when Apollo 11 landed on the Moon in 1969. In just a dozen years, technology which had only been available to a very few, is now a common object in school classrooms. This is one striking example of the rate of technological change. Businesses have had to face up to many similar changes in the time since the war.

New technology has brought changes in the way things are produced, and in the range of products and services that are produced. Before looking at the effect of these changes, *Fig 12.9* shows that in the motor industry technological change is only one of a series of problems that producers have faced. The way that car makers in this country and in Europe have reacted to these changes has been to make their methods of production more efficient and it is technological advances that have enabled them to do this. Such changes have also been happening in many British businesses. The major changes have been in:

a **information technology** where a microcomputer and word processor can store, alter, transmit and process information

b **automation** where automatic equipment, controlled by a computer, replaces the work of humans both on individual machines and on the whole production line

c improved **materials** which are often stronger or lighter than the ones they have replaced

d the introduction of **robots** to bring speed and accuracy to difficult or unpleasant tasks.

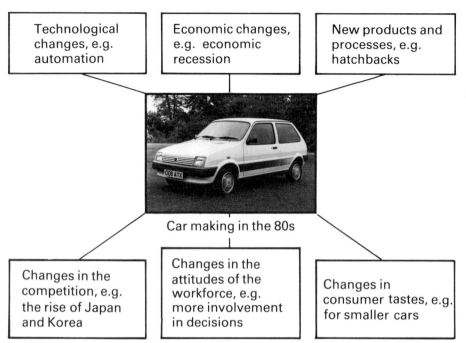

Figure 12.9 Changes in the motor industry

What are the effects of these changes? First, they should allow businesses to reduce production costs, which may lead to a lower price for the customer. Second, and linked to this, it may lead to a fall in the number of people employed as labour-saving machines are introduced. However, this is an area of some uncertainty, because new jobs might be created in the industries which provide the technology. And if a firm is able to cut costs and lower its price, then new sales might result which will allow the firm to take on extra labour.

A third change will be in the product itself. With manufactured products it should allow more 'extras' and better quality. For example, colour televisions with stereo sound, or new products altogether like the digital watch or the computer game. Information technology makes possible many services that previously could not exist, services for individuals and also more self-service. Banking provides a good illustration with the introduction of cash-points, and banking from home.

Finally, new technology should make jobs cleaner, easier, and safer for the workforce which operates the machinery. As well as providing a possible threat to the jobs of people working on the production line, advances should make the jobs that remain less physically tiring and safer. The moon shots of the 1960s and the space stations and space shuttles since have contributed to the development of technology that is safe and less likely to break down. The technology of space is again common on today's production lines.

THINGS TO DO

Short answer questions

1 Why is production important for our economy?

2 What are the three influences on a business decision about what to produce?

3 Which of these influences are most important in producing:
   a perfume?
   b nuclear energy?
   c 'throwaway' biros?
   d a space satellite?
   e trainers?
   f a feature film?

4 Which of the following businesses might be located near to their market, and which near to their raw materials?
   a refrigerator assembly
   b chemical production
   c newspaper printing
   d wholesaling
   e sugar refining
   f chocolate making
   Explain why in each case.

5 Why is 'small' sometimes 'beautiful'?

6 Why are economies of scale useful for businesses?

7 Match up the following two lists of examples of economies of scale:

	A		*B*
a	Production	*i*	Advertising agencies offer special rates for large firms
b	Marketing	*ii*	Large businesses can afford computerised offices
c	Finance	*iii*	Production lines allow greater production at lower unit costs
d	Management	*iv*	Both large and small firms can benefit from a new shipping port
e	External	*v*	The larger the business, the lower interest they pay when borrowing from a bank.

8 Explain what is meant by job, batch, and flow production.

9 Which type of production would you expect:
   a in a garage repairing cars?
   b in a factory making records?
   c in a brewery?
   d on an arable farm?
   e in an oil refinery?
   f in a solicitors?

10 Why do businesses not want their level of stocks to be
   a too low?
   b too high?

11 Why have workers become more involved in ways of improving efficiency in business?

12 Find five examples of new technology that has been employed in your school or college. Explain what the new technology has been used for.

SECTION B

Essays and structured questions

1 *a* Choose a well-known product and draw a diagram similar to the one in *Fig 12.1* showing the stages of production it passes through. You might like to illustrate each stage with a drawing or picture.
   b Explain what is happening to the product at each stage, and who would be involved in making it.

2 Read again through the information that the chapter gives about Lovells Ltd., then answer these questions:
   a What type of diaries do Lovells make?
   b What does it mean when it says that their 'sales are very seasonal'? What production problems might this bring?
   c List and explain six important factors which influenced Lovells decision to locate in Watford.
   d If Lovells were to expand what benefits in production might they be able to enjoy?
   e Suggest a new product or new market which Lovells could move into, and give reasons for your suggestion.

3 Two firms which make chess boards have the following costs of production and levels of output:

	Benson's Games Ltd.	Rowan's Games plc
Total costs	£600,000	£750,000
Total output per year	50,000	125,000

   a Calculate the cost per board for each business.
   b Which business is likely to sell the cheaper chess board?
   c Give a reason why the cost per board is different for the two businesses.
   d What factors may help the smaller business to survive in this market?

4 Which economies of scale might be possible in the following situations? Give your reasons.
  a A grocer sells three small counter-service shops and uses the money to buy a supermarket.
  b Ford takes over British Leyland in this country.
  c A building society joins forces with a large high street bank.
  d A cigarette company takes over a chain of pubs.
  e Liverpool F.C. merges with Everton F.C.

5 In a business or industry of your choice show how the introduction of new technology has affected:
  a the goods or services produced
  b the way they are produced and sold
  c the types of job in the business or industry.

SECTION C

Coursework and assignments

1 A visit to a production line

If you have the opportunity to visit a local factory, try to find out some of the following information as you are shown around:
  a what goods are produced
  b why the firm is located where it is
  c what methods of production are employed
  d how many products are finished each week
  e how many people are employed in producing the goods
  f how much the goods cost to produce
  g how the quality of the product is maintained
  h what types of work go on in the factory
  i some examples of new technology which the firm uses.

You may be able to gather some of this information by observation, but also try to talk to people who work on the production line. Write up your findings in the form of a report on the business.

2 Geesentax Limited: a production game

Geesentax Ltd. are world famous for their Paper Bricks, to be found propping up buildings from Tibet to Timbuktu. You are the management and the workers of Geesentax.

What you have to do

To start, the management must decide how to make each brick. It must then decide how many bricks to make in each production run. There will be two production runs, with a tea break in the middle. It must also decide what price to sell the bricks at, to the Paper Brick Purchasing Company.

Raw materials and machinery

These are available at the following prices:

Rulers – 20 Money Units (MUs) per period
Scissors – 50 MUs per period
Paper – 5 MUs per sheet
Sellotape – 50 MUs per roll.

Production

This is done only by the workers. It is up to the workers to negotiate their own wages. The managers must devise and keep a record of expenditure and income. All finished bricks should be delivered to the Purchasing Company at the end of each product run, and the agreed price will be paid, provided the quality is good.

Your objective is to maximise your profits!

Your product is drawn (not to scale) below. It is built to the strictest specifications.

A paper brick

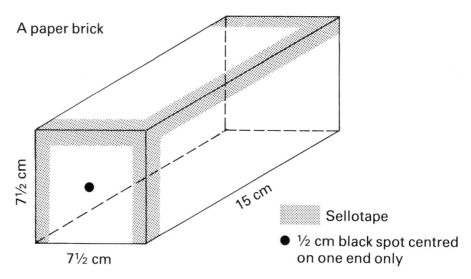

7½ cm

15 cm

7½ cm

░ Sellotape

● ½ cm black spot centred on one end only

Chapter 13

Business and community – Part one

13.1 The business and its environment

Your school is in many ways very closely linked to the local community in which it is found. It educates students who live in the local area. It employs teachers, secretaries, cleaners, etc. from the local workforce. It provides qualified and skilled school-leavers for local colleges, and for employment in local businesses and organisations. Parents and friends visit the school for plays, concerts, evening classes, and recreation. Youth clubs are often based in schools, and many are open for activities during the holidays. There are usually sporting links with other local schools, and students come together for conferences and other special events. The school is probably maintained by the Local Education Authority and the governors who control the school are representatives of local groups. Schools play an important role in their local community, and reflect the activities of that community.

In a similar way a business has its own community or **environment**. This will contain the people and the organisations who can change the business, or who can be changed by the business. *Figure 13.1a* shows some of the people and organisations which can form part of that environment.

Figure 13.1a The business environment of an oil company

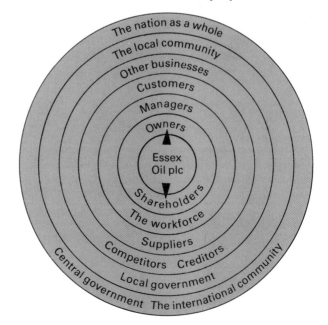

Decisions taken by this imaginary oil company, Essex Oil plc, will affect all of the groups in its environment, just as decisions taken by these groups will affect the operation of the business itself. In *Figs 13.1b* and *13.1c* there are examples of decisions which help to illustrate these relationships.

a a decision to raise the dividends paid on each share will increase the income of the shareholders

b a cut in the price of petrol will encourage customers to switch from buying a rival's petrol to buying Essex petrol

c new self-service petrol pumps will cut the number of workers in service stations by half

d by deciding to open a service station next to a new out-of-town shopping precinct shoppers will be encouraged to change their shopping habits

e by developing North Sea oil reserves. Essex will help the country buy less oil from abroad.

Figure 13.1b Decisions taken by Essex Oil

a an offer for Essex Oil shares is made to shareholders by an American oil company

b the management provoke a strike by the tanker drivers when they threaten redundancies

c a new competition, run by a rival company, loses Essex some of their market share

d planning permission for a new storage depot is turned down by the local council

e in the Budget, the tax on petrol is raised by 10p per gallon

f a new ruling by the EEC makes it necessary for Essex to develop lead-free petrol.

Figure 13.1c Decisions taken by outside groups which affect Essex Oil

There are six main groups which have an interest in what a business does:

a the shareholders who provide the finance to set up and run the company

b the lenders and creditors who provide finance for the company

c the employees who work for the company

d the customers who buy the company's product

e the local community where the workforce comes from

f the country which relies on the output of the company.

But it is quite possible that the interests of these six groups are not the same. Think about the results of a decision to buy a new labour-saving machine which a business might make. The machine could help to increase outputs and profits and this would please shareholders and customers. But the workforce would be cut, which would be against the interest of the employees and the local community. The country would benefit from the firm's increased output, but may have to find jobs, or unemployment pay for the out-of-work employees.

Businesses therefore find it difficult to please all groups at once, and they have to compromise. To make sure that their decisions do not harm the interest of one group too much the government has had to act to aid and control the business sector.

13.2 Why should the government intervene?

Just like businesses, the government, at both the national and local level, have objectives. There is a broad agreement about what these objectives should be:

Social objectives include:
a freedom of opportunity and choice
b freedom from pollution
c the protection of an individual's rights
d democratic decision-making and participation.

Economic objectives include:
a full employment
b low inflation
c an improving standard of living
d a stable balance of payments
e closing the gap of income between the rich and the poor.

It is not certain that all these objectives can be achieved at once, for the policies which might be used to obtain one objective could conflict with the policies for another objective. Should children be free to stay away from school when it might reduce their opportunities in later life? Should people be able to drink and drive when they might injure another person? Has everyone a right to know information about national defence or nuclear weapons? And on the economic side, policies which lead to low inflation might also cause unemployment; economic growth in Britain is often accompanied by a rise in imports of consumer goods from Europe and Japan which will harm the balance of payments.

It is to make sure that these wider, national objectives are achieved that the government intervenes in business activity. In the private sector of the economy the state has no automatic power over a business, but it can gain some control by passing laws in parliament. By legal, administrative, and financial controls it can make sure that businesses take social responsibilites seriously.

13.3 Social costs and social benefits

The first aim of many students when they reach their seventeenth birthday is to learn to drive. There are many costs and benefits involved in this decision. The **private cost** to the student will be the cost of a series of driving lessons, plus the test fee (and the fees for any retest!) and the time at school or college lost when lessons are taking place. The **private benefits** to the student are more difficult to estimate, but will include learning how to drive, being able to save on public transport fares, and better mobility in his or her working and social life.

But there will also be wider social costs and social benefits as a result of this decision. **Social costs** will include the traffic congestion that occurs when a learner driver is on the road, the loss to public transport of passengers, and the increased use of the road network. **Social benefits** however will also occur: benefits to the student's family from having another car driver; the employment of a driving instructor and examiners; helping to create a more mobile workforce. Every economic action in which someone engages will have some benefits and some costs, but not all these will be directly felt by that person. In the same way, not all the costs of production will be paid by a business, and not all the benefits from that production will be enjoyed by the consumers. *Figure 13.3* considers both the private costs and benefits, and the social costs and benefits involved in a decision that is very common in today's business world – the purchase of a business computer system.

Figure 13.3 Should Egham's Brewery buy a business computer?

This is the question given to a GCSE business studies class by the manager of a local brewery. The brewery wants to use the business computer for keeping accounts, to help with payment of wages, to keep checks on stock, and to record sales. The manager wanted to know all the costs and benefits that she should consider. Working together, the class came up with the following list:

SOME COSTS AND BENEFITS OF INSTALLING A BUSINESS COMPUTER

Private Costs	*Private Benefits*
The cost of the hardware	Reduction in clerical staff
The cost of the software	Data easily available
Training staff	Time and wages saved as book-keeping speeds up
Installation programming costs	Managers able to make better-informed decisions
Tranferring data to the computer	Cost savings could be passed on as cheaper beer for customers
Running costs	Increased sales
Depreciation and replacement costs.	

Social Costs	*Social Benefits*
Loss of employment opportunities	Increased motivation for workforce
Import of business computer hardware	Better trained workforce
Payment of redundancy pay and unemployment benefit	More efficient industry
Health problems due to video display screen	Employment for programmers, computer engineers, etc.
Cheaper beer might cause more drunkenness	More variety in office jobs

The manager of that brewery will be most interested in the private costs and benefits of this decision, but she will have to take account of the human results of the decision, especialy the job losses and the health aspects of using computers all day. The government may influence the decision in a number of ways. It may decide to tax imported computers and this will make the decision less attractive. On the other hand it may offer training courses for clerical staff to help the workforce to use business computers, which would make the decision more attractive. Overall the manager would need to take the social responsibilities of the business into account when she was making such a decision.

13.4 Cost-benefit analysis

What the business studies class was doing in *Fig 13.3* was a simple **cost-benefit analysis** of that project. To finish the analysis, the group would need to put some figures to the costs and benefits. This would present a number of problems. While the private costs are probably quite easy to find, the private benefits can only be **estimates** as they will happen in the future. With social costs and benefits it is very difficult to give any figures. How do you calculate the cost of lost jobs, or the benefit of better training? It is probably more important for the business to be aware of these costs and benefits, rather than having to calculate their actual effects on a decision.

The government does try to estimate social costs and benefits as well as private ones when it is taking a major decision about public spending. Projects such as the third London airport, the Newcastle Metro, and the Channel Tunnel have been studied using cost-benefit analysis, although the final decisions with such projects might be political rather than economic.

13.5 Aiding and controlling the producer

Figure 13.5 Government expenditure on aiding industry 1980–1985

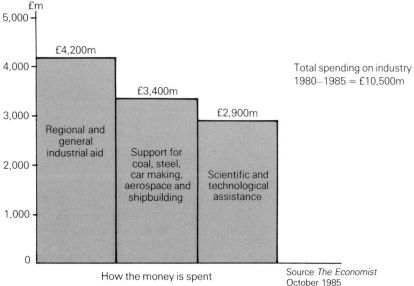

How the money is spent

Source *The Economist*
October 1985

As we have seen there are many groups which are affected by decisions which business makes. The largest private sector business in Britain, BP, employed 138,000 people and had sales of £38 billion in 1984, while the largest public sector business in 1984, British Gas, employed more than 93,000 workers and had sales of £7 billion. Such businesses are not only a very important part of the whole economy, but also their activities will affect communities, employees, and many other similar businesses. The government passes laws to make sure that these groups are protected against any unfair or criminal activity that a business might carry out. It also can influence the producer by giving financial assistance and through **taxation**. How much the government decides to aid producers will depend on how it chooses to spend the money it raises through taxation, and this will be a political decision. *Figure 13.5* shows that the amounts spent are considerable.

13.6 Helping businesses to start up

Small businesses are the acorns out of which large oaks (large producers) grow. When economic activity is declining many big firms reduce the number of their workers, and some of these may decide to use their redundancy pay to set up a small business. But a new company will find it very hard to raise enough **capital** to both set up and expand. The small businesses sector is a very important part of the UK economy. It provides a quarter of all jobs and a fifth of the country's output. You have probably done a survey of your local community and seen how many small businesses there are. Recent governments have decided that they need to help small businesses, especially when the economy is facing a **recession**, a fall in economic activity. Encouragement has come in a number of ways:

a They have been encouraging **mini enterprise** schemes in schools and colleges to give students the chance of setting up a mini-company and producing and selling a good or service to friends and parents. For an example see *Fig 13.6*.

> Six- and seven-year-olds borrowed capital from their headteacher at an infants school in Stoke on Trent to help them design mugs for an enterprise project. A Potteries factory made the mugs for them. The children sold them on a market stall and made a £275 profit to put in the bank for the next year. The managing director, aged 7, was able to declare a 100 per cent dividend from the mug-making business.

Figure 13.6 Cups of cheer!

b They have tried to cut down on the number of rules and regulations which a small business has to follow to reduce the red tape.
c The Department of Trade and Industry has set up advice centres for small firms in cities and towns, and there is also help for small businesses in rural areas.
d The Business Expansion Scheme makes it attractive for private individuals and companies to provide finance for a new small business to help it expand.
e Banks do not like to lend to new businesses because many fail in the first year. The government is now willing to provide a **guarantee** for a bank loan

to a small business which will take some of the risk out of that loan for the bank.

f People who have been unemployed for more than six months can apply for an **enterprise allowance** if they want to set up their own business.

There has been an increase in business start-ups since 1980, especially in the retailing and service areas, but while some 800,000 new businesses were registered between 1980 and 1984, some 500,000 businesses were lost due to failure and 170,000 due to merger. Starting a new business is still a risky venture.

13.7 Helping businesses to locate

We looked at how a business might choose its location in the last chapter, but since the war the government has tried to influence this decision. Although Britain is a fairly small country not all of it has been able to benefit from economic expansion. Some areas became well-known for one particular industry – shipbuilding in the north east, mining in South Wales, cotton in Lancashire, the woollen industry in Yorkshire, engineering in the West Midlands etc. But as these industries have declined, the new expanding ones have grown up in other areas, close to the large market of London and the south east. In the older industrial areas it has become more difficult for the workforce to find employment, but it is also quite difficult for the workforce to move to the new expanding areas. Problems of finding housing, of moving children from schools and of a lack of information about vacancies are just a few of the reasons.

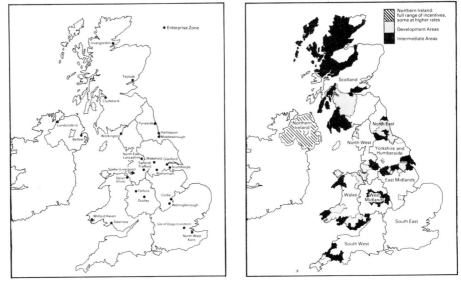

Figure 13.7a

We saw that full employment has been a major objective of governments, and so to help reduce the problem of **regional unemployment**, they have generally used a policy of trying to move the work to the workers. They have tried to persuade businesses to set up in certain areas by offering financial assistance as a 'carrot' to attract firms. The assisted areas in 1985 are shown on the map in *Fig 13.7a*. Northern Ireland is the area with the highest rate of regional unemployment and receives most assistance. Regions of Great Britain with very high unemployment like Merseyside, Strathclyde, and Newcastle are called **Development areas**. Regions with somewhat fewer problems such as the West Midlands, Plymouth, and the Lake District are known as **Intermediate areas**.

What benefits are offered to businesses to attract them to these areas? Some are shown in *Fig 13.7b*.

> *a* **Regional Development Grants** Both manufacturing and service businesses can get a grant from the government towards buying new buildings, plant, and machinery if they are located in a Development area. But for medium and large businesses there is a limit of £10,000 for each job created, so that work is attracted to the area, rather than just large automated factories, which employ few people.
>
> *b* **Job grants** A business can get £3,000 for each job created in a development area.
>
> *c* **Selective assistance** The government will give financial help to job-creating or job-preserving projects in Development and Intermediate areas.

Figure 13.7b Help for businesses in Assisted Areas

The type of business which will find these offers most attractive are ones which do not have to locate close to a particular market or raw material – the 'footloose' businesses – and ones which will be using quite an amount of labour in providing its product or service. Each firm will have to weigh up the benefits the government offers against the costs of, perhaps, being a long way from its market. Another carrot which the government can offer is an improved **infrastructure** in an assisted area; better roads, rail links, new schools and housing, shopping centres, business parks, and trading estates.

13.8 Enterprise zones

On the map in *Fig 13.7a* you will notice that there are 25 **enterprise zones** marked. These were set up by the government between 1981 and 1984 to bring new life back into very depressed areas. Within small zones businesses are encouraged to create jobs by not having to pay rates to the local council, by receiving a 100 per cent grant towards new buildings, and by being given quick planning permission and fewer statistics to collect for the government. By the end of 1984 businesses were employing some 48,000 people in the zones, but in many cases the firm had merely moved into the zone from the same county, which suggests the jobs were being shifted rather than created.

13.9 Helping with development

Research and development (R & D) is a costly activity for many businesses because the results might not bring in revenue for several years. For example, it might take 5–10 years to develop a new motor car model, and 10–15 years for a new airliner. Yet the benefits in terms of future sales, profits and employment for the company, and the social benefits of future employment for those in related businesses are clear. And so the government meets nearly half the total cost of R & D in Britain. It does this through the British Technology Group, through its own research, through university research, and by supporting research in industry. Much of government spending helps big business, especially those involved in defence, aerospace and the nuclear industry. There is also increased help for high-technology electronics and telecommunication industries.

With small and medium-sized businesses, the government has provided advice and support for innovation, especially in the area of **information technology**. Just as schools and colleges have received help to buy micro-computers, hardware, and software from the government, so businesses have received support to use and develop microelectronics in their production and administration.

Figure 13.9 Micros in business

13.10 Controlling monopolies and mergers

When you play the board game Monopoly, the winner is the one who gets to own all the properties in London. He or she would be able to charge whatever rent they liked to those living and working in London, and would be able to build hotels wherever they wished. On the other hand the owner might shut down hotels to raise rents even higher. In just such a case the government would probably intervene to protect the interests of consumers and workers. Indeed, where such monopolies did exist in Britain, the government stepped in to own them; e.g. the Post Office, gas supply, electricity supply, and television and radio transmission.

Back with the game, individual players can still have a lot of power over the market even if they do not win all of it. Indeed, ownership of about a quarter of the board would probably be enough. In the manufacturing industry of Britain this is the normal position. In one out of six markets five firms control most of that market. In the 1980s there has been an increasing rate of **merger** by companies where one firm takes over ownership of another, or where the two agree to join forces. In these cases the government has the power to investigate the merger through the **Monopolies and Mergers Commission** (MMC) if:

a the value of assets involved is more than £5 million.

b the merger creates or increases a monopoly share of 25 per cent or more of a market in part of the UK.

Figure 13.10 shows examples of the types of merger that can occur:

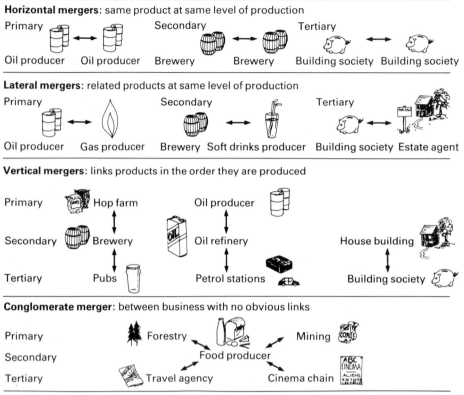

Horizontal mergers: same product at same level of production

Primary   Secondary   Tertiary

Oil producer   Oil producer   Brewery   Brewery   Building society   Building society

Lateral mergers: related products at same level of production

Primary   Secondary   Tertiary

Oil producer   Gas producer   Brewery   Soft drinks producer   Building society   Estate agent

Vertical mergers: links products in the order they are produced

Primary   Hop farm   Oil producer

Secondary   Brewery   Oil refinery   House building

Tertiary   Pubs   Petrol stations   Building society

Conglomerate merger: between business with no obvious links

Primary   Forestry   Mining

Secondary   Food producer

Tertiary   Travel agency   Cinema chain

Figure 13.10 Possible mergers

There are many possible reasons why two businesses would want to merge. It is often a quick way for a business to grow bigger. This may bring advantages in production, in marketing, in management, and in terms of profits. An owner who wants to retire may sell the business to ensure that it continues. Companies also join together to be able to compete better in overseas markets against international companies. Recently businesses have even been merging to avoid being taken over by another company!

Mergers can also bring disadvantages, especially for the people who rely on the businesses:

a for the shareholders – the price offered for their shares might not be a reasonable one, and the new company might not be as successful as the old ones.

b for the managers – it takes time and effort to combine two teams, and there might be a reduction in the number of staff needed.

c for the workers – some may lose their jobs as more labour-saving machinery is employed or as factories are closed. Some may be demoted, and some may have to move to work in another area.

d for the customers – there may be a reduction in choice of products and higher prices as the competition is reduced.

The government is often in a difficult position. It may favour mergers to help make UK production more efficient and to help firms compete abroad. But it may oppose mergers because consumers or workers may suffer. The Monopolies and Mergers Commission will look at each case it is given and weigh up the costs and benefits.

13.11 Controlling business agreements

There are some agreements between two or more businesses which the government has decided to control. These are ones where businesses co-operate to reduce output, or to divide the market, or to keep up prices. *Figure 13.11* gives some examples of these agreements. They are known as **restrictive practices** and the law now says that all such practices should be registered and agreed by the **restrictive practices court**. The court will find these agreements illegal, unless there are good reasons why the benefits to the public are greater than the costs.

> *a* Petrol companies meet in secret and decide to keep the price of petrol the same even though the price of oil has fallen by 10 per cent.
> *b* A chocolate company refuses to supply a large supermarket with its products because the supermarket is selling the chocolate at 5p off the recommended retail price.
> *c* A group of airlines agree to lower the price for six months in order to drive another airline which has been offering cheap flights across the Atlantic out of business.
> *d* Two breweries in the Midlands swap pubs so that one owns all the pubs in Leicester and the other all the pubs in Nottingham.
> *e* Book publishers are able to tell bookshops what price to charge for paperbacks to let small bookshops compete with large ones.

Figure 13.11 Some restrictive business activities

13.12 How economic policies affect business

There are not only the direct industrial policies of the government which affect business decisions. There are also the general economic policies which the government uses to reach some of the objectives we mentioned earlier. *Figure 13.12* provides a picture of this. The government has direct control over the amount of money it spends, **public spending**, and the amount of tax that wage earners, consumers, businesses, and savers pay. Changing its level of spending, or changing the rate of taxation is known as **fiscal policy** and by using these methods the government hopes to change the amount of money spent by the public on **consumption**, and the amount spent by firms on **investment**.

Consumption and investment are also influenced by the amount of money available for spending, known as the **money supply**, and the cost of borrowing money from banks or other financial institutions, known as the **rate of interest**. The government, through the Bank of England, can try to control the size of the money supply, and can influence the rate of interest. These two activities make up **monetary policy**. The government is also in charge of the country's **balance of**

payments, the difference between the amount businesses and consumers spend on goods and services made abroad (**imports**) and the amount that overseas businesses and consumers spend on UK goods and services (**exports**). To change the value of imports and exports the government has two possible 'weapons': either influencing the value of the pound against other currencies (especially the dollar), the **exchange rate**; or putting a tax or **tariff** on goods and services which are purchased from abroad. These make up the **external economic policies** of a government.

A fourth policy weapon exists which previous governments have used to try to reduce wage increases and so keep down the costs of production for a business. This is known as an **incomes policy** and it has also been combined with controls in the **prices** charged by businesses. The Conservative government from 1979 did not use these policies to control the private sector, but attempted wage and price control in the public sector.

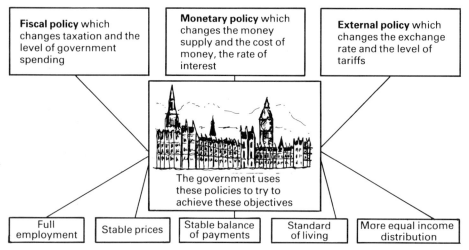

Figure 13.12

13.13 How fiscal policies affect business

This will depend on what the government is aiming for with its fiscal policy. It will be trying either to help the economy to expand or to reduce the expansion. Some examples will help to show how the fiscal decisions the government takes will affect business activity:

a   A decision to expand in order to reduce unemployment and increase economic growth.
    The decisions taken:
        increased government spending in building schools and hosptials
        a cut in **income tax** (a tax on wages and salaries) of 1 per cent
        a cut in **corporation tax** (a tax on business profits) of 5 per cent.
    The effects of these decisions on business:
        a boost to the construction industry and an increase in employment in that industry

as consumers pay less tax, they will have more to spend on buying goods and services

businesses will be able to keep more of their profits, and use them to buy new machinery and other equipment.

b A decision to contract in order to reduce inflation and the level of imports.
The decisions taken:

reduced government spending on defence and regional policy

an increase in **value added tax** (a tax paid when goods and services are bought) of 2½ per cent

a cut in the tax relief business can claim for new investment.

The effects of those decisions on business:

fewer orders for businesses that supply the defence industry, and fewer jobs

businesses in declining areas receive less assistance

consumers buy fewer goods and services because of the higher VAT

businesses postpone plans for buying new machinery.

13.14 How monetary policies affect business

Governments do not usually try to control the notes and coins which are in circulation, but credit at the·bank is the most important type of money and the government can restrict the amount of money that banks lend to customers. It can also increase or decrease the cost of borrowing money, the rate of interest. Again, some examples can show how monetary policy affects business activity:

a A decision to expand the money supply and lower interest rates to encourage economic activity.
Effect of these decisions on business:

businesses find it easier to borrow money to finance expansion and increased capital spending

businesses find it cheaper to borrow money which makes some projects worthwhile

consumers are able and willing to borrow money to buy, for example, consumer durables.

b A decision to restrict the money supply and raise interest rates to reduce inflation.
Effect of these decisions on business:

businesses find it difficult to borrow money for expansion

the cost of borrowing money increases so that some business projects are postponed

consumers prefer to save money than borrow it to buy, for example, consumer durables.

13.15 External policies

Here the effect of policies is more complicated. If the government decides to let the exchange rate of the pound against other currencies go up in value (e.g. from £1 = $1.50 to £1 = $2.00) then British exports become more expensive, while British imports become cheaper. If the government decides to let the exchange rate of the pound fall in value (e.g. from £1 = $1.50 to £1 = $1.25) then British exports become cheaper, while British imports become more expensive. *Figure 13.15* shows a simple illustration.

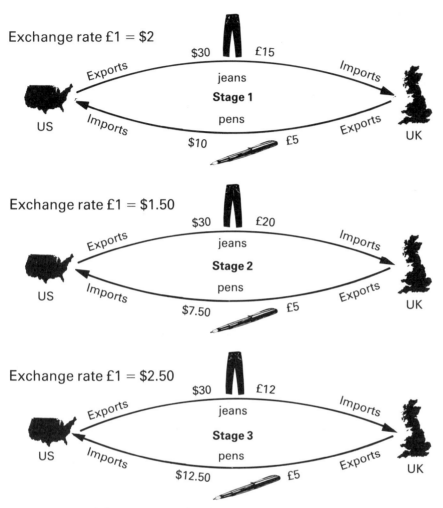

Figure 13.15 Trade between UK and USA

From *Fig 13.15* it can be seen that a falling exchange rate is likely to be good for export businesses and bad for import businesses. The higher price of imports will also help companies that make goods in the UK which compete against imports.

A rising exchange rate is likely to be bad for export businesses and good for importers. The lower price of imports will also be a problem for UK businesses which compete against imports.

The Government may also restrict the level of imports by putting a tax or tariff on imported goods, or by limiting the number of imports which can be brought in. This has been done in Britain to reduce the import of Japanese cars, and help the domestic car producers to increase their market share. Since joining the European Economic Community however Britain cannot use tariffs against goods coming from the other 11 countries who are members, while British business has free entry into their markets.

THINGS TO DO

Short answer questions

1 Select a business of your choice.
   a List five decisions it might take and explain how they would affect any of the groups mentioned in *Fig 13.1a*.
   b List five decisions that might be taken by any of these groups and explain how they would affect the business.

2 What do you think are the social and economic objectives of the present government?

3 A building firm decides to develop a piece of farmland on the edge of the town where you live. Which of the following would be social costs, private costs, social benefits, or private benefits?
   a the cost of buying the land from the farmer
   b new houses for people without homes
   c the revenue from the sale of the houses
   d the loss of farmland to the community.

4 Give two examples of projects which could use cost-benefit analysis.

5 Explain what *Fig 13.5* shows about how the aid that government gives to industry is divided up.

6 Why do new businesses find it hard to raise capital to set up and expand?

7 What help has the government provided for small businesses?

8 In their location policy the government has usually tried to move the work to the workers. Why?

9 Match the following examples of regional policy to the definitions:

a	Enterprise zones	*i*	Regions of high unemployment that receive assistance from the government
b	Job grants	*ii*	Money given to firms for job-creating projects

c	Development areas	*iii*	Small areas where businesses are encouraged to create jobs
d	Regional development grants	*iv*	Money given to firms for each job created
e	Selective assistance	*v*	Money firms get towards buying new buildings or machinery in depressed areas.

10 From the map in *Fig 13.7a* find the nearest enterprise zone to your school or college. Why does this area need special help?

11 Which type of merger is shown by the following examples which have taken place in recent years?
   a S & W Beresford (a sugar and commodity merchant) – British Sugar Company
   b Longman (publishers) – Penguin (publishers)
   c Habitat – Mothercare
   d Trafalgar House (shipping) – *Daily Express*
   e Cadbury – Schweppes
   f BPCC (printing) – *Daily Mirror*.

12 When can the government refer a merger to the Monopolies and Mergers Commission?

13 What are the four main policies that the government can use to control the economy?

14 Which of the policies in 13.12
   a involve changes in the exchange rate?
   b involve changes in government expenditure?
   c would try to control wages?
   d would try to control the amount of money in the economy?

SECTION B **Essays and structured questions**

1 *Figure 13.3* shows information about a decision which Egham's Brewery is thinking of taking. Using that information, write a report to the manager of the brewery in which you explain:
   a the private costs and benefits of the decision
   b the social costs and benefits of the decision.
   Finally, make a recommendation as to whether the brewery should buy a business computer.

2 Case Study – Sportscare

Read the case study on Sportscare and answer the questions.

Margaret McNerney worked in the marketing department of Smith & Nephew, which makes medical products like Elastoplast. She was a keen netball player and also a football fan. She came up with the idea that a company like Smith & Nephew could sell a medical bag which was specially designed for sports clubs, packed with bandages, tape, and freeze and antiseptic sprays to treat injured players. But the company ruled out producing such a bag, because they were not sure that the club would fill it with their own branded products.

So Margaret decided to go it alone. A former colleague agreed to help fund the setting up of 'Sportscare' and Margaret was able to find suppliers who would provide brand-name products (including her own former employer), and a small manufacturer to make the bag to her design. She also carried out some market research, and found several sports clubs, including Arsenal, interested. But then only weeks before beginning business, her partner pulled out. Margaret was fed up. She had a well-researched idea but couldn't find enough finance. She felt a bank would not help because she didn't have anything to put into the business. Would Sportscare fail before it got off the ground?

(Adapted from *The Guardian*, 4.10.85)

a Elastoplast is well-known as a 'brand name'. What are the advantages to a company of having a well-known brand?

b Why were Smith & Nephew unwilling to produce a sports medical bag?

c Margaret felt that a bank would not lend her money. Why do you think this is so?

d Explain a government scheme which might help Margaret to raise the money to set up Sportscare.

e What are the advantages and disadvantages for Margaret of setting up her own business rather than working for someone else?

3 *a* Why does the government encourage businesses to locate in the assisted areas?

b Explain the help that the government will give in those areas to help businesses:

   i employ more people

   ii buy new machinery

   iii keep open a factory that would otherwise close.

c What extra help do businesses in enterprise zones get?

4 Case study – Crisps and Peanuts

In 1986 the Monopolies and Mergers Commission began to investigate a proposed £1.26 billion merger between United Biscuits and the Imperial group. United Biscuits make many well-known brands of biscuits, while Imperial owns John Player cigarettes and Courage beer. However, the Commission is most concerned about their market share of the snacks market.

Present share of the snacks market

	United Biscuits	Imperial
Peanuts	50%	2%
Crisps	23%	23%
Savoury snacks	3%	17%

The only other major competitor in the snacks market is Nabisco with about 45 per cent of the total market. Together United Biscuits and Imperial would also have about 45 per cent of this market, which is worth £600 million in sales each year.

Now answer these questions:

a Is the government allowed to investigate this merger?

b What is meant by market share?

c If the new UB-Imperial company has 45 per cent of a £600 million market, what is the value of its sales in this market?

d What benefits might such a merger bring to the two companies?

e What disadvantages for the consumer of snacks might the merger bring?

f Do you think the merger should be allowed? Argue your case.

5 *Figure 13.11* gives some examples of restrictive practices in business. For each example say who would gain and who would lose from the agreement. Which ones do you think the Restrictive Practices Court would allow?

6 The government cuts its spending on defence, and raises income tax by one per cent. Explain the possible effects of these decisions on:

a a business that constructs aircraft wings for the RAF

b a business that produces washing machines and fridges

c a large department store.

7 The government raises the basic rate of interest by 1 per cent to 13 per cent. Explain the possible effect of this decision on:

a a building society which lends money for mortgages

b a large engineering business

c a chain store which sells hi-fis and televisions.

8 How would a fall in the value of the pound against other EEC currencies affect:

a A UK business which imports motorcycles from Germany?

b a car maker in Britain who sells 50 per cent of its output to EEC countries?

c a British tour operator that sells package holidays in Spain?

SECTION C

Coursework and assignments

1 A large oil company wishes to drill for oil on the Isle of Wight. It has carried out some surveys and is convinced that there are profitable oil deposits.

a Divide the class into groups. Each group is to represent one of the sectors which would be interested in this decision: the management, the employees; the customers; the shareholders; the local community; the country.

b Each group should make a list of the reasons it would support or oppose this decision.

c Each group should appoint a spokesperson who will present its ideas at an inquiry in front of a set of independent judges. The inquiry should try to produce a final decision about whether drilling should go ahead.

2 Find out a decision which your school or local council or a local business is thinking of making. Carry out a simple cost-benefit analysis of that decision similar to the one in *Fig 13.3*. Make your recommendations.

3   Choose one of the following topics:
  a help with location (Assisted areas and enterprise zones)
  b help for small businesses
  c help with new technology.
By using your local or school library, or by writing to the Department of Trade and Industry, produce a file which could tell a manager what help the government provides to assist businesses in these categories.

4 Each year, usually during March or April, the Chancellor of the Exchequer presents a Budget to parliament. This is an outline of the government's taxation and spending plans for the next year.
  a When the next Budget occurs, collect from a newspaper the reports which tell you which decisions were made. Or you might be able to record reports from the TV or radio.
  b Make a note of the decisions taken which you think would directly affect a business which you have studied.
  c Outline how the decisions taken will affect that business.
  d Why do you think the government took these decisions?

Chapter 14

Business and community – Part two

14.1 Aiding the worker: training

The most important resource that any business has is the **human resource**, the workforce. Think about the skills which this resource can provide:

a communication skills: talking, writing, listening, arguing, etc.
b numeracy skills: researching, calculating, analysing information
c problem-solving skills: sorting out, finding an answer
d decision-making skills: deciding between various choices
e social skills: helping, working together, caring, co-operating, etc.

How do we learn the skills and knowledge that we need at work? For our grandparents and parents learning and training took place when they were young. After school most would have only a short period of training at work. Some would follow an **apprenticeship** to learn a skill or craft for a few years, and a few would have further education or a professional training. But once a person learnt a job and became a postal worker, a lathe operator, a train driver, a clerk, or a teacher, he or she stayed in that job for most of his or her working life. There was little further training, and little need for it because the pace of technological change was slow.

Today people expect to change jobs much more. With fast technological change many jobs have disappeared to be replaced by ones needing new skills and knowledge, while jobs which remain might well change. *Figure 14.1* gives some examples of the way jobs are effected by technological change.

a The introduction of new technology in printing has meant that the printers who used to set type by hand can now do it using computer typesetting from a computer terminal.
b Most offices will need fewer typists because word processors can be used to produce copies of standard letters, etc., and fewer messengers will be needed as electronic mail can be used.
c Fewer draughtspeople will be needed as computer-aided design can take away a lot of the routine drawing.
d Many economic and business studies ideas can be put onto a computer programme so teachers can use an electronic blackboard rather than a chalk blackboard.

Figure 14.1 Changes in work – some examples

There is now a need for people to have the chance to learn new skills and knowledge throughout their working life. To help to produce a more flexible workforce, the government has encouraged a number of projects which try to prepare people for a changing world.

14.2 The Youth Training Scheme (YTS)

For many businesses this is becoming a major way of recruiting new staff. It started as a one year scheme, and became two years in 1986, for 16-year-old school leavers, run by the Manpower Services Commission (MSC), a government agency which is now responsible for training. *Figure 14.2* shows some of the activities which a Youth Training Scheme would involve. The scheme uses large and small businesses, as well as colleges and other training establishments, and each organisation involved gets a grant from the MSC to cover the cost of training. For every two young people taken on full-time, a business would be expected to take three extra trainees. Many firms have been able to include their apprenticeship scheme in the Youth Training Scheme. The scheme is designed to give work experience and practical training to school leavers, who would otherwise be unemployed. With the move to a two-year scheme the government aimed to provide all 16- to 18-year-olds with some practical training after leaving school.

	A training contract for one year with a firm
	A trainee allowance (at the moment £27.30 per week)
A Youth Training Scheme trainee will receive	Work experience in an organisation
	Training in skills necessary for that work
	At least 13 weeks off-the-job training in social, life, and work-related skills
	At the end of the year, a certificate showing what he or she has achieved

Figure 14.2 What happens on a Youth Training Scheme

A business after the end of the year can decide whether it wishes to keep the trainee on permanently. But if it thinks the trainee is unsatisfactory, or if there are no vacancies, then it does not have to take on the school-leaver.

14.3 Technical and vocational education in schools

Over the last ten years there has been a growing interest from a number of groups in encouraging more awareness among school students of how business and the economy works, and in the teaching of the skills which will be needed in a changing world. Politicians, managers, teachers, and trade unionists have all been in surprising agreement that there needs to be changes in what you learn at school. You are probably reading this book because you are studying for a GCSE in business studies, and that course is one result of this interest. At 16 you will have to decide whether to stay on at school, or in further education, and which courses to follow. You may decide to study for a CPVE (a Certificate of Pre-Vocational Education) which will give you general experience of the skills you will need in the world of work. You may be able to do an A-level in business studies, or craft, design and technology, or engineering. Or you may do a BTEC course (Business and Technical Education Council) at your local college or a similar **vocational** course, one that will lead to a trade or occupation.

The government has encouraged these courses, and has also introduced its own **Technical and Vocational Education Initiative** (TVEI), where a small number of schools have received money from the MSC to increase the number and quality of its technical and vocational courses. These would include computer studies, business studies, and craft, design and technology studies. In the late 1980s the government hopes to be able to develop these subjects in as many schools and colleges as possible. It has also provided money for schools to buy microcomputer hardware and software, so that all students will be aware of what micros can do, and to encourage teachers to use them in their subject teaching.

14.4 Training adults

This has largely been the responsibility of the Industrial Training Boards (ITBs), but the Manpower Services Commission has some seventy Skillcentres throughout the country where adults can train, or retrain, in a wide number of skills from carpentry to computer studies. The government is also funding Open Tech, which through polytechnics and technical colleges helps to run courses for people that 'other courses don't reach', e.g. disabled people, people who have to study from home, and courses in skills for particular trades. The Community Programme, also run by the MSC, was set up to give adults who have been unemployed for over 6 months a chance to do some paid temporary work on a project which will be of use to the community, and if possible give them better skills and greater work experience to help them gain a full-time job. *Figure 14.4* gives two examples of projects which the Community Programme has been involved with.

Figure 14.4 Community Programme projects

a **Improving a country park** Fourteen long-term unemployed people have cleared overgrown paths, created new walls, and built bridges to help the public use a country park on the edge of Dartmoor in Devon. Twenty more have been recruited to restore woodland and turn an old gatehouse into a visitors' centre. The project was organised by Devon County Council, and the MSC gave £85,000 towards it.

b **Fashion for the disabled** A workshop in Yorkshire, called Fashion Services for the Disabled, produces fashionable clothing for disabled people of all ages to meet their individual needs. Ten young people are employed in the workshop which is financed by the MSC and organised by the textile department of the local college. Some of the young people are themselves disabled and they are all involved in both design and production.

Both the Community Programme and the Youth Training Scheme were started because of the growing numbers of unemployed people, especially young people, but both are also trying to encourage work experience and training which will help both the individual and the country as a whole.

14.5 Aiding the worker – job protection

Chapter 9 has shown how the government has introduced a number of laws in recent years which have increased the protection which workers get when they are in employment. Two areas which were considered were protecting workers in dangerous or unpleasant working conditions, and against unfair treatment because of a person's sex, marital status, race, or place of birth. It is not surprising that another area where the government has tried to help the workforce in a business has been over **redundancy** and **unfair dismissal**.

14.6 Redundancy

This is when a worker loses his or her job because it no longer exists. A business will make workers redundant for a number of reasons:

a when the business is stopping trading, when it is 'going bust'
b when the business is stopping trading at the particular factory or shop
c when the work that those particular workers were doing is no longer needed: the business is reducing its workforce.

The government has set up a **redundancy fund** which is financed from National Insurance contributions to help firms make payments to redundant workers. The level of payment will depend on the employee's age, weekly wage, and number of years of continuous employment with the business. *Figure 14.6* looks at four examples to show the different compensation possible.

Figure 14.6 Payment for redundancy

Case 1	Geoff Jones, aged 18. Weekly wage £50 as filing clerk in insurance office. Employed since leaving school at 16, two years' continuous service. Insurance office closes as firm is moving away to new location and his services are no longer needed.
Payment	Geoff will receive no redundancy payment because he is under the age of 20.
Case 2	Sarah Smith, aged 21. Weekly wage £85 as bookshop assistant. Employed for three years. Bookshop is closing because of competition from a large chain store.
Payment	Sarah will receive half a week's pay for each of the three years she has worked, a total of £127.50.
Case 3	Sally Wright, aged 35. Weekly wage £125 as salesperson for a cosmetics firm. Employed for ten years. Because of a fall in cosmetic sales, the firm is reducing its sales staff in her region.
Payment	Sally will receive one week's pay for each of the ten years she has worked for the firm, a total of £1,250. *continued*

> **Case 4**   George Dewhurst, aged 52. Weekly wage £150 as a machine tool operator in an engineering firm. Twenty years' service with the firm. The firm wants to slim its workforce and has asked for voluntary redundancies and George has volunteered.
>
> **Payment**   George will receive one week's pay for the service he put in up to the age of 40 and one-and-a-half weeks' pay for the years since then. His total payment will be £1,200 for the first eight years, and £2,700 for the next 12 years, making £3,900 in all.

In *Fig 14.6* Geoff Jones was not given any redundancy pay because he was under 20. Firms also do not have to pay redundancy money to employees with less than two years' service, or to those who work for less than 16 hours per week. This helps to explain why businesses like to employ young people at school or college who are working part-time. Employees on fixed-term contracts of more than two years may also be denied their rights to redundancy pay.

Many organisations have their own redundancy agreements which are negotiated between unions and management, and these may well provide more money than the examples given above. There is also a legal requirement that management discuss any proposed redundancies with a union representative so that alternatives to redundancy can be considered. If it is agreed that staff have to leave, it may be possible to reduce the size of the workforce through early retirement, natural wastage as people move to other areas or jobs, or voluntary redundancies.

14.7 Unfair dismissal

In Chapter 9 we looked at what was meant by a contract of employment. For both a business and an employee there will be a time when they want to end that contract. The worker may wish to take up a new job, or a promotion, elsewhere. The fixed term of the contract may be complete. The employer may want to dismiss the worker because of dishonesty, drunkenness, fighting, etc., or the employee may be too ill to continue with his or her work. For many years, provided the organisation gave the employee the right period of **notice** (time before they have to leave the job), the reason for dismissal was not important. It has only been since 1971 that the government has made businesses say why they want to sack someone. Through a series of Employment Protection Acts workers are now protected against unfair dismissal. It is wrong to think that it is now impossible for a business to sack an employee. What they have to do is show that there are good reasons for the dismissal. Fair reasons for dismissal could include:

a   the employee is not capable of doing the job
b   the employee has not the right qualifications to do the job
c   the conduct of the worker on the job deserves dismissal
d   the job no longer exists (this returns to redundancy)
e   continued employment of the person would be illegal
f   other substantial reasons (e.g. an employee marries an employee from a rival firm).

Figure 14.7 shows some illustrations of these reasons. A business must also show that it has gone about the dismissal in a fair way. There should be a clear code of discipline which the worker knows about and the business follows. The employee should be given a chance to explain his or her conduct and to make an appeal. If the sacking was because of bad conduct, was it only a first offence, and was a warning given? If the employee was not capable of doing the job, has sufficient training been given? Employers cannot so easily dismiss a worker on the spot.

Case 1	An airline pilot made two unsuccessful attempts to land an aircraft full of passengers, the second one resulting in damage to the nose wheel. The pilot was fairly dismissed for incompetence.
Case 2	A salesman employed because he said he had a driving licence was fairly dismissed when he failed to pass his driving test and was therefore not qualified for the job.
Case 3	A fight broke out in a car park between an employee who had six earlier cases of fighting against him, and one with a good behaviour record and fifteen years' service. The first employee was fairly dismissed, but the second only suspended for a week.
Case 4	A supermarket manager in a small branch refused an offer of a job as an assistant manager on the same pay at a larger branch. He was refused redundancy pay and was fairly dismissed because he had been offered a reasonable alternative job.
Case 5	A chauffeur for a company who was banned from driving was fairly dismissed because to employ him as a driver would have been breaking the law.
Case 6	Two hairdressers who planned to set up nearby a rival salon in the near future were fairly dismissed by their employer who wanted them to move to another salon outside the town until they left his employment.

Figure 14.7 Some fair dismissals

Not everyone is protected against unfair dismissal. In certain occupations like the army and the police force, the employees cannot claim, and some employees are denied their rights in their contract. You must also have been working for at least 52 weeks for the business, and after dismissal put in a complaint within three months.

14.8 How does an employee claim unfair dismissal?

Figure 14.8 shows the path an employee should take if they feel that he or she has been unfairly dismissed:

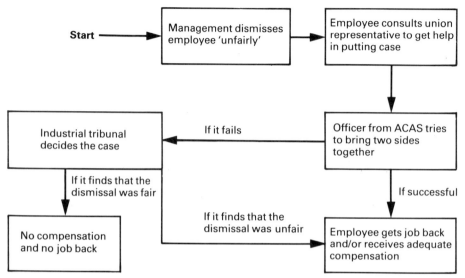

Figure 14.8 Unfair dismissal

The **Industrial Tribunals** were set up to decide on cases of unfair dismissal. Each tribunal will have three independent members; a legally qualified chairperson, a representative for management, and a representative from the union. They have an informal atmosphere, and the worker can put forward his or her own case if he or she wishes. The tribunal will decide whether or not the dismissal was unfair, and what to do if it was. The amount of compensation paid can vary, from basic levels of £1,000–£5,000 similar to redundancy, to awards of over £15,000 for serious cases.

14.9 Aiding the consumer

If we could get into Dr Who's Time Machine and travel back to 1900 what would we notice about the way goods were bought and sold? *Figure 14.9* tries to give a simple comparison between shopping for groceries in 1900 and shopping today.

	1900	*1986*
Type of shop	Probably a small business	Probably a large supermarket – a plc
Type of service	Personal service by the owner and the assistants	Self-service; supermarket run by a manager
Range of goods	Limited to groceries. Other shops would sell meat, vegetables, etc.	Groceries, fresh food, and many household goods
Where the goods come from	Mainly from local producers	Mainly national food manufacturers
Type of packaging	Some packet, tinned, and bottled. Most sold loose	Most pre-packed, frozen, tinned, or packet
Method of weighing	Done individually for each customer when buying	All groceries pre-weighed and weights and price clearly marked
Advertising	Very limited, on boxes and tins	Extensive, both on the product and in the store
Prices	Decided by shopkeeper depending on market price	Decided by food manufacturer and supermarket management
Competition	Many other small grocers	Many other supermarkets, but organised in large chains

Figure 14.9 Shopping for groceries – 1900 and 1986

There are obviously many differences between shopping then and now. But in 1900 there was some understanding that the customer needed to be careful when making a purchase. *Caveat emptor* means 'let the buyer beware', and this was the basis of the law in 1900. The customers could examine what they were buying and could check that they were getting the right weight. They could also quite easily find another shop if they were not happy. By 1900 the government had passed the first law to protect consumers, the Sale of Goods Act (1893). This laid down that goods sold must be of **merchantable quality**, that is, fit to be sold. They must be fit for their purpose, that is able to be used in the expected way, and they should match the description given of them. The Sale of Goods Act (1979) has since replaced this original Act, but the basic idea of merchantable quality remains.

The differences between then and now however mean that 'let the buyer beware' is not enough protection for the customer today. Five important changes must be noted:

a   As products have become more complicated with much greater chance of breakdown so the responsibility of the manufacturer has become as important as the retailer.
b   With more products being pre-packed and weighed, it is difficult for customers to examine the goods before they take them home.
c   With large retail chains, there is less competition in the high street so customers cannot go elsewhere as easily.
d   the growth of advertising and its power to persuade customers into buying a product.
e   People are using cash much less to buy goods, and using credit much more.

Every time a customer buys some good or service he or she enters into a **legal contract** with the shopkeeper. But all the changes listed above make it difficult for the customer to know all there is to know about the product. This is why the government, especially in the last 20 years, has introduced consumer laws to help protect the customers interests against manufacturers and retailers.

14.10 Aiding the consumer — before the sale

It has been shown in an earlier chapter that businesses use advertising to inform a customer about a product, and to persuade the customer to buy it. From TV, newspaper and magazine advertising, to posters and signs in shops, to the labels and descriptions of the goods on the boxes and packets they are sold in, a business uses every chance to tell the customers about its product, and to persuade them to buy it. But is the message which the company is passing to the customer always a true one? *Figure 14.10* gives some examples of where the advertising might be misleading.

Figure 14.10 Some misleading messages

a   'Free single with every LP bought' might appear in a music paper that you are reading, but underneath it says 'while stocks last'. There is no way for the customer to know how large the stocks are, nor who the single is by.
b   'Many reductions for children' could be a major selling point on a TV advertisement for package holidays. But these reductions might only be given on holidays at the start and end of the season when children will be back at school.
c   'Refreshing Orange Drink' is written on the label of a tin in the soft drinks part of a supermarket. But are there real oranges in the drink, concentrated oranges, orange squash, orange flavouring or orange colouring?

continued

> *d* 'Kills 99 per cent of all known germs' was a well-known claim for a lavatory cleaner, but how could a customer ever prove that this is true? This is an example of advertising 'puff'; a statement which should not be taken seriously but is used as a gimmick.
>
> *e* A bicycle is advertised by a shop '£200 reduced to £150' plus VAT and 'accessories'. It is not clear how much more the VAT and accessories will come to, nor when the bicycle was sold at £200.

The Trade Descriptions Acts of 1968 and 1972 made manufacturers, retailers, and advertising agencies responsible for the truth in the way they describe goods and services in advertisements and labels. These are the main points which the government introduced to protect the customer, and which businesses must follow:

a Any description of an item sold in the shops, whether in writing or verbally, must be true.

b The same is true for a service, like a hotel meal or the service provided by an electrician, although here the false statement must be proved to have been made deliberately.

c When two prices are shown in a shop, with the higher price crossed out, then the goods must have been on sale at the higher price in the shop for at least 28 consecutive days in the last six months.

There are other controls over advertising as well as those in the Trade Descriptions Acts. The Independent Broadcasting Authority controls the advertising shown on ITV and Channel 4, and that played on independent radio, while the advertising industry itself has its own Code of Advertising Standards and Practice. This is a voluntary code, with the Advertising Standards Authority considering complaints made by customers about advertisements which are untruthful, dishonest, or offensive. If a company's advertisement is found to be guilty of not being legal, decent, honest and truthful then it will find it difficult to find newspapers or magazines to accept the advertisement, and will probably face a lot of poor publicity.

14.11 Weights and measures

With many of the products that we buy pre-packed and weighed it is important for the government to make sure that the customers do not receive less weight than they think they are buying. Under the Weights and Measures Act of 1963 it is an offence for a business to give short weight or measure of any product on sale. Some foods, for example milk and sugar, must be sold in certain fixed weights and measures and others, like potatoes and other vegetables, must be sold by weight or volume. The Act also states the measures for selling beer and spirits in standard quantities. It is not so clear about wine, and this problem is shown in *Fig 14.11*.

Businesses also have to make it clear what is being weighed when a product is sold as a 1kg packet. Gross weight would be all the contents plus the packaging, but net weight must also appear so that customers know just how much of the product they are getting.

Q: Which glass contains the most wine? A: the third from the right. It holds nearly twice as much as the tall one in the middle. But very few places tell you how much wine you're getting.

As you can see it is not easy to know what is a glass of wine. The Weights and Measures Act listed 11 possible glass sizes, but in a survey in *Which?* magazine in 1986 fewer than six bars and restaurants told customers how much wine they were getting when they ordered 'a glass of wine'. Standard quantities for wine do not exist in the same way that a customer is served a pint of beer or a measure of spirits.

Figure 14.11 The problem with wine

14.12 Buying goods that are safe

The government has the power to stop the sale of goods that may be unsafe. Among the products that it has especially dealt with are children's toys, nightwear, electric blankets, pencils, oil heaters, and fire guards. There are also **British standards** which cover a wide range of safety hazards which manufacturers take into account when making a product. But these are voluntary controls and producers do not have to follow them. The government has not yet the legal controls to say that all consumer goods must be safe. Quite often products are imported from abroad where safety controls might be different, and frequently illegal or unsafe products find their way onto the market.

14.13 Aiding the consumer – the sale itself

Your best friend offers to swap her cassette player for your tennis racket. When you get the player home it jams after only ten minutes and destroys your favourite Madonna tape. What can you do? You must hope that your friend is a reasonable person because you cannot call on the laws of consumer protection to help you. For the law relating to the sale of goods to apply at least part of exchange must involve money. Swapping goods, or giving gifts does not count as a sale.

It does not have to be very much money, or even a reasonable amount for the product. A woman, angry at her husband, once sold the new family car for £5 through a newspaper (there were surprisingly few who were interested), but it was enough to be called a fair sale.

As was mentioned earlier, the Sale of Goods Act of 1893 was the first piece of consumer protection, and while a new Act was passed in 1979, a business selling a good is still largely bound by it today:

a The goods must match the description given of them
b They must be of merchantable quality; that is fit to be sold
c They must be fit for the purpose for which they are bought; that is able to be used in the normal way expected. If you have been told that they have a particular quality, they must have it.

Figure 14.13 illustrates how these three points would apply in practice.

a At the local furniture store, your family buys a table described on the price ticket as 'mahogany wood'. When you get it home you find it is made of chipboard with a thin layer of mahogany on top. You should be able to get your money back from the business as the furniture was not as described to you on the ticket.
b Your family buys a freezer, marked 'ex-display' model in the sale. Once home, you find it does not work. You complain to the shop assistant who just points to a notice saying 'No Exchange on Sales Goods'. But even sale goods must be of merchantable quality. 'Ex-display' does not mean that the freezer does not work. You can get back what you paid.
c In a shoe shop you tell the sales assistant that you want a pair of boots to keep out the rain. She sells you a pair, but the next time it rains, you find that they let in water. As you asked for boots fit for a particular purpose, then they should keep out the rain and you should get your money back.

Figure 14.13 The Sale of Goods Act at work

If a shopkeeper sells a faulty good, the customer is entitled to one of the following three services:

a a good replacement
b a free repair, and a temporary replacement while the repair is being carried out
c a refund. The customer does not have to accept a credit note. So a sign which says 'No refunds' has no meaning, because no business can ignore the law if it sells faulty goods.

14.14 Buying a service

The problem for a customer if a service proves unsatisfactory is that it is difficult to take a service back. The take-away that makes you ill has already been eaten; the holiday when you had to move hotel and resort is over; the haircut that is too short cannot be undone. It is only recently, with the passing of the Supply of Goods and Services Act in 1982 that a customer is protected if he or she feels that the standard of a service has not been reasonable. Some examples are shown in *Fig 14.14*.

a A dry cleaner is responsible for ruining your best dress. Even if the ticket says that the dry cleaner will not accept responsibility for damage, you should still be able to get compensation.

b You try a new restaurant. You have to wait an hour to be served. Your order of plaice and chips brings uncooked fish and burnt chips. You feel that you do not want to pay the bill, and in these conditions you would not have to pay for the meal, although the more you eat, the more difficult becomes your case. You might also be able to claim further compensation for the disappointment you suffered.

c A poorly repaired water pipe bursts for the second time and ruins the new carpet. The customer would not only expect a refund for the first repair, but also compensation for the ruined carpet and any other damage that has been done.

Figure 14.14 Problems with services

A business may again try to display a sign which says 'No responsibility for loss or damage however caused', but these **exclusion clauses** are only valid if the business can prove in court that they are fair. No business can avoid the law if the description, quality, and fitness of the service is wrong, or if negligence causes injury or death.

14.15 Buying food and drink

There are special laws which cover the serving and sales of food, drink, and drugs. The government, through the work of the Environmental Health Officers, has tried to make sure that:

a all food and drugs on sale are pure and wholesome
b food is prepared, handled, and served in hygienic conditions
c the ingredients in tinned and other processed food are clearly labelled, starting with the most substantial ingredient
d food in shops is not repriced upwards unless the first price was a mistake
e advertisers should not mislead people about the nature or value of any food or drug
f where prices are for weight (as in buying meat), then both the total price and weight of the pack should be shown, and the price per pound that is being paid.

14.16 Buying on credit

More and more people buy now and pay later, especially when buying consumer durables. Buying on **credit** has been made easier because of the number of businesses which are now willing to provide credit. *Figure 14.16* gives examples of the various forms of credit available to consumers.

a Hire purchase
Credit provided by a finance company
Goods are paid for by instalments
Customer pays interest and a service charge
Shop or finance company can take back goods if payment is not made

b Overdrafts and loans
Credit provided by a bank
Customer can decide what to spend credit on
With loan interest paid on whole amount
With overdraft interest paid on what is borrowed at any time

c Credit cards
Credit provided by Access, Barclaycard, etc.
Customer can use card for many purchases in many different places
No interest for 25 days but then interest charged higher than bank

d Shop cards
Many shops issue their own cards
Customers can only use for purchases in the particular shop or chain of shops
Interest tends to be higher than credit cards

Figure 14.16 Buying on credit

Businesses have to decide whether the benefits of letting customers buy on credit are greater than the costs. Let us look at the recent decision by Marks & Spencer plc to issue a shop card to their customers. The benefits might include:

a an increasing volume of sales as people can now buy on credit as well as cash
b building up regular customers who use the shop because they have a card
c improved competition with other stores which take credit cards
d they can now use card holders for market research and for special promotions.

The costs might include

a a worsening of their cash flow as cash will not immediately be received for all their sales
b possible loss due to bad debts when people are unable to pay off their credit
c increased losses due to stolen cards
d administrative costs and the extra time it takes to serve customers.

In addition, businesses will be aware that the government, through the 1974 **Consumer Credit Act** has tried to protect customers who buy goods on credit. This has meant that:

a all businesses that lend money for interest must be licensed
b the consumer must be told the true rate of interest that they are paying; this is known as the Annual Percentage Rate (APR)
c if the goods that are purchased are faulty, then the buyer can get compensation either from the shop or the company that has lent the money
d businesses which persuade customers to sign an agreement to buy goods at home rather than in a shop, must give the buyers three days in which to change their mind
e there are a number of agencies which keep data about potential credit customers. These customers have a right to know what data that agency holds about them.

14.17 Aiding the customer – after the sale

Many products that are bought come with a **guarantee** from the manufacturer. Although usually with consumer durables, they are often also to be found on such common purchases as chocolate bars, jars of coffee, and washing powders. Guarantees cannot take away rights which a customer has under the laws we have looked at in the last sections, but they may add to these rights.

Figure 14.17 shows two typical guarantees.

a Taken from a Mars Bar wrapper: 'This confectionery should reach you in perfect condition. If it does not, please return it to us stating where and when it was bought. We will be glad to send you a Mars confectionery voucher covering both the purchase price and the postage. This guarantee does not affect your statutory rights.'

b Taken from the guarantee for an electric kettle: 'This appliance has been manufactured to exacting standards and the company guarantees that should any defect in materials or workmanship occur within 12 months of the date of purchase we will repair, or at our option, replace the defective part free of charge – always provided that the appliance has been used for normal domestic purposes in the UK. This guarantee in no way diminishes the buyer's statutory or legal rights, but it does not cover damage caused by misuse, negligence, or damage in transit.'

Figure 14.17 Guarantees

Notice that in the second guarantee there is a time limit, and also some allowance for the way the kettle has been used, although both examples show that the normal rights of the customer remain.

The need for **after-sales service** can also be important when buying a consumer durable. Guarantees usually cover the first year, or a business includes the first service within the purchase price (as with car purchase). As we have seen there is now more protection for the consumer if servicing is poor, but it now common for people to take out insurance in case a major item like a washing machine fails after the guarantee period.

14.18 How the customer can deal with a bad buy

To finish this section let us follow a consumer through the steps that can be taken if he or she has bought a faulty good, and see also some of the organisations that exist which can provide consumer aid.

Figure 14.18

Stage 1: making the complaint

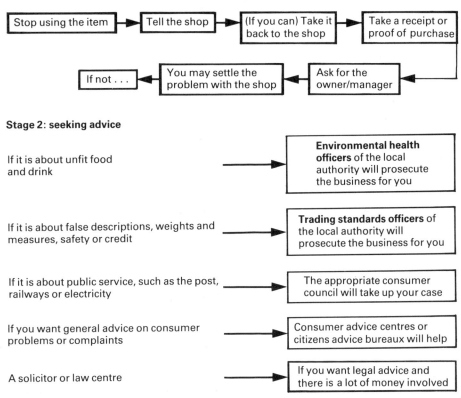

Stop using the item	→
Tell the shop	→
(If you can) Take it back to the shop	→
Take a receipt or proof of purchase	

If not . . .	←
You may settle the problem with the shop	←
Ask for the owner/manager	

Stage 2: seeking advice

If it is about unfit food and drink → **Environmental health officers** of the local authority will prosecute the business for you

If it is about false descriptions, weights and measures, safety or credit → **Trading standards officers** of the local authority will prosecute the business for you

If it is about public service, such as the post, railways or electricity → The appropriate consumer council will take up your case

If you want general advice on consumer problems or complaints → Consumer advice centres or citizens advice bureaux will help

A solicitor or law centre → If you want legal advice and there is a lot of money involved

Stage 3: widening the net

Write a formal letter stating your demands, providing evidence and stating a time limit. Write again, adding further factors or addressing someone more senior if unsuccessful
Contact **a trade association** if the firm belongs to one. They may have a voluntary **code of practice** which will support your claim. They might judge your case
Contact local local newspapers, radio or television consumer programmes, and consumer groups like the Consumers' Association which publishers Which? magazine

Stage 4: taking legal action
If the business will still not accept responsibility

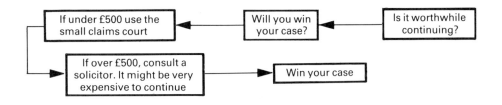

If under £500 use the small claims court	← Will you win your case?	← Is it worthwhile continuing?
If over £500, consult a solicitor. It might be very expensive to continue	→ Win your case	

THINGS TO DO

Short answer questions

1 Why is it more difficult today for someone to stay in the same job for their whole working life?

2 Using *Fig 14.2* explain the main features of the YTS.

3 What examples of technical & vocational courses exist in your school?

4 What is the difference between redundancy and unfair dismissal?

5 Which of the following would be regarded as fair reasons for dismissal?
a someone who is continually away from work due to illness
b someone who is gaoled for burglary while still at work
c someone who has a row with his or her supervisor
d someone who lights a cigarette in a non-smoking area of a chemical plant
e a woman who becomes pregnant.

6 Who sits on an industrial tribunal and what do they decide?

7 Why is 'let the buyer beware' no longer enough protection for the consumer?

8 Match the names of the following Acts with the statements opposite of what the Acts do:

a Weights & Measures Act	*i*	Protects consumers who borrow money to buy goods
b Sale of Goods Act	*ii*	Helps a customer who feels that the standard of a service is poor
c Trade Descriptions Act	*iii*	Says that goods must be of merchantable quality
d Consumer Credit Act	*iv*	Decides how much whisky makes a measure
e Supply of Goods and Services Act	*v*	States that goods and services must be advertised truthfully.

9 How do British standards help to protect the consumer?

10 Why do gifts not come under the Sale of Goods Act?

11 What should a customer do who has bought a faulty good from a shop which displays a 'No refund' sign?

12 What advantages are there for a customer who buys on credit rather than using cash?

13 What disadvantages are there for the same customer?

14 Why do businesses offer guarantees?

15 How can the following people help consumers?
  a Environmental Health Officers
  b Trading Standard Officers
  c Trade Association
  d The Consumers' Association
  e The Small Claims Court

SECTION B

Essays and structured questions

1 *'Watch out Japan, here comes Tracy Logan'*
This was the headline for a recent advertisement in newspapers by the Manpower Services Commission. The advertisement continued:

> 'Tracy Logan is a typical British 16-year-old, leaving school this year. But to Japan, and other international competitors, she's a big threat. That's because this year she'll be starting two years' paid skill training on the new Youth Training Scheme. She'll begin her course by trying out several different skills before she chooses the one she'll train for through to the end of the second year. By then she'll have a skill, a certificate to prove it, and a better chance of getting a job. Our competitors in the Far East and Europe have been training their young people like this for years . . . it's helped them take trade away from us. But from now on they're going to have to watch out.'

  a What does the Manpower Services Commission do?
  b What will Tracy gain by training in the two-year YTS?
  c Why should Japan be worried about Tracy Logan?
  d Why would the Manpower Services Commission need to advertise the YTS in a national newspaper?
  e What alternatives does Tracy have other than choosing the new YTS?

2 *a* Why do businesses make workers redundant?
  b How are payments for redundancy calculated? Give some simple examples.
  c What alternatives are there to redundancies if a business wants to reduce its workforce?

3 Look carefully at *Fig 14.8*. Explain all the stages that a worker can go through if he or she is claiming unfair dismissal.

4 Comment on the following advertisements from the point of view of the Trade Descriptions Act or the Advertising Standards Authority code that advertisements should be 'legal, decent, honest and truthful'.

a Unbeatable sale

b 'Free £50 Holiday Spending Money' was displayed on the outside of a chocolate wrapper. Revealed on the inside of the wrapper – you have to send off 25 wrappers to benefit.

c A well-known lager is described as 'probably the best lager in the world'.

d A hotel in a travel brochure is described as '10 minutes from the sea' and 'well equipped with swimming pool and bar'. In fact, there is a railway line between the hotel and the sea, and the swimming pool is cracked so never filled.

5 How does the Sale of Goods Act or the Supply of Goods and Services Act help the consumer in the following cases?

a the heels have fallen off a pair of shoes you bought this morning

b the hair dryer you bought a fortnight ago is not powerful enough to blow dry your hair

c the car repairs which were carried out last week were clearly inadequate as your car fails to start when coming home from work

d you buy a pair of gloves which the shop assistant says are 'genuine leather'. When you show them to your mother, she realises that they are made of plastic

e The new portable stereo cassette player which your uncle gave you for Christmas has jammed and refuses to work.

6 Explain what the following sign would mean, displayed in a local electrical discount store.

> *Credit at Powers*
> Instant credit available up to £2000
> No deposit needed
> APR = 30.2%
> Instant credit of 24 times your monthly payment
> Other credit cards accepted

SECTION C   **Coursework and assignments**

1 By contacting either your local Careers Office or local Job Centre find out what special training schemes are being run in your area. Choose one of the schemes and try to arrange a visit to find out:

a who the scheme is for

b how it is organised

c what skills are being learnt

d how long it lasts for.

Write up your findings in the form of a report.

2 Role Play

The Case:

Sheila Larkins worked as a bus driver for a Midland bus company. She had eight years' service and an excellent record. The buses were one-person operated, so as well as driving Sheila also collected the fares. During an inspection, her supervisor discovered that £25 in fares, which according to the ticket machine had been collected, was not in the collection tray. Sheila could not account for the money, but claimed that the ticket machine was faulty. Stealing was an offence for which drivers could be immediately dismissed by the bus company and so the supervisor sacked Sheila as soon as her shift finished. Sheila claimed the dismissal was unfair.

The role play:

In groups act out what you think would happen at an industrial tribunal which is called to decide on Sheila's case. The tribunal should have three members and there should be someone to give Sheila's side of the case, and someone to represent the bus company.

3 Choose a product or a service and find out how the various Acts discussed in this chapter are applied to businesses which make or sell those goods and services. These are some of the headings you might use:
  a What controls are there over the way the products are advertised?
  b How is the safety of the product checked?
  c How does the business make sure that the good is of merchantable quality and fit for its purpose?
  d What guarantees or after-sales service are offered?

Glossary

achievement a feeling of success at doing something well; important at helping to motivate people at work.

advertising the way businesses try to inform the public about their product, and persuade them to buy it. There are many types of **advertising media**, including television, radio, newspapers and magazines.

Annual General Meeting (AGM) a meeting once a year where the shareholders of a company receive a report from the Directors on the company's activities and performance.

Annual Percentage Rate (APR) the true interest rate that a customer pays when borrowing money or buying on credit.

apprenticeship a trainee is employed by a company and learns a skill by working with a skilled employee. Will also involve part-time study on a day-release course.

assets what a business owns. **Fixed assets** last for longer than a year, e.g. buildings, machinery and vehicles. **Current assets** are used for a short time, e.g. stocks, money owed by debtors and cash. **Other assets** come from outside the business, e.g. shares in another company. **Liquid assets** are those assets which a company owns which can quickly be turned into cash. They usually include money owed by debtors and cash in the bank, but not stock.

Assisted Area parts of the UK with high levels of unemployment where businesses are given grants and other aid from the Government to persuade them to set up a new factory or office.

attitude what somebody thinks or believes about something; it decides how that person will behave.

automation changing a job so that tasks performed by humans are now performed by machinery, often controlled by computer.

bad debt money which is owed to a business by customers or debtors but which will never be paid back.

balance sheet a 'photograph' of the financial position of a business at one point of time, showing all that it owes and all that it owns.

bankruptcy when a business no longer has the funds to pay back its debts.

batch production see under **production**

board of directors see under **director**

break-even the level of output and sales of a business when the Total Costs of making the goods equal the Total Revenue from selling them. This is often shown on a graph, the **break-even chart**, where the **break-even point** is the level of output which gives neither profit nor loss.

British Standards Institute (BSI) a non-profit making organisation which gives its 'Kitemark' to consumer goods which have reached a certain standard of quality and safety.

budget (a) a plan of the income and expenditure expected over a period of time or for a certain business activity; used to estimate profits, and as a way of reviewing activities when the budget is compared to actual results. **(b)** a plan of what the Government expects to spend, and what income it expects to raise from taxation which the Chancellor of the Exchequer presents to Parliament once a year (usually in April).

bureaucracy administration in large organisations; could be the source of 'red-tape' which slows down decision-making.

capital (a) the man made factor of production, including machinery, buildings, vehicles, tools and money. **Social capital** is provided by the state and includes roads, railways, hospitals and schools. **(b)** money provided for a business by its owners, which will not be paid back until the business is wound up.

cash the most liquid (easily usable) asset held by a business, either in the till or in the bank.

cash flow the balance between money coming into a business from sales and debtors, and money going out of a business to pay for purchases and to pay creditors. Often shown in a **cash flow statement** which covers a certain number of weeks or months.

chain of command the path that decisions and orders will follow in an organisation from the top to a particular employee.

chain of distribution see under **distribution**

closed shop where all employees in one business, or one department, have to be members of one union.

collective bargaining when management and unions negotiate over pay, conditions and job security on behalf of the employees of an organisation.

communication the sending of messages from a source to a receiver, and the feed-back that is given. Ways in which messages can be sent in business include letters, meetings, telephones, posters and notices. A **communication network (net)** is a diagram showing the direction in which messages can be sent in an organisation.

Companies Acts laws which regulate the way **registered companies** are formed and organised in order to protect the interests of their owners.

Confederation of British Industry see under **Trades Union Congress**

consumer credit see under **credit**

consumer goods products bought by households to satisfy their needs. They will either be used up within a year, **single use**, or will last for more than a year, **consumer durable**.

consumer legislation laws which protect the interests of the consumer when buying goods and services for cash or on credit. The most important have been the **Consumer Credit Act** (1974); **Fair Trading Act** (1973); **Sales of Goods Act** (1979); **Trade Descriptions Act** (1968); **Weights & Measures Acts** (1963, 1979).

contract a legal agreement between 2 or more people that they will or will not do something. Examples in business include **contracts of employment** when one person agrees to be an employee of another and **contracts for service** when the person agrees to do a job for another. Many contracts are **unwritten**, for example when consumers buy goods from a shop.

contribution the sales revenue of a product less the direct costs and expenses of making and selling that product. This amount then **contributes** to paying the overheads of a business.

co-operative a type of business organisation, with limited liability, where each owner only has one share and one vote in deciding policy. With **retail co-operatives** the business is owned by its customers; with **worker co-operatives**, it is owned by the employees.

cost-benefit analysis looking at the private costs and benefits and the social costs and benefits of a project. The private costs and benefits are financial ones faced by the businesses involved. The social costs and benefits are faced by the community as a whole. Used by the government when deciding about a major project like the Channel Tunnel.

costs what a business spends in order to provide goods or services for its customers. Costs which change directly with changes in output, e.g. raw material or labour costs, are **direct costs**. Costs which change, but not in a directly connected way, with output, e.g. energy costs or telephone charges, are **indirect costs**. Costs which remain unchanged whatever the level of output, e.g. rent and rates, or debt interest, are **overheads**.

craft union see under **trade union**

credit being given time to pay for a good or service. A builder might be given 3 months to pay for bricks purchased; an example of **trade credit**. A customer in a department store might be given 12 months to pay for a dining-room table: **consumer credit**.

creditor people to whom a business owes money, usually suppliers and financial organisations.

current assets see under **assets**

current liabilities see under **liabilities**

debt finance raising money by borrowing from people who are not owners of the business.

debtor people who owe a business money, usually customers who have purchased on credit.

delegation a manager passing down to subordinates the authority to take decisions, but keeping overall responsibility for those decisions.

demand the amount of a good or service that consumers are willing and able to buy over a time period.

depreciation the loss in value of capital goods as they get older and are used more. It is a cost to a business, and accountants spread this cost over a number of years to cover a machine's useful life.

direct costs see under **costs**

director people chosen by shareholders to represent them in the running of a company. They form a **board of directors**.

diseconomies of scale as a business becomes too big, so problems of management organisation and communication occur and cause unit costs to rise.

dismissal an employer ending the contract of employment of an employee. Workers can now appeal against **unfair dismissal** by employers.

distributed profit see under **profit**

distribution the process of getting the finished product to the consumer. A typical **chain of distribution** for a consumer good is **manufacturer – wholesaler – retailer – customer**.

dividends the amount of profit that the director's of a business decide each year to distribute to their shareholders. The **rate of dividend** is the amount given for each share.

division of labour where an activity is split up into many stages, with workers specialising in each stage. Typical of work on a production line.

economies of scale the factors which allow unit costs to fall as a business grows in size. Economies can occur in production, marketing, risk-bearing, finance and management.

entrepreneur a person who develops a new product or service, sets up an organisation to produce it, raises the finance, runs the business, and accepts the risk of failure.

Enterprise Zone a small, usually inner-city, area with high unemployment and little industrial activity where businesses are offered grants and other special incentives by the government to encourage expansion in the zone.

equity the value of the ordinary shares of a company.

exchange rate the price of a currency, expressed in another currency, often the dollar.

exports domestically produced goods (visible exports) or services (invisible exports) sold abroad.

factors of production the resources which form the basis for all business activity, land, labour, capital and entrepreneurship.

Fair Trading Act see under **consumer legislation**

feedback the final stage in communication, when the receiver shows that he/she has understood and acted upon the message sent.

fiscal policy see under **government policy**

fixed assets see under **assets**

flow production see under **production**
footloose industry businesses which do not have to locate close to raw materials supplies or their market.
formal group see under **group**
formal organisation see under **organisation**

general union see under **trade union**
goal the target that individuals, groups or businesses decide to aim at.
goods an object that is capable of satisfying human wants. Either available in abundance without cost, a **free good**, or a scarce object that is only available in exchange for another good or money, an **economic good**.
government expenditure the amount of money that central and local government spends in providing public goods, services and social capital.
government policy the ways in which government can influence the level and nature of business activity. **Fiscal policy** involves changes in **government expenditure** and **taxation**. **Monetary policy**, changes in the **money supply** and the **rate of interest**. **External policies**, changes in the **exchange rate** and the level of **exports** and **imports**.
group an important influence in the way people behave at work. **Formal groups** are set up by management for a specific purpose; **informal groups** arise among friends and often cut across formal groups.

health and safety to ensure that working conditions do not endanger the well-being of the workforce all businesses must conform to the 1974 **Health & Safety at Work Act**. It is up to the management to make sure that a machine etc. is safe and that the workforce are following the correct procedure.
hierarchy the number of levels of authority in an organisation.
hire purchase a type of customer credit where a consumer has immediate use but pays for a good in a number of instalments, and only gains final ownership after the last payment.

imports goods produced abroad but sold in the domestic market (**visible imports**) or services purchased from abroad (**invisible imports**).
incentive scheme often in the form of some financial bonus, these motivate employees to reach a certain target, perhaps increased production, increased sales, or improved quality.
income the earnings of a business or a person over a period.
indirect costs see under **costs**
induction see under **training**
industrial action called by unions or groups of workers to disrupt production in support of their claims. Some common forms of action are strikes, work-to-rules, overtime bans, and the blacking of goods or machinery.
industrial tribunal a panel containing a lawyer, a union representative and a management representative that

decides cases of unfair dismissal, redundancy or equal opportunities at work.
industrial union see under **trade union**
informal group see under **group**
informal organisation see under **organisation**
information technology (IT) computerisation of the way that information is produced, stored and handled in a business. Based largely on the use of microcomputers and word processors.
integration when businesses join together, as a result of a merger or take-over; **horizontal integration** is where firms at the same stage of production join; **vertical integration** is where firms from different stages of production join. **Forward integration** is when a producer joins with one of its customers, while **backward integration** is when a producer joins with its supplier.
interest rates the cost of borrowing money, which can vary according to the type of customer, the amount borrowed and the time scale of the loan.
investment good items purchased by businesses as an aid to production for example machinery, buildings, tools, vehicles and stock.

job description an account of what work a job would involve, used in recruiting new employees or when wages and salaries are being calculated.
job enrichment management trying to make a job more satisfying by changing the tasks and responsibilities involved in it. Used to increase the motivation of the person doing the job. Two alternative changes are **job rotation** in which people move from one job to another, and **job enlargement** where more tasks are built into an otherwise monotonous job.
job production see under **production**
job satisfaction an important source of motivation for an employee that can be gained from a job that provides both responsibility and reward.

labour the human resource used in business activity including both manned and mental skills.
land the natural resource used in business activity including raw materials extracted and crops grown from the land, and the produce of the sea and seabed.
leadership the role taken on by one or more members of a group to organise the others. A leader who consults with and involves others in decisions is a **democratic leader**. A leader who takes decisions without a discussion is an **autocratic leader**.
liabilities what a business owes. **Long-term liabilities** are debts which do not have to be repaid for over 12 months, e.g. debenture stock and long-term loans. **Current liabilities** will have to be repaid within 12 months, for example trade credit, overdrafts and tax owed to the government.
limited liability the owner is only responsible for the debts of a business up to the amount that they have put into the business. The basis of **limited companies**,

public limited companies and **co-operatives**.
liquidation see under **wind up**
liquidity how much cash a business has, or assets that can quickly be turned into cash (e.g. stock or debtors) to pay off short-term debts.
loan see under **overdraft**
long-term liabilities see under **liabilities**
loss where the revenue from the sales of a business are unable to cover the costs of producing and selling the goods or services.

market economy the type of economy where decisions about what to produce are based on demand and supply, and where the factors of production are privately owned.
market orientated where a business finds out what the customer wants before designing and producing the good and selling it. Many businesses which produce consumer goods are now **market orientated**, rather than **product orientated** where the product is designed and produced without knowing whether it is what the customer wants.
market research gathering information about the customers for a product either through **field research**, by interviews or questionnaires, or through **desk research**, by looking at information and statistics collected about that market.
market segment a part of a market which contains a group of buyers who can be clearly identified because of age, sex, class, etc. and at whom a product can be aimed.
market share the percentage of the total value or volume of sales in a market gained by a business.
marketing the process in a business which aims to bring together the product and the customer. It recognises the needs of the customer, designs and makes available products to meet those needs, at a profit, and it increases or maintains those needs for the future.
marketing mix those elements which make up a marketing plan for a business can be remembered as the 4 P's: 1) **product** – designing and producing a product which the customer wants; 2) **price** – and selling it profitably at a competitive price; 3) **promotion** – using advertising and sales promotion to inform and persuade; 4) **place** – making sure it is distributed to where the customer is to be found.
mark-up the difference between the selling price of a good or service and the cost to that seller.
merchandising the way that a business tries to pull the customer towards their product. Would include the package design, special offers and promotions, and free gifts. Also known as **sales promotion**.
merger when two companies agree to join their operations together and come under common ownership, or where one company buys the shares of the other and therefore takes over the company.
merit goods goods and services which the government think that people should have, but which it knows that not all would be willing or able to pay for. Examples are health care and education.

mixed economy where part of business activity is controlled by government decisions, and where part is left to decisions based in the free market. Some of the productive resources will be state-owned, and some will be privately owned.
monetary policy see under **government policy**
Monopolies and Mergers Commission (MMC) a body which investigates markets where one business supplies more than 25% of the goods sold (a **monopoly**) or markets where a merger between two or more businesses will create such a control, or which involves a large amount of costs. It can recommend to the government that such a monopoly is split up, or such a merger is stopped.
motivation providing an incentive to do something; especially important in the work-place today.
multi-national company a large organisation which has offices, factories or subsidiary companies in many different countries. ICI and BP are both multi-national companies based in UK.

nationalised industry those businesses which have been taken into public ownership by the government, for example British Rail and the National Coal Board.
net assets employed the total **assets** of a business less the current and long-term liabilities. Used as a measure of the value of a business.
new issues market see under **Stock Exchange**
norms the rules of behaviour that an informal group might follow in an organisation.

objectives what an individual or a business aims for. Among the obejctives that a business might adopt are **profit**, **market share**, **growth** or **survival**.
off-the-job training see under **training**
on-the-job training see under **training**
organisation a group of people who are working together to achieve a set purpose. The positions of authority that they hold are shown on an **organisation chart**, which is a picture of the **formal organisation** structure. There will also be an **informal organisation** made of friends who cut across the formal structure.
overdraft a short-term source of finance for a business, whereby it is allowed to overdraw on its bank current account by a set amount arranged with the bank. The interest rate charged is usually higher than for a bank **loan**, but is only payable on the amount overdrawn at one time.
overheads see under **costs**
overtime working for longer than the basic hours: it is usually paid at a higher rate than normal hours.

partnership a type of business usually with **unlimited liability** when between 2 and 20 people run a business together and share the profits and losses. Common in the professions, e.g. accountants and solicitors.
pay the reward for working, usually paid in weekly **wages** or monthly **salary**. **Income tax** and **national**

insurance contributions are deducted from **gross pay**, to give a person's **take-home** or **net pay**.

planned economy a type of economy where decisions about what to produce are taken by a central agency, and where the factors of production are owned by the state.

price the amount of money that a consumer has to pay for a good or service. A business decides its price according to its costs of production, and an analysis of the market conditions.

primary the first stage of business activity, when raw materials are extracted from the land or sea or grown on farms and plantations, which is known as **primary production**.

private sector that part of the economy owned by private individuals. It includes **sole traders**, **partnerships**, **limited companies**, **public limited companies** and **co-operatives**.

privatisation to place back into private ownership business activities which have previously been in public ownership or under public control. British Telecom was privatised in 1985 when the government offered its shares on the Stock Exchange. In several areas, refuse is now collected by private companies.

producer goods goods which are made by businesses for use by other businesses as part of their production process, e.g. machinery, partly finished goods, tools and equipment.

product life cycle the stages that consumer goods pass through: **development** and **launch** when the product is first introduced; **growth** when sales increase quickly as consumers try a new product; **maturity** as sales level out and regular customers are established; **decline** as sales fall and new products are launched.

product orientated a business where the design and quality of the product is more important than whether there is a market for that product.

production the process of making something. **Job production** is when each item is completed before the next is started. **Batch production** is where products are completed in stages. **Flow production** uses a production line where products will move continuously from one operation to another.

productivity a way of measuring the efficiency of **production** by comparing the amount produced with the amount of inputs used. Most often used to measure **labour productivity** where the amount produced is compared with the number of labour hours employed. It might form the basis of a **productivity agreement**, when workers receive bonus pay for increasing output per man.

profit the surplus that remains when costs are subtracted from sales revenue over a period. **Profit** can either be **retained** in a business to finance expansion, or **distributed** in the form of **dividends** to the owners. **Gross profit** is the sales revenue that a business earns from selling a product minus the direct costs of buying or manufacturing that product over a period of time. **Net profit** is the sales revenue that a business earns from

selling a product minus all the costs involved in making it available to consumers over a period of time.

profit loss account a set of accounts which show how a business has earned its income during a year and what it has done with it. It contains three sections: 1) **the trading account** which shows its day to day trading activity; 2) **the profit loss account** which shows income and expenditure from activities outside its normal trading; 3) **the appropriation account** which shows what is done with any profit that has been made.

promotion how a business tries to pull a customer towards its product, also known as **merchandising**. It would include the use of packaging and labelling, special offers, special promotions, exhibitions, sponsorship and after-sales service to persuade the customer to buy the product.

provisions when a business sets aside money from profits to meet costs like taxation or dividend payments which it knows it will have to pay in the near future.

public corporation these are provided for the use of the community by the government and paid for out of taxes, as they would be difficult to pay for individually. Defence, policing, the fire service are some examples.

public limited company (plc) organisations whose shares have been offered for sale in the Stock Exchange to the general public. They are among the largest businesses in the UK.

public sector that part of the economy that is controlled directly by the government at national or local level. It includes **central government departments**, **public corporations**, and **local authorities**.

quality control ensuring that the finished product reaches a certain standard that is acceptable to the company and the consumer.

rate of interest see under **government policy**

recruitment the stages a company will go through to get employees for their organisation. It will involve job advertisements, application forms, references, interviews and final selection.

redundancy when a person loses his or her job because that job ceases to exist as the company is closing down a factory or department, or closing completely. Employees receive **redundancy pay** according to how long they have worked for the company.

registered company see under **Companies Acts**

research and development (R & D) the efforts of a business to find new products and processes which will improve their profitability. Usually associated with technical rather than market research.

restrictive practice when two or more businesses get together to try to prevent another business from trading freely in their market. A **restrictive practices court** exists to see that any practices that exist are in the public interest.

retail co-operative see under **co-operative**

retained profit see under **profit**

revenue the amount of income that an organisation receives from its sales or other activities.

risk the uncertainty about success or failure that is associated with a particular decision or activity, like setting up a business.

Sale of Goods Act see under **consumer legislation**

sales promotion see under **merchandising**

sampling in market research when part of the population are selected for a particular survey. With **random sampling** everyone has an equal chance of being selected. **Quota sampling** is when people are selected because they belong to a certain grouping by age, sex, etc. **Cluster sampling** is when a survey is taken in certain geographical areas. In general, the larger the sample, the more accurate will be the results, but the more expensive and time consuming will be the survey.

secondary the second stage of business activity when goods are manufactured out of raw materials, known as **secondary production**.

services consumer needs which are satisfied on a personal level either by government (**social services**) or by private organisations (**professional** and **commercial services**).

shareholder the owners of a company, who receive part of the profits of that company depending on the number of shares they own. The **shareholders fund** is the total amount that the owners have invested in a company.

shop steward the representative of a trade union in a place of work, elected by the members of that union. They will do a normal job in the workplace as well as carrying out their union duties.

social benefits the gains to the community that business activity might bring, for example the provision of jobs.

social capital see under **capital**

social cost losses to the community that a business activity might bring, for example pollution and congestion.

sole trader a type of organisation owned and controlled by one person, although that person might employ several others. That person will receive all the profits of the business, but will have to bear all the losses.

solvency when a business is able to pay its debts as they become due.

span of control the number of people in an organisation who are directly responsible to a particular manager.

specialisation where individuals, groups or organisations concentrate on doing a specific job which might form part of a much larger task or operation. Specialisation can also occur in towns, regions and countries.

status a person's standing within their group/community, given to them because of, for example, the job that they perform.

stock the materials, supplies and unfinished goods that businesses hold because they are needed in production, and the finished goods that are waiting to be sold. Businesses need to balance the costs of holding to little stock with the costs of holding too much, by using careful **stock control** methods.

Stock Exchange a market for secondhand shares where traders deal in the shares of **public limited companies**. Large sums of money can be raised by businesses by issuing shares through the **new issues** market.

strike when the members of a trade union stop working because of a dispute with their employer. An **official strike** is one that has been supported by the officials of a trade union and approved by a ballot of those involved. An **unofficial strike** is one that has occurred without the official backing of a trade union.

subsidy providing a payment to the producer of a good or service so that the price charged to the consumer will be lower than otherwise, or to keep the producer in business. The government provides subsidies to **public sector** industries and to **private sector** industries like farming.

taxation the way the government raises money for individuals and businesses to finance **government expenditure**. The main **taxes** are **income tax** on people's earnings, **corporation tax** on company profits, **value added tax** on consumer purchases, and **Customs & Excise duties** on purchase of goods like alcohol, cigarettes and petrol.

Technical and Vocational Education Initiative (TVEI) a scheme in schools run for groups of 14–18-year-old school pupils to encourage the learning of more vocationally orientated subjects. As part of their course they may study Business Studies, Computer Application and Craft & Design. TVEI is funded by the **Manpower Services Commission** (**MSC**).

tertiary the third stage of business activity, the provision of the services which allow the **primary** and **secondary** stages to continue, e.g. transport and communication services. These are examples of **tertiary production**.

trade credit see under **credit**

Trade Descriptions Act see under **consumer legislation**

trade union organised groups of employees bargain collectively with management on behalf of their members. **General unions** recruit workers from several industries; **craft unions** represent workers with a particular skill; **industrial unions** recruit from within one industry; **white-collar unions** recruit non-manual, clerical and professional staff.

Trades Union Congress (**TUC**) represents individual trade unions in discussing with employers organisations like the **Confederation of British Industry** (**CBI**) and the government over economic policies, and tries to sort out disputes between unions.

training helping employees to understand their work and to gain new skills; most jobs require an initial period of training known as **induction**, and then further training throughout the period of employment, either at the workplace '**on-the-job**' training, or at a college '**off-the-job**' training.

turnover the value of the sales of a business over a period of time.

unemployment where demand for goods and services in a country is not sufficient to bring forward an output that would allow everyone to be employed.

unfair dismissal see under **dismissal**

unit costs how much it costs to make one item of output.

unlimited liability the owners of a business are responsible for all the debts of that business, no matter how much capital they put into the business. True of sole traders and most partnerships.

Unlisted Securities Market (USM) a new market in the Stock Exchange which allows growing businesses to raise finance without the expense and obligations of issuing shares in the main market.

value added the difference between the revenue that a business gets from selling its products and the costs of the materials it used to make those products.

Weights and Measures Acts see under **consumer legislation**

white-collar union see under **trade union**

wind up setting in motion the ending of a business, also known as **liquidation**.

worker co-operative see under **co-operative**

work study carrying out a scientific study of what a job involves and how long it takes to complete. Often this information is used to improve working methods or as a basis for a new payment scheme.

worker participation management trying to involve employees in the decision making of a business, from discussions on the shop floor, to membership of the **board of directors** and profit-sharing schemes.

working capital the 'life blood' of a business; the **current assets** which circulate through a business to allow production to take place and to meet the **current liabilities**.

Youth Training Scheme (YTS) a two-year scheme for school leavers organised by the **Manpower Services Commission (MSC)** to provide young people with skills that will be useful in future employment.

Index